Emerging Economies and Financial Markets

Beth Morrissey · Gary Kleiman

Emerging Economies and Financial Markets

A Career-Tested Approach to Analyzing the Markets

palgrave
macmillan

Beth Morrissey
Managing Partner, Kleiman International Consultants, Inc
Alexandria, VA, USA

Gary Kleiman
Senior Partner, Kleiman International Consultants, Inc
Alexandria, VA, USA

ISBN 978-3-031-85668-6 ISBN 978-3-031-85669-3 (eBook)
https://doi.org/10.1007/978-3-031-85669-3

This Palgrave Macmillan imprint is published by the registered company Springer Nature Switzerland AG
The registered company address is: Gewerbestrasse 11, 6330 Cham, Switzerland

Acknowledgements The authors would like to thank the many people who assisted us with *Emerging Economies and Financial Markets*. The students in our annual "Emerging Economy and Finance Analyst Professional Development" workshop in the Landegger Program in International Business Diplomacy (IBD) at the Edmund A. Walsh School of Foreign Service at Georgetown University not only inspired creation of the manuscript but also provided excellent feedback as the work progressed. The Associate Director of the IBD, Linnea Sanders, kindly reviewed an entire draft and offered thoughtful suggestions.

Cameron Brandt, Director of Research, and Kirsten Longbottom, Research Associate, at EPFR, the leading provider of fund flow and asset allocation data, regularly provided data invaluable for illustrating historical emerging markets events.

Beth Morrissey's college classmates were also instrumental as the book progressed. Melanie McDonald spent hours tracking down citations and putting them in the proper format, while Susan L. Axelrod offered organizational support through every draft.

Since our late 1980s start inauspiciously on the day of a market crash we have constantly tested our views as regular columnists in specialist media to lay the groundwork for book writing. Over the years we contributed to *American Banker, The Journal of Commerce, Financial Times, Asia Times* and BNE Intellinews among other outlets.

Finally, we wish to thank our professional clients and colleagues for their support of Kleiman International Consultants, Inc. for more than three decades as we all navigated the rise of emerging markets as an asset class and endlessly fascinating field we hope to convey to readers.

Competing Interests The authors have no competing interests to declare that are relevant to the content of this manuscript.

Contents

Abbreviations

ACW	MSCI's All Country World Index
ADB	Asian Development Bank
ADR	American Depository Receipts
AFC	Asian Financial Crisis
AFP	Administradoras de Fondos de Pensiones, Chile's Private Pension Funds
AI	Artificial Intelligence
AIIB	Asian Infrastructure Investment Bank
APP	Asia Pulp and Paper
BIS	Bank for International Settlements
BRI	Belt and Road Initiative
BRICS	Brazil, Russia, India, China, South Africa
CFA	Certified Financial Analyst
COP	Conference of Parties, United Nations Climate Change Conference
CPI	Consumer Price Index
CRISIL	formerly Credit Ratings Information Services of India Ltd.
CSRC	China Securities Regulatory Commission
DSSI	Debt Services Suspension Initiative
EBRD	European Bank for Reconstruction and Development
EMBI	JPMorgan's Emerging Market Bond Index
EMTA	Emerging Markets Traders Association
ERSAP	Economic Reform and Structural Adjustment Program
ESG	Environmental, Social and Governance
ETF	Exchange Traded Fund
EU	European Union

FDI	Foreign Direct Investment
FSB	Basel, Switzerland-based Financial Stability Board
FX	Foreign Exchange
G20	Group of 20
GDP	Gross Domestic Product
GNI	Gross National Income
HKD	Hong Kong Dollar
IFC	International Finance Corporation
IFRS	International Financial Reporting Standards
IIF	Institute of International Finance
IMF	International Monetary Fund
IOSCO	International Organization of Securities Commissions
IPAB	Mexican Institute for the Protection of Bank Savings
IPO	Initial Public Offering
IsDB	Islamic Development Bank
LDC	Less Developed Country
LIC	Life Insurance Company of India
LKR	Sri Lankan Rupee
MDG	Millennium Development Goals
MICEX	Moscow Interbank Currency Exchange
MIGA	Multilateral Investment Guarantee Agency
NBD	New Development Bank, "BRICS" Bank
NBFC	Non-Bank Financial Corporation
NSE	Nairobi Stock Exchange
NYSE	New York Stock Exchange
OECD	Organization for Economic Cooperation and Development
OFE	Polish Private Pension Funds
OPEC	Organization of Petroleum Exporting Countries
PE	Private Equity
PKO	Powszechna Kasa Oszczednosci Bank Polski S.A., Poland's largest bank
PPP	Public-Private Partnerships
RDIF	Russia Direct Investment Fund
RMB	Renminbi, also known as yuan; China's currency
RUB	Russian Ruble
SDG	Sustainable Development Goals
SDR	IMF's Special Drawing Rights
SSE	United Nation's Sustainable Stock Exchange Initiative
SOE	State-Owned Enterprise
SWF	Sovereign Wealth Fund
SWIFT	Society for Worldwide Interbank Financial Telecommunication
TVF	Türkiye Varlik Fonu, Turkish Sovereign Wealth Fund
UAE	United Arab Emirates
UTI	Unit Trust of India

UNCTAD	United Nations Conference on Trade and Development
UNFPA	United Nations Population Fund
UNITAR	United Nations Institute for Training and Research
YPF	State-Owned Energy Company in Argentina

List of Figures

1

Introduction

Whether you are a college student studying international relations, economics, or finance or an active industry professional or policymaker, we hope "Emerging Economies and Financial Markets: A Career-Tested Approach to Analyzing the Markets" will transform your understanding about the evolution of emerging financial markets and the analytical tools and secrets employed in assessing them. As founders of the pioneer independent advisor on emerging economies, Kleiman International Consultants, Inc., we offer real-life stories about proprietary techniques, explore the history and growth of each segment of the asset class, and provide case studies based on our 35 years advising investors, banks, stock and bond markets, regulators, and policymakers.

In 1987, the year we founded the firm, Latin America was in the midst of its "lost decade" and global banks were grappling with billions of dollars in unpaid debt from there and other regions. The International Finance Corporation, the World Bank's private sector arm, had developed a database of stock markets and coined the term "emerging markets" which sounded far more optimistic—and investable—than "less developed countries" or "Third World." Stock markets did not exist in Central Europe/Central Asia as the Berlin Wall had not come down, and the Soviet Union had not disintegrated. Brazil's per capita GDP was nearly three times that of China. Emerging markets largely depended on bilateral, multilateral, or commercial bank loans. There were 32 emerging stock markets with a combined capitalization of just over USD 200 billion while advanced economies' size was over USD 7.7 trillion.

B. Morrissey and G. Kleiman, *Emerging Economies and Financial Markets*,
https://doi.org/10.1007/978-3-031-85669-3_1

Fast forward more than three decades: As of 2024, the combined capitalization of emerging markets was just over one-quarter of global market cap. China's per capita GDP has surged some 4000 percent and the Shanghai Stock Exchange, launched as "an experiment" in 1991, is now the world's third largest, coming in behind the New York Stock Exchange and Nasdaq in the US. Multiple indices of measuring performance exist for emerging and frontier market stocks, emerging market sovereign and corporate bonds, and currencies as traditional boundaries between investor, development, and humanitarian causes blur.

We wrote this book to serve a dual purpose: tracing the ascent and permutations of the field over its first generation and providing specific advice applicable to candidates or professionals in finance, consulting, or policymaking careers. The content draws on our more than 35 years as independent analysts and strategic advisers for emerging markets banks and fund managers, as well as experience in financial sector development for official lenders in every emerging region. Rather than a dry "how to" analyze book, we use non-economist language appealing to a wide range of backgrounds and disciplines, and real-world illustrative case studies never as straightforward as textbook theory. For example, in the 1990s we trained market practitioners from the newly independent ex-Soviet states in "best practices" from the investment industry perspective they had never before encountered. Participants had no idea that we spoke Turkish and could understand market representatives from Azerbaijan and Uzbekistan still referring to each other as "comrade." A generation later this post-communist hangover endures with many of the Central Asian "frontier markets" still nascent.

The authors started the firm in New York City as the US stock market crashed in the fall of 1987 on the 79th floor of 1 World Trade Center and as the firm grew, we moved to 80 Wall Street, an address to impress. An early client in New York's financial district contracted with Kleiman to analyze and monitor the Nairobi Stock Exchange for the UN as a client. Calls to Kenyan bankers and brokers ran into the hundreds of dollars – and were often difficult to get through—and we anxiously waited for reports delivered by a fax machine. Later we used a bulky Mac computer to prepare analyses and then faxed or delivered them by bicycle messenger to clients.

In the early days Greece and Portugal were classified as emerging markets, and we repeatedly had to explain to clients that Italy, a member of the Group of 7 rich countries, was not. At the height of the Eurozone crisis in 2013, Greece was again demoted from an advanced to emerging market due to capital controls but a decade on had regained investment grade status. Various public and private sector entities define the emerging market universe differently. The original, and most common, definition is based on the World Bank Atlas method which for the 2025 fiscal year categorizes them as low-, lower middle-, and upper middle-income countries with gross national income per capita below USD 14,005. Some emerging markets analysts define them based on the vagaries of benchmark stock, bond, and currency indices. For example, every country in the Middle East is defined as an emerging, or its subset frontier, market in indices due to lingering restrictions on foreign investment and low liquidity, although Qatar's per capita gross national income (GNI) tops USD 110,000 as a world-beater. Giant more developed markets like South Korea are still defined as emerging by some despite per capita GNI of nearly USD 36,000, stock market capitalization larger than the economy, and early membership in the rich country OECD club.

The term "emerging markets" has come to be used generically, and its relevance has come under scrutiny. Dedicated direct and portfolio investors split the universe into "emerging" and "frontier" based on a market's level of economic and financial sector development. In Asia, for example, only Japan, Australia and New Zealand are not "emerging" or "frontier" markets. Post-global pandemic, the term "Global South" has risen in popularity with policymakers who differentiate between the US, Western Europe, Japan, and Australia/New Zealand and the "rest of the world." For the purposes of this book, the term "emerging markets" will be applied generically to encompass the broad "Global South."

Analyzing emerging markets has adjusted and tracked in line with the asset class's expansion and information availability. In the early days, investor decision-making was driven by a few fundamental macro-economic data points – GDP growth, inflation, etc. —and basic legal and regulatory issues including whether listed stocks were freely available to foreign investors who could freely repatriate income and capital. The IFC, in its annual Emerging Stock Markets Factbook, published until the database was sold to Standard & Poor's in 1999, provided basic tax and entry/exit information. In the early days of foreign portfolio investment some emerging markets refused to divulge the extent of foreign holdings of stocks and bonds citing state secrecy, and we routinely encountered prideful ignorance with the scant data and research devoted at the time. An example stands out even today of a portfolio manager who admitted flocking to a new high-yield dollar bond but had no idea where the sub-Saharan African country issuing the paper was located. We worked with the IFC to refine its initial market coverage, notably adding Sri Lanka, and methodology, and created on our own the first local currency bond references and publications as some intrepid investors began to explore high yielding Treasury bills and bonds issued in the local markets.

In contrast, three decades later we can Google withholding or capital gains tax information from virtually any country in the world. Individual company data is also readily available from local and international investment houses and brokerages, and central banks post macro-economic and financial sector data on websites, often updated weekly and in several languages. Despite easier access to information, analyzing emerging markets has become far more complex. In addition to the range of individual macro-economic and legal/regulatory issues, global "top-down" considerations are more critical with the almost seamless web of instantaneous integration early visionaries could only abstractly conceive. US Federal Reserve rate moves have always been a key driver of moving money into/out of "riskier" investments but today more complex issues like global trade agreements and sanctions and ESG – Environmental, Social and Governance issues—also factor heavily. At the same time, as particularly evident during and after the global Covid pandemic and the outbreak of war in Ukraine, the inter-connectedness of global supply chains and the impact of disruptions to traditional channels is increasingly relevant for stock, bond, currency, and foreign direct investors across the emerging markets.

From day one crises have been an organic feature and evaluation roller-coaster. Emerging market debt became an industry due to calamity, the 1980s Latin American debt crisis. Our involvement pre-dates the introduction of Brady Bonds—restructured Latin American debt first issued in 1989—as part of the standard-setting discussions that launched the fixed income Emerging Markets Traders Association. We were hard at work diverted from a conference speaking engagement on December 20, 1994 when Mexico "suddenly" devalued its currency, resulting in the "Tequila Crisis." Later that decade the "Asian Financial Crisis" was followed by Russia's default on ruble debt, and we were called upon also by the US intelligence community to weigh national security implications. More recently, the 2008–09 Global Financial Crisis, 2013's "taper tantrum," and the impact of the Covid-19 pandemic and the war in Ukraine have all battered the asset class. Policy and practical lessons always draw on these episodes, yet history has regularly repeated. Our firm monitored the run-up to and sovereign bond defaults by Argentina four times: 1989, 2001, 2014, and 2020.

The book examines tools and topics in analyzing emerging financial markets that we believe are critical and adaptable for the public, private, and non-profit sectors. It was inspired by a professional development workshop we designed and teach at Georgetown University's Walsh School of

Foreign Service for upper-level undergraduate and graduate students headed for careers in international affairs, finance, and development. The program was the first of its kind designed to certify basic knowledge and skills and included high-level guest speakers and ratings agency-trade association events.

The book opens with an overview of the beginning of "emerging markets" as a standard asset class in the 1980s. It examines the behind the scenes and frontline roles of the World Bank's International Finance Corporation and the US government in establishing recognized equity and debt markets in every region of the world. We also analyze the watershed shift in multilateral and bilateral donor funding with the implementation of macro-economic stabilization and structural reform programs, including privatization, to address the legacy of both the 1980s debt crises and the collapse of communism. Financial sector deepening was a central element of market foundation, and the second chapter previews bank and non-bank financial institution, and mutual and pension fund development. Chapters 3 and 4 introduce the specific analytical tools and topics for the public and private sectors, focusing on key economic performance, policy reform, and political and investment climate considerations. We illustrate these concepts with case studies, and then examine in detail the range and purpose of banks and non-banks as to credit access and foreign participation. Chapter 5 delves into the commercial and institutional dimensions of public capital markets and private equity. On debt it profiles corporate and sovereign insolvency procedures.

Chapter 6 examines these markets in a multi-dimensional, mutually reinforcing global context. It traces interrelationships in foreign direct and portfolio flows and fall-out at times of sudden shocks-crises including the global Covid-19 pandemic and Russia's invasion of Ukraine. The newer actors in official and bilateral financing like "the BRICS Bank"—officially the New Development Bank—are covered while reinforcing the theme of private sector dominance in capital movement. Recent trends, including the growing importance of ESG and sustainable investing and the impact of evolving technology, are explored in Chapter 7 while the final chapter offers our own and evolving industry "crystal ball gazing." The rapid move to FinTech—especially in young frontier markets where the "traditional" brick and mortar routes are often skipped—and the global economic model shift from commodities exports toward services draws on the experience of South Africa-headquartered mobile phone operator MTN. Creation of new industry benchmarks, like MSCI'S ex-China, thematic and tech indices, and hybrid investment products mixing asset classes is another future marker we lay down in closing.

Pulling together 30 + years of all aspects of "Emerging Economies and Financial Markets" in a digestible volume has literally been the challenge of a lifetime. We hope that our firsthand examples and case studies from every continent will inspire undergraduate and graduate students focused on economics and finance, regional studies, global business, and international relations to master real-world tools. Early and mid-level analysts and policy-makers will benefit from reinforcement and fresh perspectives and discover ground for revisiting old assumptions. A perpetual theme for professionals and casual observers in the field is reinvention, and we have enjoyed the sometimes awkward and painful process that comes with learning new approaches and technologies to sharpen judgment. Our writing task is to imbue readers with the same sense of intellectual and real adventure in their particular journey that carries them also for an era of periodic fright from crises but underlying fulfillment.

2

The Early Days of Emerging Market Investing

During the "lost decade" of the 1980s debt crisis and before, capital flows to emerging economies were dominated by multilateral—IMF, World Bank, regional development banks—and bilateral loans and grants for specific projects or to help close debt and deficit gaps. Remittances sent home from workers overseas were another source of foreign inflows, but the totals were negligible. For example, in 1985 funds sent to Mexico totaled USD 1.5 billion while India received USD 2.5 billion, according to World Bank data. Foreign direct investment—dominated at the time by big Western and Japanese companies building manufacturing facilities overseas to benefit from cheaper operating costs—was another source, but again was quite low. In 1985 foreign direct investment in Indonesia was only 0.4 percent of GDP, while in China it was 0.5 percent, although there it spiked to 6 percent a decade later.

Emerging markets as an asset class—debt, equity, and currencies—first appeared on investor radar screens in the mid-1980s as an ultra-specialist niche for investors targeting higher returns than were available in traditional developed markets. For equities, interest developed with the creation of the Emerging Markets Database at the World Bank's capital markets-private sector arm, the International Finance Corporation (IFC), and subsequent release of its stock market index. The launch of the Brady Plan, named after the US Treasury Secretary at the time in 1989 to end the Latin American debt crisis, jump-started activity in bonds swapped from defaulted loans. Before then the loans were traded informally between banks trying to standardize documentation and practice. As investor activity in the debt segment developed, industry professionals formed the Emerging Markets

B. Morrissey and G. Kleiman, *Emerging Economies and Financial Markets*,
https://doi.org/10.1007/978-3-031-85669-3_2

Traders Association in 1990 which was originally called the Lesser Developed Country Debt Traders Association. Foreign investor activity in currency markets developed in line with stocks and bonds, but dedicated benchmarks came decades later. Derivatives markets got lip service as an ultimate step toward futures and options, but application was premature.

International investor interest in emerging markets was a natural outgrowth of a wave of macro-economic stabilization, liberalization, and structural reform programs implemented by policymakers across economies in the aftermath of the 1980s "lost decade." Financial sector development, funded by multilateral and bilateral donors like the World Bank and US Agency for International Development, was a linchpin as privatization and bank-fund manager opening swept across post-communist and developing regions. This chapter details the original building blocks to macro-economic stabilization and market development, designed to attract adventurous foreign investors with large asset portfolios. It covers the genesis of stock markets, local and international bonds, banks and non-bank financial institutions, and mutual/pension funds from the onset of the asset class through the 1990s as the first generation of emerging markets as an accepted, mainstream asset class.

The Pioneer Era

A World Bank Dutch executive who had previously worked at an investment bank in Thailand coined the term emerging markets as a marketing pitch, and initial forays by institutional investors into these generally illiquid, lightly regulated markets were often likened to betting at a casino. Regulation developed more slowly than the markets themselves, and many were rife with insider trading as the supervisory body was also charged with promotion functions. Disclosure standards for listed companies were rudimentary—if they existed at all—and often unenforced. Markets were illiquid in a purely technical sense measured by "turn-over ratio" —trading volume as a percentage of market capitalization—and qualitative indicators. For example, in equities market makers—firms that continuously provide both bid and ask for stocks—and for bonds primary dealers that buy securities directly from the seller and resell to other investors were largely absent. Stock markets, particularly in Asia, were open to foreign investors in theory but many listed shares were still closely held by company management and entailed onerous screening processes.

As financial sector reform and deepening began in earnest in the late 1980s, bilateral and multilateral donors were confronted with the critical issue of "sequencing" securities market development. Building capital markets was seen as "trendy" and a post-communist era triumph, and every country wanted its own stock exchange with the same vigor as a national airline. In the early 1990s, we joined experts in training market participants, regulators, and exchange authorities on what foreign investors desired as it related to the integrated context. Instructors explained that shiny new computers for the exchanges were a sideshow unless the economy was growing, inflation contained, liberalization moving forward, and a legal/regulatory regime in place to protect investor rights. Workshops concentrated on the former Soviet states, including Kyrgyzstan where an exchange was launched with much fanfare in 1994. That year inflation topped 180 percent on an annual basis and the economy contracted 20 percent.[1] The banking sector was still dominated by state-owned institutions and domestic institutional investors were lacking. The Kyrgyz Stock Exchange remains tiny with only 231 listed stocks and market capitalization of just over USD 1.6 billion as of September 2024.[2]

Stock exchange development was often driven by privatization which was both a key "structural adjustment" policy and practical exchange volume driver. Emerging market governments were urged to offload budget-draining, inefficient state-owned companies through direct sale or public offerings. Privatization was contentious in most countries as workers feared job losses and the process was subject to corruption and abuse. Governments often backtracked on privatization programs designed with donor funds fearing social unrest which could not only destabilize the ruling administration but would also derail foreign investor interest as political risk is a major factor in assessing a market's attractiveness. (See Russia case study below). Through the 1980s and 1990s, one study summarized the main methods used and ranked them in descending order based on economic growth and development favorability:

- Sales to high-quality foreign firms
- Sales on domestic capital market via an initial public offering (IPO)
- Sales to domestic businesses/business groups
- Sales to existing managers and/or workers
- Free distribution of shares to the population known as mass privatization[3]

The World Bank until 2008 had a useful privatization database that was discontinued as global activity faded from its heyday. Chile was a leader with its large-scale program launched in 1974 under dictator Augusto Pinochet's business friendly policies, later to include debt-equity swaps for state-owned companies with the 1980s crisis. Latin America and Central and Eastern Europe were the leaders in state company divestitures. Argentina, Peru, and Mexico were in the top 10 from 1988 to 1997 as measured by privatization revenue/average GDP. Argentina alone raised nearly USD 28 billion, while Brazil was ahead if measured by cumulative proceeds.[4] In Central Europe, state ownership fell to 15 percent of GDP by 1999 as Poland's divestiture program brought in close to USD 12 billion, about 10 percent of its GDP, during the 1990s.[5]IMF program conditions were a core catalyst for privatization programs throughout the period. By comparison state selloffs in Asia lagged until the aftermath of the 1997 Financial Crisis. Then they too turned to the Fund for emergency rescue and were faced with cleaning up and offering nationalized banks, a process that lasted another decade. Decades later, after the global Covid-19 pandemic and with the start of the war in Ukraine, privatization of state enterprises again became a feature of IMF programs, with countries ranging from Egypt to Sri Lanka returning to sell-offs to narrow debt and deficit levels. This time, companies are being sold on a case-by-case basis in contrast to some earlier programs that were designed to divest numerous companies all at once through voucher programs or other mass sell-off schemes.

Case Study: Russia's Privatization Pose: The Rise of the "Oligarchs"

Russia's main privatization method was the "mass voucher program" without a previous securities market history like Communist bloc neighbors. It was built on coupon rationing familiarity from Communist times, and every citizen was offered a privatization voucher for a nominal fee of RUB 25 (5 US cents at the prevailing exchange rate). The vouchers were available at local savings banks between October 1992 and January 1993, with almost 97 percent distributed and fully tradable at the outset.[6] Insider investors, often former senior executives—today described as oligarchs—and Kremlin officials, acquired huge blocks allowing them to buy sprawling state commodity companies at huge discounts. The vouchers were actively traded on the many, largely unregulated securities exchanges and the largest at the time, Moscow-based Russian Commodity and Raw Material Exchange, had a volume approaching 100,000 vouchers/day in the first year of trading.[7]

The mass privatization program through 1994 transferred nominal ownership of more than 15,000 state-owned firms with no experience with minority shareholder rights or corporate governance.[8] The ambitious and hasty effort advised by hundreds of Western experts did not accomplish its goal of genuinely spreading share ownership. The head of the privatization program, Anatoly Chubais, had to "compromise" with managers who were given 20 percent stakes in big companies, while employees were awarded an estimated

40 percent, leaving only 20 percent freely sold at the voucher auctions.[9] The state held the remaining 20 percent "golden" share to swing control. The sales did manage to transfer ownership from the government monopoly and met its goal of shedding money-draining enterprises,

As the firms were transformed into private joint stock companies with tradable shares, a market culture emerged. Prior to the end of 1992, shares of the first joint stock companies—banks, investment companies, and merchandise/commodities exchanges—were the only listings in Russia and volume was thin.[10] The first exchanges were established in late 1991, the Moscow International Stock Exchange and Moscow Central Stock Exchange. A year later there were 120 "licensed" stock exchanges throughout the country with no standardization or professional certification.[11] Regulation was lax as the Ministry of Finance and Bank of Russia shared duties for licensing, securities registration, and trading. The same year, the Bank of Russia and Russia's largest commercial banks established the Moscow Interbank Currency Exchange (MICEX) which originally provided a platform to auction and trade short-term government bonds, and later added stocks and foreign exchange.

The voucher program was followed by a more targeted "loans for shares" privatization scheme in 1995 for the country's twelve biggest companies, including half the oil industry in the waning days of the Yeltsin administration.[12] In short, state stakes were offered through tender auctions where the group or person who "promised" to invest the most in the future won control, with up-front cash not the decisive factor. "New money" oligarchs were the runaway winners, tapping bank loans from their own institutions and later reneging on pledges with no government or shareholder accountability mechanism.

Functioning securities commissions with independent mandates for transparency and enforcement were lacking in most emerging markets in the late 1980s/early 1990s. Transparency is a fluid and sometimes qualitative concept but presumes timely and adequate release of basic company balance sheet and management information, and communications with shareholders and creditors. At the same time, markets courting foreign investors had not adopted internationally accepted accounting and auditing standards. Often accounting regimes were barely standardized locally. In 2000 the International Accounting Standards were replaced by International Financial Reporting Standards (IFRS), developed and maintained by the International Accounting Standards Board, which govern how particular types of transactions and events should be reported in financial statements, according to the Certified Financial Analysts Institute. Today these standards are used by more than 100 countries.[13]

One of the prime examples of the rise of a stock exchange without an adequate legal and regulatory environment was Indonesia. In the earliest days of emerging markets investing, it was a popular destination and was regularly described in awkward metaphor as the "Wild West." Insider dealing was routine, and shares rose and fell on rumors rather than company fundamentals. Prior to 1992 when the Jakarta Stock Exchange was privatized, the market was overseen by a supervisory agency, Bapepam, which reported directly to the Ministry of Finance. Post-privatization "Bapepam" became the nominally autonomous Capital Market Supervisory Agency and automated trading was introduced in 1995 as a further advance.[14]

Technology and market infrastructure are also critical components in market development. In the 1990s the "newest" stock and bond markets, largely in Central and Eastern Europe, generally had the best technology and market infrastructure as Western vendors vied to sell state-of-the-art trading and settlement systems. They were funded almost exclusively through bilateral and multilateral donors including the World Bank and the US Agency for International Development, and often in Central and Eastern Europe high-tech trading platforms were purchased off-the-shelf despite incomplete financial sector legal and regulatory reforms, and macro-economic stabilization more broadly. In Romania, for example, donors paid for the purchase and installation of a NASDAQ system with full bells and whistles, and consultants were brought in to train the local investment community on the spanking new RASDAQ. The automated, off-the-shelf system was established in 1996 specifically for Romania's mass privatization program. Under the program's privatization law, privatized companies had to be listed on a stock market and by end-1999 there were more than 5000 listed companies. Domestic and foreign investors had little, if any, knowledge about the profitability or management of these companies. As a result, trading was thin, and the market was ultimately "de-commissioned" two decades later and the listed companies either were bought out by owners or migrated to the Bucharest Stock Exchange which had 85 stocks, and 122 bonds listed by the end of 2023.[15]

While Central and Eastern Europe benefited from donor-funded trading and settlement systems as part of the region's broader transition to a market economy, in many countries trading was done manually with paper and post-trade facilities for settling and securing shares were often dismal. Fund managers preoccupied with safekeeping were known to rent a safety deposit box at the "best" hotel in the city and keep share certificates there between trips. Settlement and registration of ownership was often backlogged for months, which also harmed market liquidity as shares could not be sold. For example, in India as recently as the late 1990s there were delays in verifying shareholding of up to six months despite a two-month maximum period required by law as compared with a T+3 (Trade day+3 days) less than 1-week cycle for most developed markets.[16]

In addition to regulatory and trading obstacles, taxation issues were also a regular challenge for investors. The IFC's early versions of its stock market fact book struggled to keep track of rules for foreign and domestic buyers in updated tables. Often foreign investors were charged higher levies on instruments than domestic investors, or equities were taxed while Treasury notes and longer-term government bonds were exempt as cash-strapped governments raised funds to plug budget gaps. This was referred to as the state "crowding out" the private sector as the government securities offered higher returns. Tax regimes were constantly changed in some markets, which investors saw as a sign that broader economic problems were deeper than officially reported and policymaking was erratic. Whopping headline tax rates, sometimes as high as 30–35 percent, obscured other advantages like high yields.

For example, in 1989 Chile imposed a 35 percent tax at the upper extreme on interest, dividends, and long-term capital gains on listed shares.[17] Despite the high levy investor interest in Chile remained strong in early years as it was about the only market where international institutional investors had large domestic private sector counterparts with which to trade. Chile was the leader in establishing private pension funds in the 1980s and active participants were able to complete large transactions and exercise corporate governance as fiduciaries with their stated responsibility to act in the interest of their investor clients. In Asia, in contrast, institutional investors were generally state-owned pension and insurance companies with the bulk of their assets in commercial bank deposits.

Banks/Non-Bank Financial Institutions

In the late 1980s banks dominated the financial sector in most emerging economies in a lopsided contest with securities markets as measured in standard fashion as a portion of GDP. Access to finance for the private sector was limited largely to conventional bank loans, often through an uncompetitive cartel of state-owned institutions, which stunted economic development. The banks had a large percentage of non-performing loans from state-owned enterprises as government directed lending to these firms and interest rate controls were common. Commercial banking services had yet to embrace fee lines, and investment business was nascent. Local banks and state-owned social security systems and insurance companies were the most prominent institutions alongside retail investors at stock market takeoff stage. Banking sector reform and privatization complemented capital market creation and revival. In Central Europe banking development was most rapid in the then-Big Three—then Czechoslovakia prior to its "Velvet Divorce" in 1993, Hungary and Poland—as large European financial institutions had often started operations even before the fall of the Berlin Wall and maintain controlling system stakes today (See case study-Hungary).

Case Study Hungary: Banking Sector Development

Hungary's banking industry transformed rapidly in the post-communist vanguard both in legal and operational terms. Before then the system was in the hands of a commercial and supervisory monolith formed decades earlier. In 1947 after the Socialists came to power banks and the central bank were nationalized and then liquidated, and a year later the National Bank of Hungary became the sole institution for both business and oversight. On January 1, 1987, the country returned to a two-tier banking system, with multiple commercial arms created over time spun off from the central bank as part of the country's broader transformation to a market economy preceded by experimentation under so-called "goulash communism," named after the dish as communism mixed with free markets.[18]

The state-owned banks created from the earlier era's National Bank were burdened by legacy non-performing loans and meager supervision and regulation through the early 1990s. A 1993 crisis spurred mass privatization the following year with foreign strategic investors able to acquire local banks for the first time. Austrian and Italian lenders had a head start with an established presence, catering the previous decade to their domestic corporate borrowers with cross-border cash and barter trade. These regional giants, including Austria's Raiffeisen and Italy's Unicredit, bet that Hungary's economy would grow quickly as they followed existing clients "eastward," and the country became a launch pad for wider Central Europe franchises.

Even before the landmark breakup and deregulation in the late 1980s, 19 financial institutions were allowed to operate.[19] US giant Citibank opened the first foreign bank in 1985 to conduct East–West business as a specialist niche. In 1990 only 5 percent of the banking system was foreign owned but by the end of the decade the level reached about 70 percent.[20] Foreign banks merged with small domestic counterparts during the privatization process while others established their own operations. While the early 1990s focus was on the corporate sector, they quickly began competing for retail customers. At the time, the Hungarian authorities prioritized and welcomed the so-called "knowledge transfer" from the more sophisticated overseas-based institutions as much as their capital to diversify the financial sector's product and technology base and provide more credit to the productive economy. The Bank for International Settlements—the so-called "bank for central banks" based in Switzerland—in a retrospective, noted that by allowing foreign banks entry and participation in the privatization process, the sector's "operation resembled that of developed economies in many aspects by the end of the 1990s."[21]

Banks and non-banks were "stuffed" with central governments' bonds and Treasury bills as few investment alternatives were available, and official prudential guidelines mandated these government paper holdings. Banks were routinely told which sectors they should lend to, typically zombie, highly indebted state-owned enterprises. The mandatory lending—which still occurs in China as the biggest and most notable example—has since been phased out, but institutional investors in many major markets still must maintain large government asset weightings. As the 1980s privatization impetus inspired by the United Kingdom's Margaret Thatcher took hold across the developing world, bank clean-up and stabilization was heavily geared at first to allowing new domestic and foreign entrants. The regulatory framework needed upgrading both in terms of outside inspection and internal risk management, with a flurry of new generation banking laws introduced.

Emerging Market Bonds

Bonds, sovereign and corporate, from emerging economies date back centuries. In fact, our office has a bond from Istanbul's famous Pera Palas Hotel—Agatha Christie wrote "Murder on the Orient Express" there—from 1922. However, after the world wars through the mid-twentieth century, most were in default, although there are numerous collectors of paper certificates as true works of art. Investors can still be found who have not given up on ancient payment promises, and they organize to press governments now in power. For example, after the Russian revolution in 1917 the Soviet government defaulted on Czarist bonds which had been widely bought in France. After the collapse of the USSR, Moscow wanted to market new bonds in France and the French government negotiated a settlement with Russia requiring Moscow to repay a portion of the defaulted bonds and French citizens in 2001 received a share of the recovered debt.

Today's vibrant emerging bond markets date from Latin America's "lost decade" of the 1980s. "Less developed countries" (LDCs), as they were then derisively called, in the region and elsewhere—including Cote d'Ivoire and Nigeria—were unable to service billions of dollars in loans owed to so-called "money center" commercial banks, mainly in the US and Europe. High interest rates in double digits and low commodity prices had resulted in regular rounds of loan rescheduling, with the hope over the decade that economic growth would bounce back to allow regular debt servicing. By the end of the decade, it was clear that repeated reworking of bank loans was not going to succeed, and that outright debt relief was the only answer. In

March 1989, then US Treasury Secretary Nicholas Brady unveiled the "Brady Plan." The program expanded on an earlier one launched by Brady's predecessor James Baker in 1985 by including options for voluntary debt and debt servicing restructuring.

The Brady Plan entailed restructuring bank loans into tradable securities with both principal and interest guarantees, and the exercise was linked to parallel IMF economic reform programs to ensure debt sustainability. Brady bonds were officially launched when Mexico introduced the first batch in March of 1990. (See case study) Although each country had a different experience, essentially banks had two basic choices: Par bonds with below-market interest rates or Discount bonds which offered the exchange at 30–50 percent below the value of the loans. Banks bought the idea as both 30-year options were denominated in US dollars and partially backed by US Treasuries.

Case Study: Mexico's a la Carte Brady Bonds

Mexico's Brady bond exchange in 1990 came after eight years of struggling for a comprehensive Latin America sovereign bankruptcy solution. In 1982 the country told its international bank creditors that it could not meet its loan obligations. Foreign exchange reserves were perilously low with only enough cash to cover 2.9 months of imports, below the internationally accepted critical 3-month threshold deemed adequate. In 1981 alone external debt surged nearly 50 percent to USD 75 billion, 45 percent of GDP, with 30 percent due in less than a year.[22] Mexico's announcement in 1982 marked the start of the "Lost Decade" for the region. The next 10 years were spent negotiating with banks and seeking official assistance which included advance payment for oil sales and bridge loans. The country rescheduled USD 1 billion of its bilateral "Paris Club Debt" with 15 developed countries.[23]

By 1987 external debt/GDP had surged to 75 percent. Late that year the government announced a voluntary debt conversion program to exchange defaulted loans for a newly issued 20-year bond with the principal backed by US Treasury bonds in an early trial of the technique. The exchange was widely seen as a failure as it raised less than the USD 10 billion level the government had planned.[24]

Two years later then-US Treasury Secretary Nicholas Brady proposed the framework for what came to be known as "Brady Bonds." After a year of negotiations with bank creditors in global financial centers grouped as the "London Club," USD 48.9 billion in Mexican debt was exchanged for three options in newly issued 30-year bonds:

- "Par bonds" at face value in one of 10 Western currencies paying 6.25 percent
- "Discount bonds" paying a market-based interest rate but at 35 percent less than face value in the same 10 currencies[25]
- "New money" bonds issued at par conditional on fresh money to Mexico public sector borrowers or to a trade credit facility.[26]

The par and discount bonds were the most popular, with banks holding 47 percent and 40 percent of the debt choosing them, and only 13 percent taking the "new money" option.[27] The lack of enthusiasm for the last choice was a reflection of years of failed efforts when it featured as the main tool in an analogy to US corporate bankruptcy "debtor in possession" financing.

Principal payment on the new securities was backed by 30-year US Treasuries placed in escrow at the New York Federal Reserve Bank, and the first 18 months of interest payments were also collateralized there. The escrow account totaled about USD 7 billion, financed in part by loans from the World Bank, IMF, and Japan, with the rest coming from Mexican government reserves.[28]

In the first full year of trading in 1991, Mexico's Brady bonds returned 38.95 percent, and then 13 percent and 31 percent the next two years before full-fledged indices tracking emerging market bond returns were developed.[29] Ultimately 17 countries undertook these restructurings with the stock of USD-denominated Brady bonds peaking at USD 156 billion in March 1997.[30]

As the first Brady bond issuer, Mexico was also the first to "retire" the instruments after buybacks and exchanges for fresh Eurobonds issued in the global market in US dollars without a guarantee. The first non-secured Eurobonds were issued in 1999, when it sold EUR 400 million in 7-year paper. When Mexico first issued its Brady bonds its sovereign debt rating from Moody's—one of the "Big Three" global credit ratings agencies along with Standard & Poor's and Fitch—was firmly in the "junk" category at Ba2, indicating the potential threat of inability to repay the bond. As they were phased out it was rated Baa2 with a "positive" outlook, in the "safe" investment grade category as of 2000.

The launch of liquid "safe" Brady bonds was the catalyst for the development of emerging market fixed income as an entire asset class. Banks took the lead in finalizing trading procedures under the auspices of the industry body EMTA. Ultimately Brady bond success was underscored as they were retired and exchanged for cheaper Eurobonds that did not require US Treasury guarantees as economies transformed with sovereign credit ratings raised to match. Brady bonds dominated emerging market debt trading in the 1990s—accounting for 61 percent of the USD 1.68 billion total in 1994—but a decade later their share in turnover had dropped to about 2 percent[31] and today there are none.

After the launch of Brady bonds in US dollars, global bond investors expanded their search for yield to securities issued in emerging markets' local currency. At the time no private or public organization tracked this "sub-asset class" or compiled a rough reference, and our firm was the first to publish a domestic instrument guide before the IFC also expanded into the area. Mexico, at the time the biggest and most liquid and researched market, was the first to attract overseas buyers to its local bond market. The Mexican peso was seen as virtually risk-free under its "crawling peg" exchange rate against the dollar, and foreign exchange reserves were ample at first. By end-1993 foreign investors held 70 percent of double-digit-yielding cetes, short-term treasury certificates denominated in pesos. A year later they held 87 percent in Tesobonos, which were short-term public debt instruments redeemable in pesos but denominated in dollars.[32] During this period of growing local debt market interest some investors also ventured much further afield in their search for yield. For example, we had adventuresome clients investing in treasury bills in copper-rich Zambia (See case study).

Case Study Zambia: Local Treasury Bills

Following the election of the Movement for Multiparty Democracy in Zambia in 1991, years of state domination over the economy under independence leader President Kaunda were overturned under strict IMF loan guidance. The foreign exchange market and interest rates were liberalized in 1992/3 and treasury bill auctions introduced in January 1993 with rates market determined, rather than set by the authorities.[33] With inflation in triple digits—peaking at an annual rate of 183 percent in 1993—the government acted to bring down prices with newfound austerity by introducing a "cash budget" to cover all spending except for debt service, enabling a primary balance—a surplus before debt payments—which burnished its fiscal credentials.

In early-1994 a London-based client trading at his bank's proprietary desk—to make money internally and not for clients—called to ask about investing in short-term Zambian Treasury bills which could soar in value with fiscal turnaround. By then the economy had partially stabilized with inflation into double digits. At the same time, global copper prices—Zambia's largest export and source of foreign exchange—were rebounding sharply after falling a year earlier and had surged 18 percent in just a few months.[34] The rally in copper prices buoyed the local currency, the kwacha, as well as the country's budget balance. Although numerous inquiries poured in about investing in local T-bill markets in Latin America and Central Europe which inspired our firm to compile dedicated publications, Zambia was in a different geography with a tiny market compared with Mexico or Poland which were by far the most popular due to their size and liquidity.

The country offered paper with maturities of 28, 91, and 182 days. Investors were attracted to both the high yields and strengthening currency. T-Bills were sold weekly through a competitive auction, and the local banks were virtually the only buyers and foreign investors had to work through them to overcome all the purchase and settlement complications. Despite a 15 percent withholding tax, the 85.4 percent yield on 91-day bills was enticing for a small band of first movers on falling inflation and a strengthening currency.[35] While the market was illiquid with buyers typically holding investments until maturity, occasionally large-scale traders joined for yield pick-up as winning strategy. Along with South Africa's post-apartheid turn after the racist regime was dismantled in the early 1990s, it inspired exploration of the wider Sub-Sahara investment universe.

Stock Exchanges

Many emerging markets—including Brazil, Egypt, India, and Turkey—have stock exchanges that date back to the 1800s. However, by the early 1980s most were nascent and foreign and domestic investor interest was absent. The World Bank's International Finance Corporation (IFC) in 1981 developed the Emerging Markets Database, the first to provide detailed statistics. Based in the Capital Markets Department, it was designed to meet the IFC's mandate "to promote the economic growth of its developing member countries through private investment."[36] Originally the IFC indices covered only 10 markets and the 10–20 most traded companies in each, with the individual country and composite indices calculated only once a year based on month-end prices. By 1987 the IFC had increased coverage to 17 markets, revamped it methodology from equal company to market capitalization weighting, and was publishing Latin American and Asian regional indices monthly with a 30-day lag.

The IFC was not the only game in town, as other index providers and investment houses rushed to develop benchmarks to measure stock market performance as investor interest grew. In January 1988, MSCI launched its Emerging Markets Index (MSCI EM) with ten countries. The group, in its 20-year retrospective, noted that "it was the first comprehensive and consistent investable benchmark index for this component of global equity markets."[37] Only 10 markets were included at first, dominated by Malaysia which accounted for almost 20 percent. When the MSCI EM Index was launched, the stocks included less than 1 percent of the world's investable equity market capitalization.[38] Today the main MSCI EM Index covers 24 markets with more than 1400 companies.

In the 1980s stock exchanges had numerous legal restrictions on foreign investors. At end-1989, for example, only six markets offered international buyers unlimited investment and free repatriation of income and capital.[39] Buying stocks in certain "strategic" industries—often including financial sector shares—required registration with a government agency and capital had to stay in place for a set period. Some markets allowed only approved custom foreign funds or designated special classes of shares. For example, the Korea Fund was launched in 1984 to offer foreign investors access to stocks in the growing economy and today the Allianz Global-managed vehicle still trades on the New York Stock Exchange. As with market development and coverage more broadly, the World Bank's IFC arm was instrumental in working with private sector counterparts to broaden investment opportunities. In addition to assisting with creation and launch of the Korea Fund, the first global emerging market equity fund was launched with IFC assistance by Capital Group for institutional investors.[40] The first global emerging markets fund for retail investors was launched in 1987: the Templeton Emerging Market Fund was listed on the NYSE, managed for years by the legendary investor Dr. Mark Mobius. A 2022 interview referred to the now octogenarian Mobius as "the Michael Jordan of emerging market investing," noting that if emerging markets investing had a hall of fame, he would be "a first ballot, unanimous entry."[41]

By the early 1990s interest in emerging stock markets had taken hold with soaring returns. In 1991 five markets in the IFC Global Indices had annual returns in triple digits in US dollar terms, topped by Argentina which advanced 393.3 percent on expectations of the imminent privatization of its oil giant YPF which was listed in Buenos Aires and New York in 1993. YPF was renationalized in 2012 as part of a broader reimposition of state control over the economy which included a government take-over of the private pension system (Fig. 2.1).

Foreign institutional investors launched dozens of mutual funds and the era of firsthand "kick the tires" research—visiting government officials, company management, and stock markets in "exotic" locales—began in earnest. Long-term institutional money from global pension funds and insurance companies was reluctant to embrace the asset class due to both fiduciary guidelines—most managers did not have the required management track record, usually three years, due to the asset class's recent emergence—and their generally slower decision-making process. Startup exposure was folded into a non-traditional "global" bucket, as a separate category had yet to

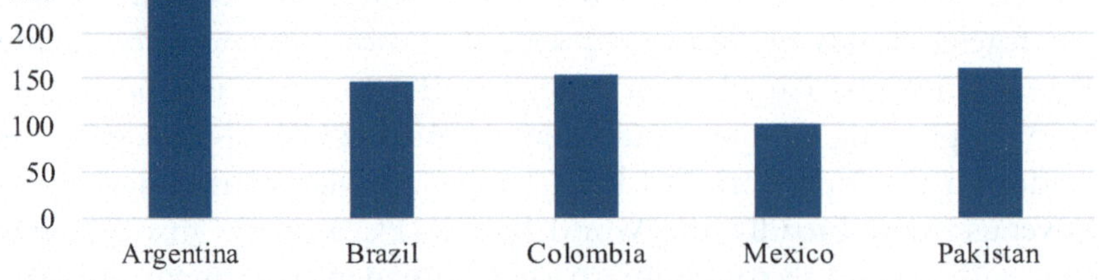

Fig. 2.1 1991 IFCG Price Index (annual % change in USD) (*Source* Emerging Stock markets Factbook 1996, International Finance Corporation)

appear for the fringe allocation. Regular conferences on investing in emerging markets attempted to draw in this audience as a cottage industry. Standing events were held in New York, Washington, London, and elsewhere. Despite successive crashes from the mid-1990s—from the "tequila" crisis in Mexico, to the Asian Financial Crisis through Russia's debt default—the number of mutual funds exploded, more than doubling from the mid-1990s through the end of the decade.[42] By 2024 there were 5605 mutual funds and Exchange Traded Funds with USD 2,75 trillion in assets under management targeting single country, regional and global emerging stock markets, according to fund tracker EPFR.

Institutional Investor Private Base

In the late 1980s, domestic institutional investors in the emerging economies were mainly state-owned insurance companies and pension funds. Regulation for these groups was uneven, often with overlapping supervisors and regulatory frameworks, or non-existent outside an extension of central bank normal duties. Latin America and Central Europe leapfrogged Asia with the launch of new, private contractual savings schemes. The two regions were aided by vast amounts of donor funding and technical assistance to develop private pension, insurance, and mutual fund industries. Poland and Hungary were the first in Central Europe to pilot private pensions to replace budget-draining, state-run social security regimes. In Poland proceeds from the privatization of 50 state-owned companies were used to underwrite the pension reform strategy, and by 2001 there were 21 private pension funds with assets under management at USD 2 billion as active institutional investors. Warsaw also inaugurated mutual funds in the region, as the aptly named Boston-based Pioneer Group brought a popular vehicle for retail investors in the early 1990s and quickly became the top equity market holder. The Pioneer First Polish Trust Company was created, introduced, and managed by Polish-American Alicja Malecka, who had extensive experience managing funds in Tokyo and New York and was recruited to head the company's Warsaw office. Several years after launching the first retail mutual fund, the group created the country's inaugural venture capital fund designed to encourage foreign institutional investors to invest in small- and medium-sized companies. Poland and Hungary designed commercial and regulatory features in line with European Union norms as they waited to become EU members in 2004.[43]

Across Latin America the insurance sector was and largely continues to be dominated by local and international banks. They either own their own insurance subsidiaries or sell products from major global giants like MetLife. In Mexico, nearly a decade after the banking sector was nationalized in 1982, the state re-privatized the sector. After licenses were awarded, the big banks—Bancomer, Banorte, etc. —established full-service groups which included pension funds and insurers. In Brazil, the pension and insurance industries did not take off until hyperinflation was contained: inflation hit 2700 percent on an annual basis in March 1990.[44] In the mid-1980s as the country grappled with debt and deficit crises, the insurance and pension market combined totaled only 0.8 percent of GDP, and by the end of the 1990s it was still small at just over 2 percent.[45]

In Asia, domestic institutional investors have a long history of state control and pervasive influence. In the private sector, they can be part of a complex cross-shareholding structure, as in the chaebol in South Korea, but regularly follow official portfolio allocation instructions. As a result, most pension and insurance fund assets were placed in bank deposits. In addition to owning pension, insurance, and mutual fund companies, governments in the region actively intervened in the stock and bond markets through the 1990s through dedicated support funds. The state was a major player in the mutual fund industry as it developed. In Malaysia there were 35 fund management companies with total net assets of just over 10 percent of stock market capitalization by the end of the 1990s. The government ran 30 of the funds which accounted for about 70 percent of the industry's net assets.[46] India was an extreme case of a duopoly state-run insurance sector—Life Insurance Corporation (LIC) and General Insurance Corporation—in the 1980s and 1990s. The two companies were the only participants and their own regulators, a recipe for conflict of interest and securities market distortions. India's life insurance market was liberalized in 2000 with private players allowed, but it was not until 2022 that only a tiny portion of LIC's shares were floated on the local stock exchange.

Conclusion

This brief overview of the trailblazing experience intends to serve twin purposes of introducing concepts and themes for later exploration in separate chapters and conveying a sense of the excitement and trial and error at the foundation that has carried through over three decades. For professionals present at the creation career-long relationships were formed, and the field's regular re-invention offers that chance for successive cohorts. The signature dates of Brady Bond and first country stock fund launch are recalled to this day, and the pillars of sound economic and monetary policy and market infrastructure/institution building are constants guiding evaluation whether the goal is to make money or spur economic development change. A delicate balancing act of drawing lessons from the past as frameworks constantly evolve is in order that will reach full illustration over the course of this book, so that readers absorb both the pioneer spirit and sober reflection that characterize lengthy, successful analyst track records.

Key Take-Aways:

- Prior to the rise of emerging markets as an asset class, capital flows were dominated by commercial bank loans, bilateral and multilateral lending, foreign direct investment by developed country-domiciled manufacturers, and remittances from citizens working overseas.
- Early development of emerging stock and bond markets, and the asset class as a whole, was instigated by policymakers seeking to spur broader economic transformation. The US Treasury Department's moves to address the 1980s "LDC" debt market crisis resulted in emerging market bonds, while attracting foreign capital for private sector development underpinned the International Finance Corporation's work on stock market creation.
- Foreign institutional investor interest surged in the early 1990s with dozens of mutual funds launched although the asset class was not fully embraced by long-term investors from global pension funds and insurance companies for nearly another decade.
- Many early macro-economic and market liberalization moves were ultimately undermined and/or totally dismantled by domestic political considerations. However, some like privatization of zombie state-owned companies, have been re-introduced to address gaping debt and deficit issues in the wake of the global pandemic and war in Ukraine, with IMF programs again a distinct factor.

Notes

1. The World Bank, Kyrgyz Republic, "GDP Growth (annual %)," https://data.worldbank.org/country/kyrgyz-republic?view=chart.
2. Asia Frontier Capital, Kyrgyzstan Factsheet, September 2024, https://www.asiafrontiercapital.com/

3. Saul Estrin and Adeline Pelletier, "Privatization in developing countries: what are the lessons of recent experience?" *World Bank Research Observer* Vol. 33, (2018) 65–102, www.eprints.lse.ec.uk/87348/1/Estrin_Privatization.
4. Paul Cook and Yuichiro Uchida, "Privatisation and Economic Growth in Developing Countries," Centre on Regulation and Competition: Working Paper, No. 7, 29 pp. University of Manchester, UK, October 2001, https://assets.publishing.service.gov.uk/media/57a08d6140f0b64974001816/CRCwp7.pdf.
5. Ladan Mahboodi, "Recent Privatization Trends," Corporate Affairs Division, OECD, 2000, p.49, www.oecd.org/daf/corporategovernance
6. Maxim Boycko, Andrei Shleifer, and Robert W. Vishney, "Privatizing Russia," *Brookings Papers on Economic Activity* 2 (1993): 139–192, https://scholar.harvard.edu/files/shleifer/files/privatizing_russia.pdf.
7. Boycko, Schleifer, and Vishney.
8. John Nellis, "Time to Rethink Privatization in Transition Economies?" *Finance & Development: A quarterly magazine of the IMF*, Vol 36, Number 2, June 1999, https://www.imf.org/external/pubs/ft/fandd/1999/06/nellis.htm.
9. Anders Aslund, "Let's Get Privatization Right this Time Around," Op-ed in *Moscow Times*, re-printed by Peterson Institute for International Economics, August 18, 2010, https://www.piie.com/commentary/op-eds/lets-get-privatization-right-time-around.
10. Boris Rubtsov, "The Russian Securities Market: 20 Years of Development," Financial University under the Government of the Russian Federation, November 2013 https://publishup.uni-potsdam.de/opus4-ubp/frontdoor/deliver/index/docId/6640/file/EFC_Rubtsov_105_118.pdf.
11. Rubtsov.
12. Aslund, "Let's Get Privatization Right".
13. https://cfainstitute.org
14. Corporate Finance Institute Team, "Jakarta Stock Exchange (JSX)," updated January 30, 2021, https://corporatefinanceinstitute.com/resources/knowledge/trading-investing/jakarta-stock-exchange-jsx/.
15. Federation of Eurasian Stock Exchanges Yearbook 2023, https://feas.org/yearbooks/
16. Kleiman International Consultants client analysis prepared February 2000.
17. International Finance Corporation, *Emerging Stock Markets Factbook: 1990* (Washington, DC, 1990).

18. Magyar Nemzeti Bank, Central Bank, "The history of the central bank," https://www.mnb.hu/web/a-jegybank.
19. Heike Jons, "Foreign banks are branching out: changing geographies of Hungarian banking, 1987–1999," Transformations in Hungary: Essays in Economy and Society, Physica-Verlag, January 2001, www.repository.lboro.ac.uk/articles/foreign_banks_are_branching_
20. Adam Banai, Julia Kiraly and Marton Nagu, "The demise of the halcyon days in Hungary: "foreign" and "local" banks—before and after the crisis," Bank for International Settlements, BIS papers No. 54, p. 195–199, www.bis.org/publ/bppdf/bispap54.pdf
21. Banai, Kiraly, and Nagu.
22. Claudio M. Loser and Eliot Kalter, Mexico: The strategy to achieve sustained economic growth, February 15, 1992, International Monetary Fund, pp. 98, https://doi.org/10.5089/9781557753120.084.
23. Loser and Kalter.
24. Loser and Kalter.
25. Jean-Claude Berthelemy & Robert Lensink, "An Assessment of the Brady Plan Agreements," OECD Development Centre, Working Paper No. 67, May 1992, www.oecd.org/development/pgd/1919358.pdf.
26. Berthelemy and Lensink.
27. Berthelemy and Lensink.
28. Berthelemy and Lensink.
29. www.jpmorgan.com
30. Rhoda Weeks-Brown & Martin Muhleisen, "The IMF 30 Years After Brady," IMF Blog, April 11, 2019, The IMF 30 Years After Brady.
31. EMTA: Trade Association for the Emerging Markets, "The Brady Plan," https://emta.org/em-background/the-brady-plan/
32. Nora Lustig, "The Mexican Peso Crisis: The Foreseeable and the Surprise," Brooking Institution, June 1, 1995, https://www.brookings.edu/research/the-mexican-peso-crisis-the-foreseeable-and-the-surprise/.
33. Martin Brownbridge, "Financial Policies and the Banking System in Zambia," Institute of Development Studies Working Paper 32, 1996. https://www.ids.ac.uk/download.php?file=files/Wp32.pdf
34. Reuters, "Copper prices jump again, rising 18% since January," *The New York Times* (Business, March 17, 1994): D15. www.nytimes.com/1994/03/17/business/futures-markets-copper-price-jump-again-rising-18-since-january.html.

35. Martin Brownbridge, "Financial Policies and the Banking System in Zambia," Institute of Development Studies Working Paper 32, 1996. https://www.ids.ac.uk/download.php?file=files/Wp32.pdf
36. International Finance Corporation, *Emerging Stock Markets Factbook: 1990* (Washington, DC, 1990).
37. MSCI Barra, "Emerging Markets: A 20-year Perspective," 2008, https://www.msci.com/documents/10199/dbc19f82-595d-4a2c-bd2d-22b593d611e5.
38. Ben Johnson, CFA, "The Dramatic Evolution of Emerging Markets," Morningstar, January 26, 2021 https://www.morningstar.com/articles/1018645/the-dramatic-evolution-of-emerging-markets
39. The markets were: Indonesia, Jordan, Malaysia, Portugal, Turkey, and Argentina. Source: International Finance Corporation, *Emerging Stock Markets Factbook: 1990* (Washington, DC, 1990).
40. https://www.capitalgroup.com/institutions/gb/en/strategies/em.html
41. Afshin Molavi, "The Michael Jordan of Emerging Markets Investing: A Conversation with Mark Mobius," Emerging World, January 9, 2022, https://eworld.substack.com/p/the-michael-jordan-of-emerging-markets.
42. Data provided directly by request, 401 funds 12/31/1996 and 966 12/31/1999, https://financialintelligence.informa.com/epfr
43. Kleiman International client analysis prepared June 18,2001.
44. James Brooke, "War on Inflation Gives a Quick Jolt to Brazil Economy," *The New York Times*, March 23, 1990: 1.
45. Ministry of Economy, Brazilian Insurance Market Overview, www.susep.gov.br/english-susep/insurance
46. Kleiman International client analysis prepared May 18, 2001.

3

Framing the Analysis Basics: Economic Performance, Policy, Institutions

In this chapter we introduce the basic tools, qualitative and quantitative, essential to understand for investors, multilateral lenders, and industry practitioners assessing emerging economies and financial markets. The range of macro-economic issues to consider—most easily tracked—is vast and we winnow to the core cross-section. The subjective factors like the legal and regulatory framework from both written laws/regulation and actual implementation are not as hard and fast but often decisive in identifying below the radar screen vulnerabilities. As seen in Poland in recent years under the ruling right-wing Law and Justice Party (PiS), an historic record of structural reform efforts including private pensions can be undone by a shift in politics. (see case study below).

Investors, donors, and ratings agencies evaluate markets for different reasons, but work from a common foundation. Rating agencies seek to estimate the probability of default and willingness to pay. In addition to running out of cash to service debt, some countries have been forced into default by international sanctions. A recent example is Russia where sanctions due to its war in Ukraine resulted in a default on its external debt in June 2022 for the first time since 1918. While not typical, countries have defaulted despite having adequate funds to service obligations. In 2008 Ecuador defaulted on external debt payment having declared the obligations "illegitimate" since they were incurred under earlier administrations.[1] In a unique move, a year later the Ecuadoran government bought back almost all of the defaulted debt at a very discounted rate so it could resume relations with commercial and official creditors. Raters' basic sovereign assessment covers income levels, growth prospects, and economic diversity/volatility, and calculations

B. Morrissey and G. Kleiman, *Emerging Economies and Financial Markets*,
https://doi.org/10.1007/978-3-031-85669-3_3

drill down into external liquidity and fiscal flexibility. Donors—including the World Bank, IMF, regional development banks, and bilateral providers such as the US Agency for International Development and the UK's Department for International Development—focus in a broad sense on economic programs in order to deliver budget and balance of payments and project/technical assistance. The IMF is called in as lender of last resort when a country runs into trouble, while other organizations target specific sectors and foreign trade priorities. Investors' mission is the simplest but often most confounding in practice: to make money for themselves and clients in local and international stocks, bonds, derivatives, and currencies.

Case Study: Poland's Private Pension Puncture

In 1999 Poland introduced compulsory private pension funds (OFEs) based largely on the successful Chilean model created nearly two decades earlier. In the first decade of Central Europe's transition to a market economy, the funds were viewed as key to the development of vibrant, local capital markets by regional governments and bilateral and multilateral donors. The government transferred cash to the new funds that were converted into Treasury bonds, and the 21 new vehicles were also given a portion of the 19.5 percent social security payroll tax. They were not perfect: citizens complained of high management fees and managers objected to strict regulations which they said discouraged risk-taking.[2] From 1999 through 2012 the OFEs grew, spurring development of the country's stock and bond markets. By 2013 OFEs had assets under management of 17 percent of GDP, and they held about 30 percent of total assets in listed stocks on the Warsaw Stock Exchange which had become the biggest and most liquid in the region.[3] The exchange was planning to become a regional center and was working toward attracting numerous listings from Ukraine and elsewhere.[4] At end-2012, the 14 remaining OFEs held 51.1% of assets in government bonds.[5] A real net return on a contribution made in 1999 and held through 2012 averaged 6.6 percent annually, according to a government analysis in 2013.[6]

In September 2013, then Prime Minister Donald Tusk, running for re-election and confronted with public debt level reaching the constitutionally mandated ceiling of 55 percent of GDP and a massive 4.8 percent of GDP budget deficit, announced the government would seize the USD 51 billion of government bonds held by the OFEs. The securities were transferred from the private funds back into the state-run pay-as-you-go system and then canceled. While the move did return the budget to surplus in 2014, it drew sharp criticism from the financial industry and the architect of the country's post-communist economic reforms, Leszek Balcerowicz, who said seizing private pension savings to "cure public finances is a medicine that is worse than the illness."[7] In 2019, the ruling nationalist Law and Justice Party totally reversed the final vestiges of private pension funds. All private pension fund assets were transferred to 15.8 million individual retirement accounts worth some USD 43 billion with a fee of 15 percent. As under the previous regime, the move helped the government balance the budget and meet campaign promises to pay a "bonus" 13th month pension.[8]

The reversal of immediate post-communist liberalization under two ideologically opposite political parties after the turn of the century dried up both foreign investor interest—most OFE managers were subsidiaries of global financial services giants like MetLife—and stock market liquidity. Although the end of the private pension scheme solved immediate funding needs for the government, it did not remedy the pension crisis in one of the countries with the lowest birthrates in the European Union. As the population ages, the government will have to scramble to fund pensions that are now the state's responsibility.

Quantifiable Macro-Economic Issues: The First Step in Economic Assessments

Assessing emerging markets begins with basic macro-economic data falling into two broad categories—domestic and external. Donors, investors, ratings agencies, and policymakers routinely use both for assessing the overall health of a country, although the relative importance of the buckets and their components have constantly shifted the past few decades. Typically, emerging markets economies grow faster than developed country counterparts. Gross domestic product—the total value of goods and services produced by a country—is the headline measure. It is readily accessed, with governments releasing numbers on a monthly or quarterly basis, generally with short time lags. Growth of 3–5 percent is the current standard, half the early heyday of the asset class with routine near double digit takeoff as economies were reformed and liberalized. A September 2022 World Bank study warned of the risk of a global recession which did not occur and "a string of financial crises in emerging market and developing economies that would do them lasting harm" as central banks around the world raise interest rates with "a degree of synchronicity not seen over the past five decades." Despite the inflation-induced warning, the study's historical data show that when global GDP records a 0.5 percent contraction, emerging economies outperformed advanced counterparts with growth of 1.4 percent versus contraction of 1.3 percent, respectively. Even during the Covid downturn in 2020 when advanced economies contracted 4.6 percent, the downturn in emerging markets was far less severe at 1.6 percent. Despite higher inflation and advanced country post-Covid interest rate hikes, the World Bank projects that emerging economies will grow about 2 percent faster than developed counterparts in the coming years.[9]

In some countries fortunes are hostage to natural events, and the composition of GDP in terms of industry, services, consumption, and investment provides the broader context. For example, in Morocco economic growth or contraction is a function of good rains or drought in any given year, although agriculture accounts for just over one-tenth of economic output.[10] Similarly in India annual monsoon rains drive results. More than half the population is employed in the agricultural sector, which accounts for almost one-fifth of GDP. Weather is already an overriding factor for many commodity producers and will be for the rest of the group as climate change worsens.

The "informal" economy is often ignored even as it is about one-third of GDP in emerging markets and not included in official data, according to the World Bank.[11] [12] As a result, many emerging economies are far larger than official data indicates. In South Asia, more than 80 percent of workers and 90 percent of companies are in the category and often prefer it to avoid paying taxes.[13] In addition to avoiding government levies, workers in the informal economy traditionally have not had access to the formal economy, notably the financial system. The rapid adoption of fintech this decade is, however, enabling a much larger portion of the population—notably rural residents often far from established institutions—to access finance.

A second perennial macro-economic data series monitored closely by public and private sector analysts is inflation. Historically many emerging markets have suffered from rising prices, often from the feed-through from depreciating currencies which makes imported goods more expensive. The composition of the basket in consumer price indices (CPI) is a key determinant. Turkey has long suffered from regular bouts of high inflation. It is an energy importer and fuel, housing, and transportation together account for 30 percent of CPI.[14] In India food and beverages account for more than 45 percent.[15] Coverage of India's annual monsoons regularly extrapolates for food inflation, with some analysts predicting CPI data based on the price of onions in major cities across the country. Over decades central banks have adopted inflation targeting—long a standard in developed economies—with the preferred range in the low single digits, but volatility in key components can frustrate the task (See case study: Turkey).

Case Study: Turkey's Endless Inflation Saga

As with serial defaulter Argentina's runaway inflation, Turkey's history tends to repeat itself. One of the authors was a high school foreign exchange student in Turkey in 1979–80, living with a family in Izmit on the bay of the Sea of Marmara. With no knowledge or understanding of economics at the time, crisis gravity was missed. The foreign exchange program gave each student 1,000 Turkish lira a month for spending money. In September of 1979, the amount allowed frugal students to splurge on street vendor snacks, the occasional Nescafe, and even the "International Herald Tribune" or "Time" magazine. Nescafe had replaced traditional Turkish coffee entirely as it was all exported because the government was broke, and reserves were near zero. By year-end 1979 inflation had reached triple digits and essential goods from abroad disappeared, with the lira fixed at 35/dollar.

Turkey had been through a succession of coalition governments through the 1970s and in late 1979 a new one came to power amid regular worker strikes and rising street violence between leftist and nationalists which killed 5,000 people.[16] Inheriting economic chaos, the government's first move was to devalue the lira from 35/USD to 70/USD, with intent to regularly adjust the exchange rate to reflect the difference between domestic and foreign inflation.[17] This experience with cost spiral and loss of purchasing power was personally crushing before they entered professional calling. By the time of departure in July of 1980 the entire group of international exchange students was as insolvent as the country. Two months later the military overthrew the elected government, the third coup since the country's independence in 1923.

Economic crises since then feature constantly with inflation and exchange rate entanglement. President Erdogan is a self-described "enemy of interest rates." He erroneously believes that high interest rates cause inflation, and in less than three years fired three central bank governors after they hiked rates in defiance to foster price and currency stability. As we write, inflation hovers in the 50 percent range and the lira has lost nearly 500 percent against the US dollar since the start of the decade. The currency depreciation and inflation level continue to deter many investors even after President Erdogan, re-elected for a third term in mid-2023, appointed a "market friendly," Wall Street-respected, economic team (Fig. 3.1).

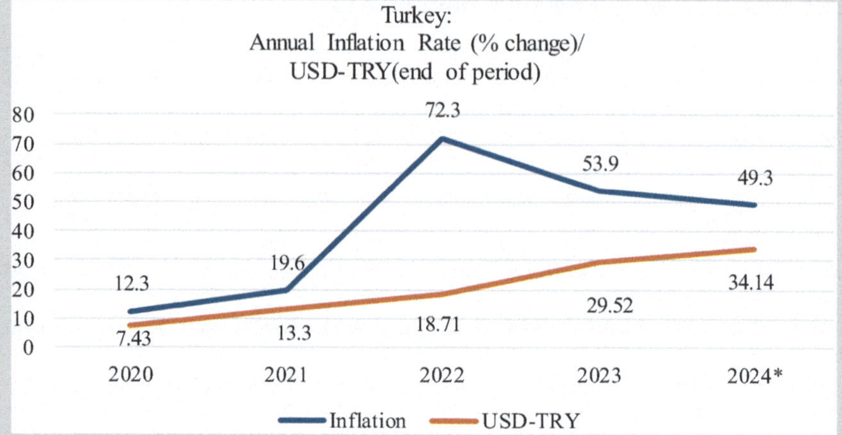

Fig. 3.1 Turkey: Annual Inflation Rate (% change)/USD-TRY(end of period) (*Sources* IMF DataMapper, Bloomberg)

Turkey is hostage to fossil fuel imports: 93 percent of oil and 99 percent of gas are sourced from abroad.[18] Prior to the outbreak of war in 2022, it bought 70 percent of wheat from Russia and 15 percent from Ukraine with the supply squeeze also cramping inputs as Turkey is one of the largest flour and pasta exporters globally.[19]

After assessing growth and price data for a country, public and private analysts and policymakers examine fiscal and monetary policies. During the 2020 global pandemic, fiscal deficits ballooned as the IMF retreated from its traditional conservative stance and encouraged countries to ramp up spending to lessen the impact of the crisis on the population. Deficits spiked for healthcare and social transfers, as Brazil for example suspended deficit rules and handed cash to poor citizens. (See case study). Fiscal indicators are readily available through government and donor websites, including the primary balance, the deficit or surplus excluding interest payments on government debt. A fiscal deficit of 3 percent of GDP was viewed as an "acceptable" and sustainable threshold pre-pandemic, the same level as agreed in the European Union's 1992 Maastricht Treaty. The primary number is ideally flat or positive. Tax collection ratios, with less than 15 percent of GDP a red flag warning, and government borrowing for payroll versus productive investment are also broken out. Boosting spending—and the deficit—for construction of critical infrastructure or education is viewed more positively than, for example, building new "bridges to nowhere" for the sake of raising the headline GDP number or reducing unemployment as various countries have resorted to in recent years.

Case Study: Brazil's Fevered Fiscal Pump

As the Covid-19 pandemic gripped Brazil in March 2020, Congress declared a "state of public calamity" through year-end. The declaration was needed to suspend the primary fiscal balance target and at the same time the government ratified a constitutional amendment allowing creation of a "war budget" that separated Covid costs from the ordinary budget.[20] The measures allowed a massive emergency stimulus package, focused on cash transfers to the poorest citizens, worth more than 8 percent of GDP.

Spending in 2020 more than doubled the general government deficit to 15 percent of GDP from 6 percent pre-pandemic as the primary deficit hit a record 10 percent of GDP. Public debt, most issued domestically in local currency, neared the critical 100 percent of GDP mark. A year later Congress approved another, smaller emergency aid package of USD 8 billion, 1.4 percent of GDP, consisting of cash transfers to the poor, employment support, and dedicated funds for healthcare. Investors and the IMF welcomed the new program which also triggered spending limits.[21]

While investors and ratings agencies monitored debt and deficit levels closely, the Covid package—one of the biggest in emerging markets—did contain the hit to the economy in 2020 despite its impact on inflation. Prices rose 4.5 percent in 2020, the highest in four years. Brazil's massive spending limited GDP contraction to 4.1 percent, while its Latin peer Mexico, where stimulus was only about 1 percent of GDP, saw its economy shrink 8.3 percent.

After assessing the government's fiscal policies, investors, analysts, and policymakers turn their focus to the central bank. The central bank manages the money supply and interest rates through either expansionary—lowering rates to spur bank lending and consumer spending—or contractionary policy with hikes to control inflation. Investors seek a monetary authority independent from government interference, with that power enshrined in law, to concentrate solely on price and currency stability. Turkey's central bank had a past history of able technocrats, but political masters had in recent years cramped its autonomy as described above in Case Study B. Brazil's central bank was granted independence in 2021—and held firm against government calls to slash interest rates as inflation fell just two years later—while China's People's Bank is firmly controlled by the ruling Communist party.

After assessing a country's domestic economy, analysts then turn attention to its external accounts, focusing on its ability to service debt, pay for needed imports, and allow foreign investors and regular citizens to freely transfer money in and out of the country. International reserve details are easily found on central bank websites, and adequacy is measured against months of import coverage payment, with three as the recommended minimum. After the global Covid pandemic many countries experienced a significant drop in reserves, forcing them to turn to the IMF. For example, in 2021 Ghana's reserves covered four months of imports, according to the IMF, but a year later the level had dropped to 2 months. The fall was due to a surge in the price of imported oil and fertilizer due to the war in Ukraine, and a drop in exports. The drop in reserves forced Ghana to default on its local and external debt obligations and turn to the IMF for a USD 3 billion bailout in 2023 (Fig. 3.2).

International reserves are not only needed to buy goods and services from abroad, but they are also critical for foreign debt payments. Sufficient reserve capacity is also measured against the ability to repay all short-term debt (less than 12 months). Some countries, like Colombia, base the currencies in their reserve holdings on trade patterns. The US, for example, its largest trade partner, accounts for about one-quarter of the total, so the same portion of its foreign currency reserves is in US dollars. Globally, 149 countries report their reserve holdings to the IMF on a quarterly basis. In the second quarter of 2024, of the USD 12.3 trillion in reserves tracked, 54.2 percent were in US dollars with the Euro in second place accounting for 21.5 percent of the total.[22]

In contrast, countries under sanctions like Venezuela and Belarus without dollar access typically hold more gold than foreign currencies, with the latter reporting official reserves in 2024 of less than one month of imports. Despite international sanctions, Russia's foreign reserves top USD 630 billion, with nearly USD 190 billion in gold in 2024. Others base assets against the IMF's Special Drawing Rights (SDR). The SDR is the IMF's synthetic denomination which is exchangeable for five major currencies. After adding China's RMB to its SDR basket in 2016, SDRs are in USD (41.7 percent), EUR

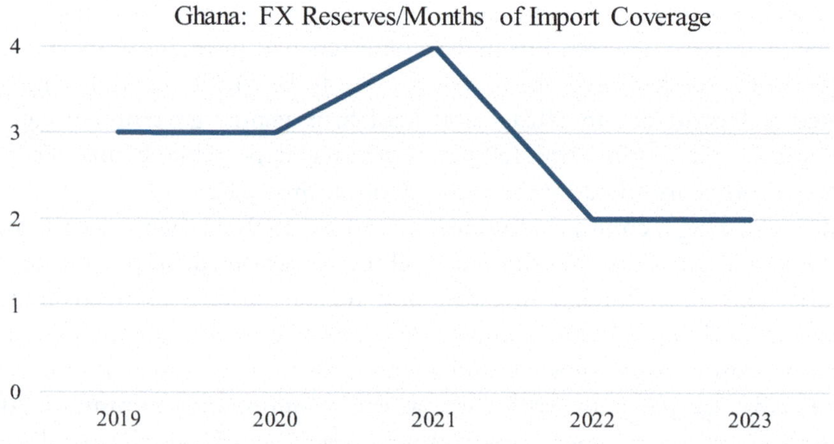

Fig. 3.2 Ghana: FX Reserves/Months of Import Coverage (*Source* IMF)

(30.9 percent), RMB (10.9 percent), JPY (8.3 percent) and GBP (8.1). The composition is reviewed every five years to reflect the relative importance of currencies in the world's trading and financial system.[23]

Another key factor in assessing a country's external accounts is balance of payments data, which are generally reported monthly or quarterly. The data cover all transactions—government, corporate, and resident—in a country with the rest of the world. There are two sides: the current account (goods and services trade, cross-border investment earnings, and remittances) and the capital account, comprised of direct and portfolio inflows and official aid and loans. The current account is reported as a percentage of GDP, with a deficit of 3 percent of GDP or more a traditional warning sign that trouble with meeting payment obligations may occur. The export and import dimensions offer a sense of sales diversification and high-cost input reliance to guide judgment beyond the headline number fluctuations. Following Russia's invasion of Ukraine, emerging markets investors scrambled to determine which countries were most reliant on Russian and Ukrainian goods. Before the Russian invasion US Department of Agriculture data put global exports of Russia and Ukrainian wheat at one-third of the global total, and together they accounted for more than three-quarters of sunflower oil. Lebanon, already reeling from years of economic and political crisis, imported half of its wheat from Ukraine, and already lacked the cash to purchase food and energy. Similarly, Pakistan, under an IMF program and with inflation already running in double-digits, imported the bulk of its grains from Ukraine.

The Asian Financial Crisis in 1997 was spurred by a massively high current account deficit in Thailand. For several years, the gap had trended as high as 8 percent of GDP, far above the 3 percent seen as a danger threshold. The deficit was driven by the combination of imports far exceeding exports and a rigid uncompetitive exchange rate with the baht pegged to the US dollar (see case study). These balance of payments crises are often historic turning points for a country's overall economic model. India, for example, had a balance of payments crisis in 1991 when its foreign reserves were depleted, which resulted in stark turnaround from its post-independence all-pervasive state control. More recently in South Asia, Sri Lanka's managed exchange rate regime—a so-called "currency band" which is when the central bank intervenes to keep the currency within a set range against either the US dollar or a basket of currencies—was dismantled in 2023 to win IMF backing.

Case Study: Asia's Splintered Peg Era

In the decade before the Asian Financial Crisis (AFC), the "Asia Tiger economies" —Thailand, Indonesia, Malaysia, Philippines, and South Korea—were the fastest growing countries globally. Foreign investment poured into the region. The Asian markets attracted almost USD 100 billion in 1996, almost half of total capital inflows to global emerging markets.[24] There are numerous domestic economic and financial sector reasons for the AFC, including stock and property market bubbles and lax lending standards and oversight of local banks. However external imbalances are often cited as the proverbial "straw that broke the camel's back." (Fig. 3.3).

Fig. 3.3 Thailand: Current Account Deficit/GDP (*Source* Federal Reserve Bank of St. Louis)

Currencies in the region had long been pegged to the US dollar at levels which favored export sectors. The US Federal Reserve began raising interest rates sharply in 1994, sending the US dollar higher, leading to appreciation of the Asian currencies tied to the greenback and making exports less competitive globally. The Fed moves—which doubled rates in just over a year—resulted in stock and bond investors offloading emerging market holdings to return to the safe-haven dollar.

The "Tiger" economies had funded their strong economic growth with hefty foreign borrowing, but by the mid-1990s foreign investor enthusiasm was waning and export receipts were slowing as China replaced the region as a low-cost production and export base.[25] Foreign investors began to question the sustainability of the region's external deficits and pressure on the currencies mounted as they retreated from the region. By July 2, 1997, Thailand's foreign reserves were almost depleted after the central bank tried to support the pegged baht and the country floated its currency which lost about half its value by the end of the year, marking the beginning of the AFC.

Qualitative Factors

After assessing the key quantitative factors of an economy, public and private analysts turn to "qualitative" issues that cannot be measured or compared across markets with statistics. Analysis generally focused first on so-called "structural reforms." This is a catchall subjective field the IMF describes as "inherently difficult to measure as they often involve policies or issues that are not easy to quantify."[26] While raising growth and reining in inflation and deficits are key features in IMF reform programs, the structural changes are implemented to turn around economic performance for the long term. The G20 finance ministers and central bank governors in 2015, after coordinating rescue from the 2008 global crash, recognized the essential role of structural reform in ensuring strong, sustainable, and balanced growth. Success turns on evidence that economic liberalization—including deregulation and elimination of subsidies—is progressing in policy decisions and on the ground application and embraced across the political spectrum. Analysts also prefer that the reforms are embedded in law and even constitutionalized so that a shift in government leadership cannot immediately derail progress.

Attention to structural reform progress has been revisited in historical waves over the past three decades, with renewed focus as economies recover from the effects of the global pandemic and endure the economic impacts of the war in Ukraine. With numerous poor and lower-middle income countries having run up massive debt and deficits from 2020–2023—resulting in a wave of countries in debt distress and a handful of fresh sovereign defaults—the IMF and other donors have reverted to earlier playbooks to assist with reforms that will benefit over the longer-term. Earlier, Latin America's programs commenced with the resolution of the 1980s debt crisis, and after the fall of the Berlin Wall and break-up of the former Soviet Union, bilateral and multilateral donors rushed to assist with transformation from communist/socialist systems to market economies. These reforms embraced a top-to-bottom laundry list, including tax and subsidy changes, removal of labor market rigidities and insolvency law overhaul, and financial sector deepening—creation and/or expansion of local stock and bond markets—which we examine in depth in the next chapter.

In the first round of reforms in the 1990s, notably in Latin America and Central and Eastern Europe, identifying and sequencing necessary changes was an exercise in trial and error, especially if mixed with outside insistence on quick private sector makeover. The European Bank for Reconstruction and Development (EBRD), founded in 1991 to "foster the transition towards open market-oriented economies and to promote private and entrepreneurial initiative," admitted in its 2010 Transition report that "measuring transition is difficult."[27] In 1994 it took a first crack at ranking progress in the region through six original indicators, and the number of gauges expanded with refinements through the years.[28] Nearly two decades later, the EBRD admitted that its core methodology for measuring the impact of success of reforms was too simplistic and did not consider the need for public institutions to have a regulator to enforce rules and fair competition. Too much emphasis was on reducing the role of the state and encouraging private ownership and market forces in a broad sweep, and not enough on developing complementary legal and regulatory imprints needed to keep investors and citizens protected.

In Central Europe, as in other regions, the first advice from donors was privatization of state-owned enterprises (SOEs). Selling state companies would in principle stop budget drain and introduce efficiency and competition. Through the 1990s divestiture of state companies took many forms and often degenerated into scandals giving the process a bad name. For example, as described in the case study in Chapter 1, Russia's rapid voucher privatization program in 1992–93 enabled get rich quick schemes for "oligarchs" who bought private citizen shares and used them to scoop up the country's crown jewels—notably mining and oil companies—at bargain rates. A legal framework with well-defined ownership and property rights was not in place and the commercial banking system was nascent. The MICEX (the Moscow Interbank Currency Exchange) as a suitable trading platform for the privatization vouchers was established the same year and was barely developed. The successor Russian Trading System, modeled on NASDAQ's trading and settlement system, was not rolled out until 1995, after the voucher privatization was complete.[29]

Privatization has also been contentious in Egypt, as programs to sell state companies have been promised for three decades. (See case study) The US Agency for International Development spent much of the 1990s assisting the country with divestiture preparation, but by the time of the "Arab Revolution" in 2011, there were still hundreds of state-owned enterprises. A decade later, despite receiving widespread praise for other structural reforms backed by the IMF—including energy subsidy rollback—17 state-run holding companies remained in control of 180 smaller ones despite 2018 plans to sell minority stakes.[30] Although their net profits after tax quadrupled over a 3-year period pre-pandemic, the World Bank noted that "the widespread presence of SOEs across the economy affects competition and distorts market outcomes."[31] The most recent efforts to divest state companies have focused on selling them to wealthy buyers from the Gulf States as

Cairo attempts again to rein in state involvement. There have also been some sales through the stock market, but these have generally been small stakes.

Case Study: Egypt's Privatization Hieroglyphics

As Egypt battled growing trade and fiscal deficits and its debt/GDP level hit 150 percent, in 1991 it turned to the IMF, World Bank and other international financial institutions for assistance. A rescue package of USD 562 million was agreed with lending linked to the government's agreement to launch major economic and structural reforms under an Economic Reform and Structural Adjustment Program (ERSAP). The key areas of the program included liberalizing foreign trade and removing price controls, floating the currency, lowering and removing a range of subsidies, and privatization.[32] The following several years bilateral donors joined their multilateral counterparts and poured economic and financial market consultants into Cairo to advise relevant government agencies. We spent several months in 1993 working on a US Agency for International Development privatization program, contracted as part of a team to assess efforts, review the legal/regulatory framework, and analyze the prospects for state-owned enterprise selloffs on the local stock market.

The Kleiman International consultants found that despite our experience with privatization in emerging markets in transition in Central and Eastern Europe, in Egypt there were experts at the biggest investment bank—who were educated and worked in the US and Europe—and were far more familiar with the domestic economic/investment climate, capacity of the stock market, and legal and regulatory regime. It was often difficult to arrange meetings with counterparts in the government and financial sector as there were dozens of consultants from other donor agencies attempting to undertake the same analyses. Privatization was deeply unpopular with Egyptians fearing job losses. From 1991 through 2004 the average number of state company divestitures was only about 15/year, with the pace finally picking up a bit in the following two years to an average of 25 annually.[33] However, through 2006, employment declined in almost 75 percent of the privatized companies.[34]

The privatization program was suspended after the Arab Spring revolution in 2011, and Egypt did not re-engage with the IMF until 2016. Instead, it relied on loans and grants which did not have conditions for reform or liberalization from wealthy Gulf Cooperation Council states. That year as foreign reserves dried up and investment sank, the IMF approved a USD 12 billion, 3-year package. Before the outbreak of the global pandemic Egypt had climbed out of its 2016 crisis but despite repeated promises and timelines since then, the long-delayed privatization program remained largely stalled.

After the war broke out in Ukraine in 2022, the Egyptian government, scrambled to secure another IMF agreement as the currency sank as foreign investors fled emerging market stocks and bonds globally, inflation spiked, and growth slowed. The government once again dusted off privatization plans and announced that it wanted private investment in the country, estimated then at about 30 percent of the total, to more than double within three years. Some USD 15 billion in assets were identified to be offered largely through share sales in 2022, despite no advancement in offloading the minority stakes in 23 state-owned enterprises identified four years earlier.[35] While there have been some recent successful divestitures, Egypt's traditional Gulf allies have made clear that they now expect a solid return on their investments.

Tax reform is another qualitative indicator that is assessed. It may entail simplifying an existing regime or creating a system from scratch to boost collection. In 2019 rich country OECD member countries took in an average of 33.8 percent of GDP in tax revenue, with Mexico and Colombia the laggards at 16.5 percent and 19.9 percent, respectively.[36]India introduced its biggest overhaul since independence in 2017 with launch of a comprehensive Goods and Services Tax which replaced the value added, sales, and 11 different indirect levies at the central and state level. It was long overdue and made a splash among investors drawn to Prime Minister Modi's modernization narrative but was unnecessarily complex with various rates and exemptions that continue to shift more than half a decade later.

Spending on subsidies is also analyzed. Direct government support through subsidies, generally to keep the price of goods competitive in international markets or low at home, is most often directed toward export industries, agriculture, oil, or increasingly "new economy" or "green" sectors. China is a prime example. In 2015 the world's biggest car market announced it would end subsidies to new energy vehicles (NEVs) —electric, plug-in hybrids, and hydrogen fuel cars—in 2020. Instead, government aid was reduced and extended as the country strives to meet its 2025 target for NEVs to account for 20 percent of car sales. China also offers subsidies and tax incentives for renewable power to meet its goal of carbon neutrality before 2060. Egypt slashed subsidies in November 2016 under a 3-year, USD 12 billion IMF agreement. Fuel, water, and electricity subsidies were removed but most food ones stayed, notably on bread, as past price rises provoked widespread riots. In 2024 the government upped the price of subsidized bread for the first time since the 1980s and the country's 2024/25 budget allocated USD 2.65 billion for bread subsidies, with subsidies accounting for about 11 percent of spending.

Currency regime modification is also keenly assessed as it encompasses both exchange rate policy and liberalization. A major change in the regime is initially generally devastating to the country's income and output. In the 1990s the Mexican and Asian crises allowing the currencies to freely float at market-determined levels were painful for citizens, investors, and donors on the ground through the first 12–24 months. Prior to December 20, 1994, Mexico's peso was pegged to the US dollar, its current account deficit soared, and fiscal policy was loose. On that date the peso was effectively devalued

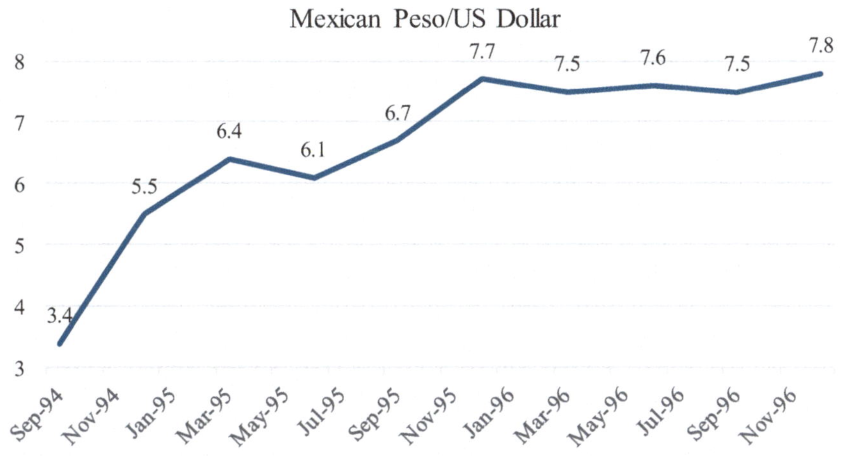

Fig. 3.4 Mexican Peso/US Dollar (*Source* Bloomberg)

by 15 percent, and the central bank hiked short-term rates to 32 percent in a failed attempt to stem capital flight. Two days later the peso was floated outright, with the market determining its level. Shocked foreign investors with large holdings of local government debt, many of whom were already celebrating the holidays and had to return to their offices, fled the Mexican market adding even more pressure on the currency. The peso sank more than 30 percent against the US dollar within a year, inflation soared to over 50 percent and the economy contracted more than 6 percent (Fig. 3.4).

Bailouts from the IMF and the US followed but just a few years later economic growth was nearly 7 percent annually and Mexico's fiscal house was largely in order. So, although painful at first, the removal of foreign exchange controls and the end of central bank intervention to support the fixed level have proven that the shift to a market-determined rate boosts growth and investment over the longer term.

Investment Climate Considerations

Most emerging markets drew on lessons from earlier economic crises and donor prodding to adopt free-market rates, but exceptions remain as a main complication in the overall investment enabling environment. For example, in Nigeria investment value and profit repatriation were routinely threatened by devaluation and a hodge-podge of foreign exchange curbs prior to the election of President Tinubu in 2023. Three rates were quoted: the official fixed government transaction one, the Nafex for investors and exporters as a "managed float," and a parallel or "street" market rate.[37] The government adopted the Nafex rate in mid-2021, but the central bank continued to intervene in the market. This multiple exchange rate practice was criticized by the IMF discouraging it in its charter, and the World Bank withheld a loan to push for change. Foreign investors had largely exited the local stock market with this logjam. One of President Tinubu's first acts in office was to sack the longtime central bank governor and float the currency. While the naira sank some 40 percent within days, foreign investors gradually began to return to the country, but within months an informal "parallel" exchange rate was again active due to lingering hard currency shortages.

Another example of a "fixed" exchange rate is China. The Peoples Bank of China allows the renminbi to trade in a 2 percent range around a midpoint it fixes daily against the USD. While the central bank rarely intervenes directly in the currency market, it directs the country's state-owned banks to buy and sell to keep the currency within its daily band and maintains strict capital controls on outflows.

Other qualitative issues assessed by public and private analysts encompass a broad array of legal and regulatory topics. These include insolvency/bankruptcy, corporate governance, reporting/compliance, judiciary independence, equal foreign and domestic investor tax treatment, corruption/bribery, and minority investor protection. However, clarity of regulations and equal and timely enforcement are as important as the existence of rules "on the books." Until mid-2021, the World Bank's annual "Doing Business" report was a flagship reference regularly used by analysts to determine gaps in this area. It ranked 190 countries for performance in a dozen commercial categories, before a temporary halt after data manipulation and reporting irregularities were uncovered.[38] (Case Study) In the aftermath of the scandal, the Bank conducted an internal audit and external review and has rolled out a replacement.[39] The new "Business Ready"—B-Ready—is designed to replace and improve on the original "Doing Business." Instead of the original composite score, it breaks out rankings in three areas (regulatory state, public services, and operating efficiency) based on tens of thousands of company interviews in multiple cities across each county. Public and private analysts also cite Transparency International as another go-to for insights. It grades 180 countries' perceived levels of public sector corruption according to experts and the business community. In 2023, Estonia and Uruguay were the only emerging economies to place in the top 20, with the United States ranked 24th while Venezuela joined war-torn South Sudan, Syria, Somalia, and Yemen at the bottom of the list.[40]

Case Study: Bretton Woods Flagship Publications Weave Checkered Reputation

In October 2021 the IMF and World Bank convened largely virtually for their annual meetings, but the traditional October release of annual/semi-annual publications was relatively uninterrupted by the immediate pandemic. The annual publications are widely read by public and private sector analysts seeking insights on and projections for the global economy and include "World Economic Outlook" and "Global Financial Stability Report" among others. Global growth disparities, elevated debt levels, the vaccine divide, and climate change were dominant themes. Analysts reviewed the hundreds of pages with content and process in mind, distressed over the IMF's board decision to retain Managing Director Georgieva after she was involved with artificially inflating China's ranking in the discarded "Doing Business" report during her tenure as CEO of the World Bank from January 2017-September 2019.

The private sector, in particular, was outraged and argued that country research distortions from World Bank top officials documented in the independent legal review of "Doing Business" were unacceptable. The absence of regret and accountability at the Bretton Woods institutions prompted calls for immediate and widespread revamping of ethical and practical structures to prevent a repeat episode. Internal integrity was breached despite both the World Bank and IMF offering easy reporting of lapses on their websites. Following the board's decision, MD Georgieva stated that "the problem was on the other side of 19th Street" —referring to the IMF headquartered across the street from the World Bank in Washington—as if she bore no responsibility as chief operating executive at the time.

Hundreds of IMF and World Bank professionals produce the annual prominent references by compiling and crunching statistics, writing/editing, and peer reviewing. An equal number provide technical assistance and guidance to policymakers in emerging and frontier markets. Under the rules some reports—on specific countries or issues—are never released due to member objection, often when findings are unfavorable. For example, for several years Laos refused publication of its annual Article IV review—standard reports for every member after Fund representatives meet with country officials to discuss and review fiscal, monetary, and financial issues—presumably due to the IMF's negative commentary about lack of promised reforms and liberalization. While the Bretton Woods institutions conclusions and policy recommendations may ultimately prove to have been mistaken, prior to the "Doing Business" saga the basic data-information collection and formulation process was not in question. Those named in the investigations should have at least temporarily stepped aside from analysis function oversight, and a longer-term fix could permanently separate it from other management duties. An immediate reputation balm could also come from developing a formal analyst code of conduct with enforcement as a model for all official lenders.

There are numerous examples of inadequate and un/underdeveloped legal and regulatory environments across the emerging market universe. An example most longtime analysts regularly cite was Indonesia in the 1990s. It was in the spotlight for poor corporate governance, minority shareholder rights, insolvency procedure, and reporting/compliance. The stock exchange was described by numerous emerging market fund managers as "the world's biggest casino" due to its reputation as a haven for insider trading and volatility, an "unpredictable" court system and difficulty in recovering funds after corporate defaults.[41]

A key example was the long-running saga of Indonesian conglomerate Asia Pulp and Paper (APP). In February 2001, the company declared a moratorium on its USD 13.9 billion debt, half in outstanding USD bonds. Founded in Indonesia in 1972, the company consolidated holdings and moved its headquarters to Singapore in 1994. It was listed on the New York Stock Exchange in 1995, with its American Depository Receipts (ADR) priced at USD 11/share and was then removed when they plummeted to USD 0.12. Prior to default, APP stocks and bonds were underwritten by the world's top financial institutions, including Goldman Sachs and JP Morgan, and its books were audited by "Big 5" accounting firm Arthur Andersen.[42] The sign-off by leading global firms provided a level of comfort for investors even as APP's debt climbed, and they assumed reporting and compliance were up to internationally accepted standards, particularly with the NYSE listing which is seen by emerging markets investors as a "seal of approval." After the depth of misrepresentation set in, creditors spent nearly a decade in court proceedings trying to recoup losses.

APP belatedly disclosed USD 220 million from previously unreported swap contracts—a financial agreement between two groups to exchange assets with cash flows for a set period of time—and the auditor resigned. Corporate governance and minority shareholder rights were ignored, and accounting/compliance norms trampled despite both US and Singapore listing clearance. In addition to institutional investors, export credit agencies in the US, Canada, and EU were owed nearly USD 1 billion at the time of default and had to pursue their own remedies.

Another key qualitative factor that has arguably returned as a top consideration in the wake of the war in Ukraine is political, and broader geo-political, risk. Political risk can never be ignored whether around a shift in government form or election cycle outcome. In individual countries a candidate can pledge outright to undo structural reforms. For example, in Mexico the year prior to the 2018 presidential poll, the peso depreciated 5.5 percent against the US dollar with leftist, populist Andres Manuel Lopez Obrador (Amlo) the presumptive heir. After his landslide victory, the anti-establishment platform included canceling construction of an airport that was already one-third completed on corruption grounds. Free market constitutional reforms enacted in 2013, notably opening the energy and telecom sectors to private investment, were anathema to Amlo. Government control over debt-laden national oil company Pemex was expanded on a vision of return to its early glory, as the Mexican economy underperformed neighbors and peers during his term in office. In 2024 history repeated with the peso and stock market plummeting as Amlo's Morena party swept presidential, parliamentary, and local elections with a near supermajority to revise the constitution at will. President Sheinbaum as his successor singled out direct voting for judges and reining in private industry regulators as priorities.

The definition of political risk has changed over the past few decades. In the early 1990s political risk was seen as either a sudden change in policies or the removal of a government. In the aftermath of the Asian Financial Crisis in the late 1990s, the definition became broader and focused as well on confidence in the government's ability to manage economic growth and push forward with structural reforms. Following the September 11th attacks on the United States, global issues—economic, political, and security—became a major focus for emerging markets debt, equity, and currency investors. Today investors define it even more broadly as an assessment of both a government's stability and security as well as its ability to manage the economy and be fiscally responsible while steering a reform course, which has become a new subjective standard.

There are numerous factors that are included in the broad definition of political risk. For investors allocating funds to emerging markets debt, equity, or currencies, they include both individual country considerations as well as broader geo-political concerns. For example, dedicated investors have long indicated that investment in South Korea has been somewhat constrained by worries about an attack from the North. Every time the North launches a missile, Seoul's stocks, bonds, and currency tumble as both foreign and domestic investors trim their holdings. While the selloffs are short-lived—generally a few days at most—the threat of political risk hangs over market participants in the volatile region.

The definition of political risk in individual emerging market countries has broadened in recent years. Long-time factors such as coups or social unrest, as well as peaceful political transition continue to be factors. Newer issues that investors are monitoring closely include: central bank independence, resource nationalization, relations with trade and investment partners, sanctions realignment, and government stability as it specifically relates to fiscal responsibility and reform.

Even before the global Covid-19 pandemic and Russian war in Ukraine, global geo-political factors were emphasized in public and private sector analyses both for their impact on individual country/company/credit investments and the potential for such an event to slow global economic growth. A rise in risk aversion from a global event causes immediate damage to emerging market debt, equity, and currencies. They are hit from knee-jerk falls in markets across the globe, so-called "contagion," as investors flee to traditional safe havens, mainly US dollar and Swiss franc assets.

While analysts agree that global geo-political risk factors can threaten outflows from emerging markets in every region as happened when Russia invaded Ukraine in 2022, they also recognize that more nuanced views will settle in after a seismic event to straightforwardly adapt the previous business model (Fig. 3.5).

An example of an overarching theme revisited is resource nationalization, which began in the wake of Russia's Yukos saga in 2003 and continues more than twenty years later as Chile's leftist president nationalized the world's largest lithium reserves, the commodity critical for electric vehicle production. The move came just a year after the Mexican government took over its country's lithium deposits.

Resource nationalization is seen by investors as an indication of a country's overall investment climate even though moves may not immediately impact portfolio investment holdings. Zambia after four years in bond default, to be explored in a later chapter, envisions stricter state control of its copper industry in the future, and after private operators reneged on their own promises holders may be inclined to give authorities the benefit of the doubt on better management. Outright government takeovers of privately held

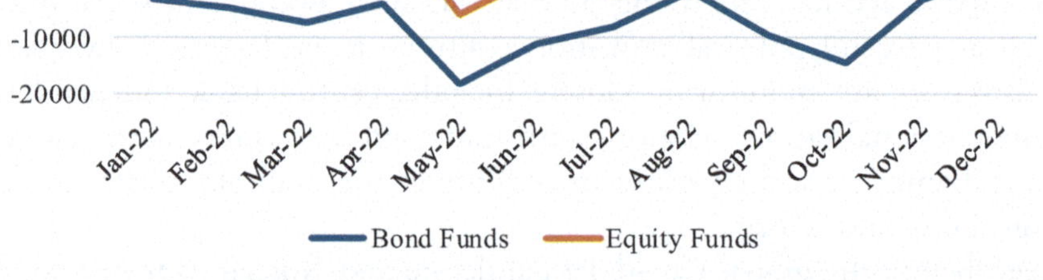

Fig. 3.5 Emerging Market Stock & bond Fund Flows in 2022 (USD millions) (*Source* EPFR)

assets do, however, over the longer term reduce foreign direct and portfolio investor confidence and can threaten external accounts with outflows.

The addition of monetary authority independence as a critical issue in the political risk category came to the forefront of investor attention after the Turkish government's month-long standoff in 2006 over appointment of a central bank governor. It heightened worries not only about the institution's independence, but also about the growing number of disputes between the secular establishment and governing AK Party of then Prime Minister, later President, Recep Tayyip Erdogan. Following the crisis—and as the currency tumbled and inflation remained high—foreign investors retreated from the once-popular market on repeated central bank head replacement and low double-digit interest rates against higher inflation. Following the 2023 election which resulted in another term for long-serving Erdogan, investors and analysts were relieved with the appointment of a respected industry practitioner to head the monetary authority.

The addition of these new political risk considerations has not diverted attention from the traditional emphasis on political and regime stability as evidenced by the selloffs in Thailand following the coups in 2006 and 2014. Political transition periods receive similar attention, as evidenced in 2021–23 by the myriad of elections in Latin America which brought leftist regimes to power in Brazil, Chile, Colombia, and Peru.

While market reaction to a single country or global political event is often sharp and sometimes deep, thirty years of recent history indicates that ones that are resolved quickly often have only a minor impact on prices. In fact, short-term "shock" events are often seen as buying opportunities after prices dip. One long-time emerging market investor regularly advised clients that often the best time to buy is "when there is blood in the streets." In general, emerging market investors are less concerned with democracy than policymakers, and instead seek stable environments in growing, reforming economies.

"Unorthodox" policies from authoritarian/democratic hybrids are in vogue in Hungary and Turkey in the 2020s. The former's right-wing nationalist Fidesz government dismantled the private pension system as one of transition Europe's proudest achievements which created large institutional investors in the stock and bond market. It deliberately reduced foreign bank presence with their efficiency and product contributions in favor of state champions. In Turkey, President Erdogan's unconventional and erroneous monetary policy belief that high interest rates result in inflation is matched in foreign policy adventures around the Mediterranean and Africa. Their political tinge may preserve power but not necessarily investor votes, particularly when both leaders waffled after Russia invaded Ukraine. Hungary's stock market is barely in positive territory over the past decade and Turkey's down 4 percent with respective double and triple-digit currency depreciation.

Key Takeaways:

- Analyzing both quantitative—easy to measure and compare economic indicators—and subjective qualitative factors is critical for investors, multilateral lenders, and industry practitioners.
- Domestic and external data along with qualitative issues such as structural reform and legal and regulatory conditions are core components in the mix.
- Political/geopolitical risk factors drive individual country and emerging market universe fund flows. The definition of political risk has expanded from simply government stability and security to cover the ability to manage the economy and be fiscally responsible in a discipline hybrid. Geopolitics in turn has morphed in the past five years to cover supply chain integrity, sanctions bloc realignment (BRICS +), and environmental/social/governance (ESG) dimensions to be elaborated in later sections.

Notes

1. Reuters Staff, "Ecuador defaults on foreign debt," December 13, 2008, https://www.france24.com/en/20081213-ecuador-defaults-foreign-debt-.
2. Jonathan Kandell, "Can Poland's Private Pension Funds Survive Government's Bond Grab?" Institutional Investor, May 2, 2014, https://www.institutionalinvestor.com/article/b14zbl2m808dyf/can-polands-private-pension-funds-survive-governments-bond-grab.
3. European Bank for Reconstruction and Development (EBRD), "Poland's new pension measures," September 13, 2013, https://www.ebrd.com/news/2013/polands-new-pension-measures.html.
4. The Warsaw Stock Exchange contracted with Kleiman International to perform an assessment and recommendations in 2012.
5. EBRD, "Poland's new pension measures.".
6. Kandell, "Can Poland's Private Pension.".
   EBRD, "Poland's new pension measures.".
7. Norma Cohen & Jan Cienski, "Poland Pension Reform Reversal Highlights Public Disillusion," Financial Times, February 4, 2014, https://www.ft.com/content/8ddeb5bc-6293-11e3-bba5-00144feabdc0

8. Reuters, "Poland to transfer all private pension funds to individual accounts," April 15, 2019, https://www.reuters.com/article/poland-pensions-idUSW8N20901C.
9. The World Bank, "Global Economic Prospects," June 2023, pg. 4 https://openknowledge.worldbank.org/server/api/core/bitstreams/6e892b75-2594-4901-a036-46d0dec1e753/content
10. www.data.worldbank.org
11. The International Labor Organization definition: Work in the informal economy is often characterized by small or undefined workplaces, unsafe and unhealthy working conditions, low levels of skills and productivity, low or irregular incomes, long working hours, and lack of access to information, markets, finance, training, and technology. Workers in the informal economy are not recognized, registered, regulated, or protected under labor legislation and social protection. The root causes of informality include elements related to the economic context, the legal, regulatory and policy frameworks and to some micro level determinants such as low level of education, discrimination, poverty and, as mentioned above, lack of access to economic resources, to property, to financial and other business services and to markets. www.ilo.org
12. Shu Yu and Franziska Ohnsorge, "The Challenges of informality," World Bank Blogs, January 18, 2019, https://blogs.worldbank.org/developmenttalk/challenges-informality.
13. Maurizio Bussolo, Siddharth Sharma, and Hans Timmer, "COVID-19 has worsened the woes of South Asia's informal sector," World Bank Blogs, December 7, 2020, https://blogs.worldbank.org/endpovertyinsouthasia/covid-19-has-worsened-woes-south-asias-informal-sector.
14. Turkish Statistical Institute, "Turkey Consumer Price Index (CPI)," Trading Economics, https://tradingeconomics.com/turkey/consumer-price-index-cpi.
15. Government of India, Ministry of Statistics and Programme Implementation, India Consumer Price Index (CPI), Trading Economics, https://tradingeconomics.com/india/consumer-price-index-cpi.
16. Reuters Staff, "FACTBOX—Turkey's 1980 coup and its aftermath," Reuters, April 4, 2012, https://www.reuters.com/article/uk-turkey-trial-1980/factbox-turkeys-1980-coup-and-its-aftermath-idUKBRE8330F320120404
17. Rudiger Dornbusch and Sebastian Edwards, eds., *Reform, Recovery, and Growth: Latin America and the Middle East,* (Chicago: University of Chicago Press, 1995), chap. "Partial Adjustment and Growth in the

1980s in Turkey", https://www.nber.org/system/files/chapters/c7662/c7662.pdf.
18. International Energy Agency (IEA), *Turkey 2021: Energy Policy Review*, IEA, Paris, March 2021, https://www.iea.org/reports/turkey-2021.
19. Hürriyet Daily News, "Turkey not to suffer shortage in grains: Ministry," February 26, 2022, https://www.hurriyetdailynews.com/turkey-not-to-suffer-shortage-in-grains-171811.
20. International Monetary Fund (IMF), "Brazil: 2021 Article IV Consultation," IMF Staff Country Report No. 21/217, September 22, 2021, https://www.imf.org/en/Publications/CR/Issues/2021/09/22/Brazil-2021-Article-IV-Consultation-Press-Release-Staff-Report-and-Statement-by-the-466076.
21. IMF, "Brazil 2021 Article IV.".
22. International Monetary Fund, Currency Composition of Official Foreign Exchange Reserves, Q2 2024, https://data.imf.org/?sk=e6a5f467-c14b-4aa8-9f6d-5a09ec4e62a4
23. International Monetary Fund (IMF), "Factsheet: Special Drawing Rights (SDR)," July 29, 2022, https://www.imf.org/en/About/Factsheets/Sheets/2016/08/01/14/51/Special-Drawing-Right-SDR.
24. International Monetary Fund (IMF), "The Asian Crisis: A View from the IMF—Address by Stanley Fischer," First Deputy Managing Director of the IMF at the Midwinter Conference of the Bankers' Association for Foreign Trade," Washington, D.C., January 22, 1998, https://www.imf.org/en/News/Articles/2015/09/28/04/53/sp012298.
25. Michael Carson and John Clark, "Asian Financial Crisis: July 1997-December 1998," Federal Reserve History, Federal Reserve Bank of New York, November 22, 2013, https://www.federalreservehistory.org/essays/asian-financial-crisis.
26. International Monetary Fund (IMF), "Structural Reforms and Macroeconomic Performance—Initial Considerations for the Fund," Policy Papers, October 14, 2015, https://www.imf.org/en/Publications/Policy-Papers/Issues/2016/12/31/Structural-Reforms-and-Macroeconomic-Performance-Initial-Considerations-for-the-Fund-PP4995.
27. European Bank for Reconstruction and Development, "Recovery and Reform," 2010 Transition Report, Chapter 1, pg. 2, file:///C:/Users/Admin/OneDrive/Downloads/transition-report-2010-english-web%20(1).pdf.
28. The original 6 indicators covered three broad aspects of transition: enterprises (small- and large-scale privatization and enterprise restructuring); markets and trade (price liberalization and competition and

trade and foreign exchange system): and financial institutions (banking reform).

29. www.bloomberg.com/profile/company/RTSX:RU
30. Patrick Werr, "Egypt's buoyant state enterprises leave private sector in the shade," Reuters, January 19, 2021, https://www.reuters.com/article/egypt-economy-int-idUSKBN29O1DJ.
31. Werr, "Egypt's buoyant state enterprises.".
32. Omar Ghannam and Mohamed Gad, "From the 1990s until Now: The IMF Loan and Exacerbating the Crisis," Egyptian Center for Economic & Social Rights, September 22, 2016, https://ecesr.org/en/2016/09/22/from-the-1990s-until-now-the-imf-loan-and-exacerbating-the-crisis/.
33. Karim Badr el-Din, "Privatization: A key to Solving Egypt's Economic Woes," World Bank Blogs, Arab Voices, March 11,2014, https://blogs.worldbank.org/arabvoices/privatization-key-solving-egypt-s-economic-woes.
34. Badr el-Din, "Privatization.".
35. Momen Saeed Atallah, Yasmin Hussein and Moataz Mohammed, "Egypt outlines broad plans to sell state assets," Reuters, May 15, 2022. https://www.reuters.com/world/middle-east/egypts-pm-wants-boost-private-sector-investments-2022-05-15/
36. OECD Global Revenue Statistics Database, https://www.oecd.org/tax/tax-policy/global-revenue-statistics-database.htm
37. BNP Paribas Team, "Nigeria: Exchange rate regime under pressure," FX Street, April 14, 2021, https://www.fxstreet.com/analysis/nigeria-exchange-rate-regime-under-pressure-202104140835.
38. Doing Business Legacy (worldbank.org).
39. The World Bank, "World Bank Group Statement on Doing Business Data Corrections and Findings of Internal Audit," December 16, 2020, https://www.worldbank.org/en/news/statement/2020/12/16/world-bank-group-statement-on-doing-business-data-corrections-and-findings-of-internal-audit.
40. Transparency International, "Corruption Perceptions Index 2023," https://www.transparency.org/en/cpi/2023
41. Olivia Rondonuwu and Sara Webb, "Indonesian supreme court rules on bonds, overturns APP ruling," Reuters, October 31,2008, https://www.reuters.com/article/indonesia-app-idUKJAK19746820081031.
42. Arthur Andersen collapsed following accusation of obstruction of justice in 2002 after it was found to have shredded papers for Enron,

the US energy company that was found to have committed one of the biggest accounting frauds in history.

4

The Importance and Diversity of Financial Market Participants

Banks and non-banks as an awkward generic term define financial sectors, with so-called universal groups blurring both categories, and often tied to an industrial parent as a complex conglomerate for a regulatory nightmare. Typically, as an economy develops, access to credit for households and corporates is initially through mainstream banks, leaving aside informal savings channels that are also prominent. While countries have forged sizeable non-bank institutions, commercial banks remain the main funding source through the standard measure as a percentage of GDP, often at ratios in the 100% range twice the average for securities intermediaries. The profiles below outline historic evolution and business lines, and the sound legal and regulatory frameworks specialists recommend and investors assume are in place. Banks, micro-finance institutions, insurance, pensions, and collective investment funds are highlighted. Full treatment would include less-followed pillars like leasing and factoring firms, and dedicated consumer and mortgage lenders that are covered in passing (see case study).

Non-Bank Financial Institution Spotlight: India

Although China's non-bank financial institutions, commonly referred to there as "shadow banks," dominate Asia, India's non-bank financial corporations (NBFCs) were found by the Basel, Switzerland-based Financial Stability Board (FSB) to be among the fastest growing in the world in 2018. The more than 10,000 institutions provided almost 20 percent of total lending in the economy—up 4 percentage points in just three years—and their combined assets exceeded USD 370 billion.[1] However, not all were required to be

B. Morrissey and G. Kleiman, *Emerging Economies and Financial Markets*,
https://doi.org/10.1007/978-3-031-85669-3_4

licensed by the Reserve Bank of India, the central bank, and most were not subject to its oversight and supervision.

The NBFCs grew rapidly through the 2010s as state-owned public sector banks, burdened by massive amounts of non-performing loans, were unable to lend after the RBI banned them from further advances until balance sheets were cleaned up. Estimates put more than 70 percent of NBFCs loan portfolios in infrastructure, commercial real estate, and residential housing by 2018.[2] They were also key lenders to sectors deemed "priority" by the government, including agriculture and small and medium-sized enterprises. The sector was a key source of finance until the collapse of Infrastructure Leasing and Financial Services Ltd. (IL&FS) in 2018 which resulted in nearly USD 13 billion in investor losses. IL&FS was massive, with hundreds of business lines. In a nutshell, it was brought down by three basic issues:

- Reliance on short-term funding to invest in long-term infrastructure projects, referred to as maturity mismatch;
- IL&FS consisted of hundreds of inter-connected businesses, many of which were off-balance sheet special purpose vehicles and therefore not disclosed;
- Huge dividends were paid to shareholders from 2015–2018 despite negative cash flow.[3]

Just four months after the collapse of IL&FS, another NBFC, Reliance Home Finance, defaulted on a bank loan repayment, followed several months later by one of the leading housing finance companies.

The sector's downfall came following years of 20-percent-plus annual growth and rippled through the entire financial sector. Listed NBFCs sank in value, debt mutual funds saw massive outflows as they were a major funding source for NBFCs, and bank stocks dropped sharply as lending to NBFCs was estimated at 10–15 percent of total loan books. In the wake of the IL&FS failure, the Reserve Bank proactively revoked licenses of small NBFCs and introduced a citizen awareness campaign. The monetary authority also reiterated that depositors at NBFCs are not covered by the bank deposit insurance facility.

Banks

China's banks are the prevailing intermediaries at home and in 2024 they were the world's four largest by assets.[4] It also has the second largest onshore bond market which commercial and policy lenders control as both issuers and investors. In 2023 banks held nearly three-quarters of the government bond market, nearly 90 percent of bonds issued by heavily indebted local governments, and of the top 10 names by issuer size in corporate bonds, 8 were banks.[5] The "big 4 banks" are majority-owned by the state, with partial stakes floated on the Shanghai, Shenzhen, Hong Kong, and overseas stock exchanges. Global giant Industrial and Commercial Bank of China is the only emerging market-based bank designated as systemically important—failure would have an impact on the global economy—on a list compiled by the Basel, Switzerland-based Financial Stability Board, and it is 73 percent owned by the government.[6] The Financial Stability Board is made up of senior policymakers from central banks, ministries of finance, and supervisory/regulatory authorities from the G-20 plus Hong Kong, Singapore, Spain, and Switzerland (Fig. 4.1).

Asia has a legacy of state-owned banks that remains intact despite the post-1990s financial crisis divestiture strides under IMF programs and recommendations. India had its own debt and balance of payments crash that spurred home grown reforms, but public sector banks as vaunted post-colonial channels to this day still account for about 60 percent of system assets despite chronic non-performing loans and capital deficiencies.[7] Private sector banks, most domestically owned, are far healthier with their relatively fresh entry

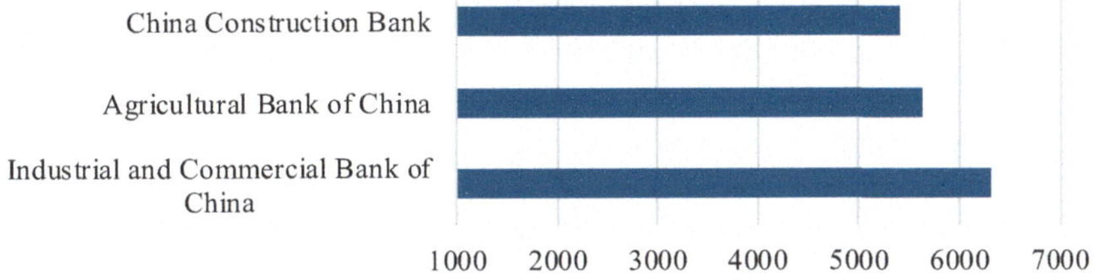

Fig. 4.1 The World's 5 Largest Banks by Assets (USD billions) (*Source* The world's 100 largest banks, 2024, S&P Global Market Intelligence)

and franchise divergence from government lending mandates. Indonesia has four state run banks, each with a specific niche. Bank Rakyat targets medium-and-small enterprises, Mandiri corporates and Islamic finance, Bank Negara is internationally focused and state savings bank Tabungan Negara offers mortgages.[8] After the regulator, the Financial Services Authority, announced stricter capital requirements in 2021 to spur consolidation among the deliberately fragmented groups, 35 mergers and acquisitions followed, with buyers from Japan, South Korea, and Thailand buying Indonesian counterparts.[9]

State banking monopolies faded as the emerging markets developed deeper financial systems, but a heavy presence often lingers that interferes with commercial orientation, efficiency, and corporate governance. Foreign and local private banks are routinely superior by financial ratios of profitability and return on assets/equity, as they can lend to higher-margin borrowers and do not have to follow as closely government directed lending like state-owned counterparts. Efficiency is the ability to provide high-quality products and services at the lowest costs, and their management and operating overhead expense is lighter with technology and knowhow comparative advantages.[10] Competition is measured by total number of institutions in smaller economies, but proliferation is logical in giant markets like China and India, and then the concentration ratio in terms of a few participants' stranglehold over assets or loans/deposits becomes paramount. As noted in the first chapter, in Central Europe the sector is a mix of foreign, private, and state-owned banks. In Poland, the largest bank, PKO, is state-controlled but branches and subsidiaries from Western Europe parents make up about half of the top ten banks.[11] This hybrid model is the norm, with private banks as the driving force rare exceptions. National development banks, once in fashion but later dissolved as unrestrained money losers, have also come back in modern versions to reinforce official banking sway. For example, in mid-2022 Ghana launched the Development Bank Ghana, with initial capital of USD 800 million from the government, World Bank and other donors. Its mandate is to stem the traditional funding shortage for small- and medium-sized enterprises. It will lend "longer-term funding" to local banks and micro-finance providers which will in turn provide much needed affordable finance to smaller businesses.[12]

Microfinance

This grassroots tiny amount lending has long been a favorite in the development field, with its own data collection and good practice global association. The nonprofit London-based Microfinance Association offers training to lenders and regulators. Microfinance dates back to the late 1970s when Bangladeshi professor, later the country's Prime Minister, Muhammad Yunus undertook research to determine how to get credit to the rural poor. The "Grameen Bank Project" was granted a license in 1983 and today is 90 percent owned by the provincial customers it serves, with the government holding a 10 percent stake.[13] (Case study) Overall the industry's record is mixed on reducing extreme poverty and marking a first step toward formal financial inclusion, but it has exploded in size since its inception in South Asia. According to a recent book, an estimated 200 million people worldwide now access microfinance providers.[14]

Case Study: Microfinance's Nobel Cause

Microfinance was launched in the mid-1970s by Professor Muhammad Yunus, then-head of the Rural Economics Program at the University of Chittagong in Bangladesh. He was awarded a Nobel Peace Prize in 2006. Microfinance began with a research project examining design of a system to provide banking services to the ignored rural poor.[15] At the time, Bangladesh was regularly cited as one of the poorest countries in the world, famously called a "basket case" by former US Secretary of State Henry Kissinger.

Professor Yunus's project was named the Grameen Bank, "rural" or "village" in the Bangla language, with five objectives:

- Extend facilities to poor men and women;
- Eliminate exploitation by money lenders;
- Create self-employment for the large jobless population;
- Bring the disadvantaged, mostly uneducated women, into arrangements they can understand and manage by themselves;
- Reverse the age-old vicious cycle of "low income, low savings and low investment," into virtuous circle of "low income, injection of credit, investment, more income- savings."[16]

Less than a decade after its launch Grameen became an independent bank, with the government holding a 10 percent share while borrowers held the rest. In the early years of the spread of microfinance throughout the developing world, non-governmental organizations were the sponsors. The IFC in the 1990s started promoting it as a business case to private investors. Its website notes that microfinance is a "key first intervention in frontier and conflict countries to spur economic growth."

Four decades later providers offer loans, savings, and insurance to 200 million people globally.[17] Micro-insurance became another product line drawing attention from the relevant overseer. Crises and insolvencies over the years with lack of experience and supervision forced institutions under formal prudential structures, as they evolved from simply making loans with non-government and official lender funds to deposit-taking institutions. Unlike traditional commercial banks which assessed loan applications by the assets pledged as collateral, the field is distinguished by identifying cash flows in informal trade turnover and "intangible attributes" including reputation, honesty, and attitudes.[18] It has leapfrogged and diversified beyond the founding mission of providing tiny, often under USD 100 loans. In remote areas the inauguration of physical branches has been a festive occasion. As with mainstream banks, technological changes like mobile banking have prompted virtual makeover, against the harsh reality of sparse internet connection (Fig. 4.2).

In the early days, non-governmental organizations were the sole players in the microfinance sector. The institutions were fully funded and did not take deposits. As interest grew, new institutions were formed that offered not only loans but also took deposits. They were owned by "members" and outside investors to accelerate industry growth in the 1980s and 1990s. Failures occurred in every region, including in pioneer Bangladesh.[19] Throughout those decades numerous crises arose as poorly regulated providers "over-lent" and customers "over-borrowed." Today these institutions are commercial and

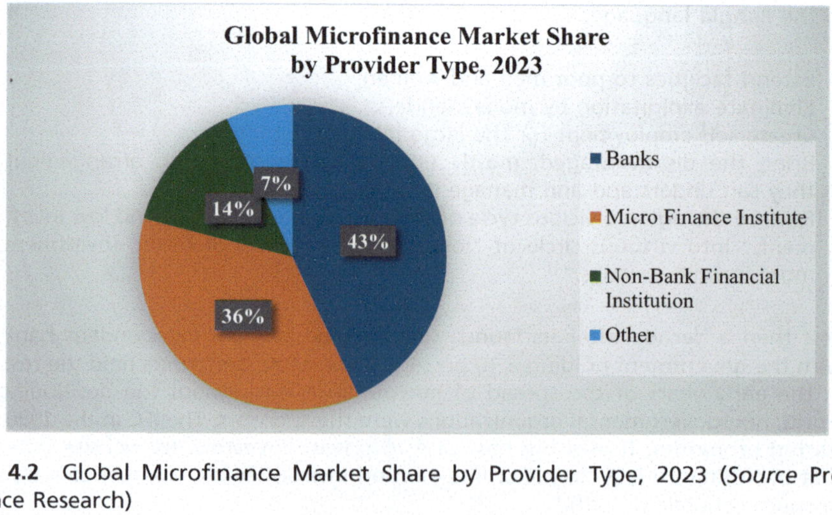

Fig. 4.2 Global Microfinance Market Share by Provider Type, 2023 (*Source* Precedence Research)

regulated as a banking prudential category subset subject to rules of conduct and usury lending rate limits.[20]

The rise of mobile phones and internet banking is again transforming the microfinance industry and putting it in direct competition with digital and business point-to-point platforms. Successful micro-finance houses now go for full mainstream banking licenses and sell shares on stock markets. In the other direction big banks, often at government behest, open their own dedicated small-scale units as in South Africa. They have a track record as an overlooked profit center, with the original purpose residing along a financial services spectrum. Today, for example, South Africa has some 1300 registered microfinance credit providers who have their own industry association. Several of them, like African Dawn Capital, are listed and traded on public stock exchanges.

Insurance/Pensions

Pension funds and insurance companies are large institutional investors, with long-term patient investment time horizons in their legal and practical responsibility as contractual savings providers. As holders of decisive securities blocks, they also have a reputation for shaping innovation and good corporate governance. [21] East Asia has world ranking state pension schemes after decades of savings accumulation. South Korea's National Pension Fund is the third largest public fund globally after Japan and Norway, with assets under management of USD 775 billion as of end-2023, while Malaysia's Employees Provident Fund for private sector workers is the 15th largest.[22] They are charged by their governments with broad market development policy and allocation roles such as building local bond foundations after the 1990s Asian Financial Crisis, and stepping in as equity buyers to support local stock markets during the global financial crisis in 2008.

During the Covid-19 pandemic, governments in the region, as elsewhere, allowed citizens to tap retirement savings from these pools. In Malaysia more than 6 million citizens drew down their accounts four times from 2020–21 to soften the impact from the pandemic. In each instance the Employee Provident Fund was forced to sell domestic and overseas assets into turbulent markets. In addition, employee contributions to the Provident Fund were cut from 11 percent to seven percent of salaries. Early withdrawals were rationalized as a stopgap income boost, but in cases of consecutive depletion may undermine system soundness and viability as Asia comes to regret a consensus to forego private backstops with equal heft.

Globally, China's Ping An Insurance is the largest with assets of USD 1.5 trillion while its main competitor China Life Insurance comes in 8th with USD 665.3 billion.[23] Ping An has a range of subsidiaries including life and property/casualty insurance, banking, and securities. The group's investment portfolio is more than two-thirds in bonds, with equities less than 15 percent.[24]Bonds, concentrated in state-owned transportation, finance, utilities, and energy companies are three-quarters of China Life's holdings, with equities 17 percent.[25] Life insurance differs from non-life in asset-liability matching, with both tending toward conservative fixed-income but the former with the longer payout formula favoring maximum maturities. With China's population rapidly aging, the central government, after years of false starts, is rolling out a national pension system to standardize underfunded and poorly designed provincial plans. Beijing in 2022 also announced that citizens can contribute up to RMB 12,000 (USD 1860) annually on their own with incentives to supplement accounts, the first time a private pillar was officially endorsed. The capital markets cheered on projections that private pensions could top USD 1.7 trillion by 2025.[26]

India's pension system offers a wide range of options but caters to only a small portion of the population, missing the elderly and informal workers. Coverage under private pensions is only about 6 percent of workers, with 90 percent of jobs in the informal sector.[27] The insurance industry in India was liberalized in the 1990s under an initial opening wave that was not repeated until 2022. The life segment is dominated by Life Insurance Corporation (LIC) of India as one of the country's biggest institutional investors. In 2023 it held 37.45 percent of its USD 550 billion-plus portfolio in Indian government and state enterprise bonds and 24.7 percent in equities, nearly 4 percent of India's market capitalization.[28] Holdings are concentrated in large companies, with financial and energy accounting for 23 percent and 16 percent, respectively.[29]

India's state-owned life insurance giant came to market in 2022, with foreign investors permitted to own up to 20 percent. Previously LIC was off limits, but overseas portfolio and direct investors turned to dozens of other competitors. They could first take a 26 percent stake in life insurers in 2000, which was further raised to 49 percent in 2015 and 74 percent in 2021. The initial public offering for LIC was disappointing, with doubts over franchise value after prospectus review as stocks were in correction mode more broadly. The state divested a 3.5 percent stake and raised USD 2.7 billion, one-third of its original target.[30] It was the country's largest IPO ever despite timing delays around the Russia-Ukraine war, and non-resident participation was lackluster after 6 months of net outflows from the local stock market.

In Latin America, the private pension fund industry that was a showcase for years (See case study-Chile) is still the linchpin institutional investor, with assets under management estimated at nearly USD 1 trillion. As in Asia, the industry shrank during the pandemic when governments in Chile, Colombia, and Peru allowed citizens to tap their savings to fund essentials. While an immediate liquidity infusion for citizens, the base accumulated over decades was eroded with double-digit portfolio leakage as a portion of assets that will be difficult to recoup over the medium term, especially since populist Presidents in all three countries favor full-circle return to old-style government-run social security protection.

Prior to the pandemic Chile, the leader in private pension fund creation, saw widespread social protests demanding reforms to the system. Citizens protested meager payouts and high fees. Leftist President Gabriel Boric's 2022 victory was attributed to that anger, and he has announced a "reform" plan for the private pension system. The change would allow citizens to keep their individual contributions. However, it would gradually increase employer contributions with the state initially funding a newly created Guaranteed Universal Pension Plan.

Three consecutive authorized withdrawals from private pension funds (AFPs) during the global pandemic in 2021–22 amounted to USD 44.2 billion, and by mid-2024 pension savings dropped from 83 percent of GDP to 62 percent, USD 188.1 billion.[31] Although they were eviscerated by the emergency pullouts, the AFPs are still bigger in comparison with Chile's stock market capitalization of USD 168 billion, but their influence will be a shadow of former glory with the establishment of the new state system.

The private heyday has passed for Latin America, as in Eastern Europe when Hungary and Poland dismantled their compulsory versions for fiscal contingencies at the time. Future contributions in Chile, even if partially voluntary, will likely be surpassed by Brazil's as a standout example of plans that are visible securities market actors, with a professional association to promote self-regulation and product acceptance. After decades of political debate, in 2019 Brazil reformed its pension system as it became clear the costs of the public, pay-as-you-go system was crippling the economy. A year earlier social security outlays accounted for 44 percent of the federal government's budget and totaled 8.6 percent of GDP. The reform increased the retirement age for men from 56 to 65 and for women from 53 to 62, saving an estimated USD 194 billion over the next decade.[32] In addition to the General Social Security Regime, there is a separate one for government workers and a private system offered by companies and for individuals as active investors mirroring the US 401 K voluntary retirement contribution model.

Case Study: Chile's Private Pension Pendulum

For decades, Chile's replacement of its public pay-as-you-go pension system with privately managed individual accounts (Administradoras de Fondos de Pensiones, AFPs) was a model for emerging markets. It was replicated in Mexico, Central and South America, and its champion, the brother of later President Pinera, advocated for the cause globally. Private pension funds were seen as such a popular innovation in the 1990s that they nearly spread as far as Zambia as the US Agency for International Development wished to pilot and guarantee them there. They asked for our advice, and we recommended waiting until the local capital market was better prepared.

Chile's mandatory personal accounts were introduced in 1981 and immediately were controversial since they did not cover self-employed workers as a large component. The AFPs were regularly criticized for high administrative fees to compensate for the unknown risks of the experiment. Contributions were set at 10 percent of the monthly salary and tax deductible.

In 2008 a new pension law was enacted that provided benefits for more workers, encouraged greater competition (and lower fees), and ensured more gender equity in retirement practice. It set up a basic universal minimum pension for all citizens as a supplement to the individual accounts.

As the industry grew, AFP investment rules were liberalized in stages by the superintendent in charge of the industry. Initially, portfolios were restricted to government and financial institution bonds, and a few corporate debt instruments. Within four years, as the capital markets and client familiarity developed the government bond investment edict was halved to 50 percent and up to 30 percent of assets could be invested in equities on a step-up schedule. By 1996 restrictions were further eased and AFPs could hold up to 6 percent in foreign assets, a level that was hiked to 45 percent in 2008.[33] Alternative investments were also gradually allowed and the most recent guidelines in 2020 featured private equity, real estate, and infrastructure funds.[34] This progression from predominant captive safe fixed income to riskier equities and unconventional asset classes is the prototype. In 2021 new regulations had the AFPs report how they assess climate and ESG criteria in their process, in line with Chile's regional leadership as a sovereign bond issuer in the sphere.

Collective Investment Funds

As described in chapter two, the earliest mutual funds targeting emerging markets were launched for international investors in the 1980s. As capital markets developed across the emerging universe, retail investor interest took off both at home and abroad. Before these innovations choices were limited to bank deposits, gold, and real estate, which remain asset class competitors.

In 2020, the World Bank found the average size of 71 countries' mutual fund assets was 182.14 percent of GDP. The industry encompasses a size and popularity range based on investor culture and the relative position of other contractual savings channels. In Brazil assets under management have tripled since the turn of the century to top 75 percent of GDP. In contrast, Poland's mutual fund industry is tiny despite its early start in the region with the tradition of private pensions and retail investors acting on their own. At its peak before the 2008 Global Financial Crisis holdings were only 10.6 percent of GDP and pre-pandemic stood at only 6.8 percent and have since rebounded slightly to 9 percent, according to ECB data. In Asia, Indonesia boasts 97 licensed fund managers, but the ten largest dominate the industry with more than half of assets[35] (see case study).

Case Study: Mutual Funds Collective Takeoff

China has seen its mutual fund industry surge in recent years in line with its growing economy and broader financial sector opening. At year-end 2000 there were 34 funds and by 2005 49 fund management companies had USD 57 billion under management, of which more than 20 were joint ventures with foreign investment houses. In 2005 ownership restrictions were relaxed and foreigners were permitted a 49 percent stake in joint ventures with domestic firms, up from 33 percent previously. By 2011 foreign commercial banks, including giants HSBC and Citigroup already present in the country, were granted permission to distribute mutual funds, and in April 2020 the China Securities Regulatory Commission (CSRC) fully opened the mutual fund industry to foreign asset managers. In 2024, the mutual fund industry had just over USD 4 trillion in assets under management in nearly 10,000 funds, almost double the amount from three years earlier.[36]

In Malaysia 37 approved mutual funds managers managed 381 vehicles with total assets of USD 29.95 billion in 2006. By end-2023 38 locally incorporated managers offered 740 funds with total assets of USD 212 billion.[37] Two-thirds of the assets under management are invested domestically, with nearly 50 percent directed to equities. However, the industry is concentrated, with the top five managers accounting for more than half of the assets under management. Although the ESG/sustainable segment is growing, only 68 of the investment vehicles offered are qualified as Sustainable and Responsible.[38]

In India, the mutual fund industry has expanded dramatically over the past two decades as the private sector and foreign joint ventures have dissolved Unit Trust of India's former monopoly which was launched in 1963 as a joint initiative by the government and the country's central bank, the Reserve Bank of India. As recently as 2003, UTI controlled two-thirds of the industry but now it is not even in the top ten as measured by assets under management. Today the industry has 44 asset management companies offering more than 2500 funds. Total assets under management stood at USD 505.5 billion in the fiscal year that ended March 2022, and topped USD 800 billion in the third quarter of 2024, according to the Association of Mutual Funds in India. Over a decade assets under management in the industry surged 500 percent.[39] Nearly 13 million citizens are invested in local mutual funds; however, that is less than 3 percent of India's population.[40]

In Latin America Brazil has by far the largest fund industry and it has surged in size in recent years. In 2006 there were more than 3000 funds with total assets topping USD 308 billion, most in fixed income funds due to high inflation in the early 2000s. A decade and a half later there were 773 asset managers managing more than 25,000 funds with assets under management of USD 1.3 trillion, more than 50 percent of GDP.[41] The number of managers is up due to plethora of new small, boutique firms offering a wide range of products.

As in developed markets, the mutual funds cover all asset classes with offerings in equities, bonds, money markets, mixed variable/fixed income, and Exchange Traded Funds (ETFs). ETFs have overtaken the once omnipresent closed- versus open-end fund structure, where either a set number of shares is issued or continuously redeemed following investor preference. Indonesia and Malaysia feature Islamic finance with Sharia compliant alternatives like sukuks—bonds that do not pay interest, but a risk shared guaranteed return in compliance with Islamic law—and stocks screened by religious authorities excluding listings like pork producers.

While Islamic finance is generally thought to be used only in countries with predominantly Muslim populations, it is increasingly being embraced in Western markets with many, including the Bank of England, arguing that it inherently aligns with ESG.[42] One tenet of Sharia finance is that it should do no harm, with for example, investments in alcohol and tobacco banned. It emphasizes fairness and encourages partnerships which underpin sustainable investment. In 2024 Islamic finance was a USD 3.9 trillion industry spread over more than 80 markets, although only ten countries account for nearly 95 percent of the world's Sharia compliant assets, led by Saudi Arabia and Iran with a 25–30 percent share each.[43] Issuance of sukuk bonds was expected to reach USD 170 billion in 2024 as compared to USD 168.4 billion a year earlier and total global outstanding sukuks are estimated at USD 875 billion, issued in 27 currencies, according to ratings agency Standard and Poor's.[44]

Legal/Regulatory Regimes

Since the early 2000s the IMF and World Bank, working with the relevant industry groups, have promulgated international codes and standards to manage capital markets risks and ensure good governance. They conduct regular financial sector assessments based on these technical criteria posted on their websites, juxtaposing laws and rules on the books against actual supervision and enforcement.

The first, and most basic, assessment is whether the central bank is independent. An independent central bank with decision-making not subject to interference by the government is a first tenet of the Bank for International Settlements' (BIS) Core Principles, the longstanding rulebook dating to the 1980s when only advanced economy central banks set cross-border guidelines for multinational lenders. The BIS—known as the bank for central bankers—pioneered the concept of risk-adjusted minimum capital adequacy ratios as a portion of assets, and consecutive iterations have added complex formulas to cover liquidity and operations safety cushions. Emerging market authorities are now full members of the club, but often lag a generation behind at 3 or 4 in the so-called Basel (BIS headquarters city) numerology now 5 for the state-of-the-art regime. Some members insist on the right to adapt their own provisions in line with local habit such as experience with formal deposit insurance, and often bridle at the home-host country tug of war over monitoring and resolving problem institutions, an exercise in "joint cooperation." For example, issues may arise when a developed country-based bank runs into trouble with its operations in an emerging market. Conflict centers on whether the parent bank or the country's bank resolution fund should rescue the institution and/or reimburse domestic savers. Regional and sub-regional supervisors have forged their own understandings and collective practice, and Europe's emerging market banks fall under the comprehensive EU edifice.

Insurers are guided by the International Association of Insurance Supervisors' Core Principles. The International Organization of Securities Commissions' Objectives and Principles set the standard for regulators and broker-dealers. Pension funds in turn have a separate body and norms. The danger is a stovepipe approach of separate overseers not appreciating the entire commercial and prudential picture and sometimes working at cross purposes. Originally the proliferation made sense as financial institutions evolved over time, but now these simultaneous elements are commonplace, and financial intermediaries exploit the interrelationships in their business model. An umbrella non-bank institution menu features pension and insurance products along with standard mutual funds and managed accounts. It may be a separately capitalized subsidiary of a multifaceted banking group, or stand-alone organic structure. In these situations, central banks typically take the lead in setting the course for system protection, with the array of modern financial services increasingly combined under a single overseer as well for easier collaboration.

The IMF divides financial sector standards into four core components.[45]

- "Regulatory governance" covers the independence, enforcement authority, and decision-making arrangements.
- Practical application of laws, rules, and procedure falls under the "regulatory practice" heading.
- "Prudential framework" encompasses internal controls and corporate governance.
- "Integrity and fairness/safety net" is the final component including protection of depositors, investors, and policyholders in times of stress or crisis.

The Fund assessments typically rank performance of the financial sector's legal and regulatory regime on a scale of 1–10 in the areas and present a priority roadmap for corrections.

The IMF's codes presume the presence of basic company, bankruptcy, contract, consumer protection and private property laws, and internationally accepted accounting and auditing standards. They wave a red flag in nascent areas. For example, the Fund conspicuously criticized El Salvador's bitcoin legal tender embrace without safeguards as an overriding financial stability issue. The popular "buy now, pay later" firms that proliferated with the e-commerce revolution have also set off alarms as non-deposit takers escaping central bank scrutiny.

A key standard the IMF seeks for every market is a bank deposit insurance scheme. It is normally funded by the banks themselves, but amounts can be purely symbolic and inadequate to compensate clients in the event of failure. Even in developed markets deposit insurance funds can be quickly depleted if a large institution fails. In Mexico, the Institute for the Protection of Bank Savings (IPAB) guarantees bank deposits and addresses solvency issues. The Mexican Congress allocates funds to IPAB annually and the insurance scheme is also funded by the banking industry, and it sells Savings Protection Bonds on the local market.[46] Similarly capital market participants and insurers should have investor and policyholder guarantee pools in cases of insolvency, fraud, or manipulation such as insider trading. In the US, the well-known counterparts are the Federal Deposit Insurance Corporation (FDIC) and Securities Investor Protection Corporation (SIPC).

Financial sector information disclosure and reporting rules have expanded to include "ESG," environmental, social, and governance factors as detailed in the concluding chapter. Global attention may be on US SEC and EU blueprints, but the emerging and frontier market members of IOSCO have been equally active on this front, with markets like Kenya undergoing epic drought on the frontlines of climate change. The balance in designing and elaborating core principles has tipped away from advanced economy bias at their origin, which caused investors to downplay standard-setting exercises in their everyday allocation routine as the elaborate checklists were rolled out. In their due diligence fund managers incorporate headline indicators such as Basel capital minimum adherence as a basic safeguard against bad loan danger but tend to ignore the complex hierarchy of ratios and standards where the IMF has the technical lead in determining the "good housekeeping seal. It received this mandate after the Asian financial crisis, which spurred the "codes and standards" movement (see case Study Kenya).

Case Study: Kenya's ESG Edict Safari

Back in 2008, then Kenyan President Kibaki launched Vision 2030 to create a "newly industrializing middle-income country providing a high quality of life to all its citizens by 2030 in a clean and secure environment."[47] Five years later the Bankers Association launched the Kenya Sustainable Finance Initiative, supported by donor agencies, to provide training for employees at all levels on ESG issues through online training courses for 46 participating banks. The central bank governor stressed its importance as "developing countries like Kenya are being disproportionately hit by global warming despite being among one of the lowest polluters on the planet."[48] In advance of the UN's COP 26 climate summit in 2021, the World Bank warned that climate change will force tens of millions of East Africans to abandon their homes within the next three decades "even if schemes to reduce its impact on the region are rolled out."[49] These countries heavily rely on agricultural exports and in recent years have been hit by severe droughts, massive flooding and even locust infestations, directly attributed to environment swings.

The Nairobi Stock Exchange joined the ESG push as a member of the Sustainable Stock Exchange Initiative in 2015, a United Nations funded program for 115 stock markets where more than half offer training on ESG topics. A Green Bond module was launched in 2016 with assistance from the World Bank's IFC and the Dutch Development Bank as an inaugural pilot.

After the Finance Ministry announced investor exemption from paying withholding tax on green bonds, a corporate "green bond" debut listed for trading on the Nairobi bourse. Property developer Acorn Holdings raised USD 42.5 million (equivalent) to build environmentally friendly student housing in Nairobi. The bond was structured as a "restricted public offer," targeting only sophisticated institutional investors. The shilling bond was later cross-listed in London, the first placement from a Kenyan company on the dedicated International Securities Market. Both the Nairobi and London listed bonds are guaranteed by outside credit insurance provider Guarantco, established in 2005 by a handful of bilateral donors. It protects principal and interest payment for ESG bonds funding infrastructure development in Africa and Asia.[50]

The Nairobi Stock Exchange (NSE) in late 2021 published its own detailed ESG guidance manual for listed companies. It intends to align reporting with incipient international standards outlined in UN and global professional bodies, and most correlated regionally with the EU's comprehensive directive. The NSE granted companies a one-year grace period to implement disclosure, but blue-chips were ahead of the game. The biggest, most actively traded stocks on the USD 20 billion exchange—telecom operator Safaricom, financial services group KBC, and East African Breweries—started publishing annual sustainability reports several years before. The exchange has also announced plans to launch a stand-alone Climate Transition Index to attract more international investors, and specifically sustainability ones.[51] ESG guidelines have also been introduced in Nigeria, Tanzania, South Africa, and Botswana in the sub-Saharan region.

Next door in Tanzania the Dar es Salaam Stock Exchange (DSE) released its own issuance, listing, and reporting regime for sustainable bonds in early 2022. Months later the country's second largest bank, National Bank of Tanzania, floated the continent's first gender bond, aided by non-profit Financial Sector Deepening (FSD) Africa, an arm of the UK development agency. It was nearly 300 percent oversubscribed and proceeds go to banks and corporations committed to women's empowerment through financial inclusion, leadership positions, and labor market equality.[52] Further South, Botswana's Absa Bank listed the exchange's first sustainable bond in 2024.

Although sub-Saharan markets remain small and are often not on investors' radar screens, their location and demographics propel the embrace of ESG and sustainable financing instruments and reporting. They are among the most battered by climate change, and the young populations—in Kenya more than 60 percent of citizens are under age 25—are pushing leaders to act. The need to develop the "S" and "G" components was highlighted during the worst of the global pandemic when authorities were criticized for deficient testing and vaccinations and sweeping lockdowns in the absence of basic healthcare buildup. With tens of million suffering starvation due to climate change and conflict across Kenya and the Horn of Africa, UN programs are severely underfunded. The so-called impact investor community is working with select mainstream developed and emerging market-based banks and fund managers on partial capital market models that can secure long-term commercial funding, where homegrown ESG qualitative and quantitative criteria can be incorporated.

Key Takeaways

- Banks remain the dominant actors, and even as the old government-mandated directed lending model has fallen by the wayside state-controlled intermediaries are frequently in pole position versus private and foreign competitors. By the roughest estimate of financial system depth that places size against GDP their footprint can be double securities players.

- Micro-finance, originally created to get credit to the rural poor, has surged across the globe and today these institutions are commercial and regulated as a subset of the banking sector. They have also appeared in nascent securities markets as issuers with examples including Bolivia and Cambodia.
- Non-bank institutional investors are the linchpins of capital markets, including broker-dealers with underwriting functions, and mutual-pension-insurance funds that conduct large transactions and exercise corporate governance. Latin America and Eastern Europe were in the vanguard of private pension creation, but fiscal contingencies and system atrophy over time undermined an in-built advantage.
- Voluntary global organizations and codes govern regulation and conduct in banking, securities, insurance, and pensions which emerging markets rarely duplicate since standards were originally geared more toward advanced economies, and local professional capacity is stretched thin. The central bank routinely has the outsized oversight role across the financial intermediary range, and although a single body for all non-banks is the recommended global trend this design is impractical in under-resourced supervisor experience.

Notes

1. Cindy Li and Sean Creehan, "India's Non-Banks Emerging from the Shadows," Pacific Exchange Blog, Federal Reserve Bank of San Francisco, May 31, 2019, https://www.frbsf.org/banking/asia-program/pacific-exchange-blog/indias-non-bank-financial-companies-emerge-from-the-shadows/.
2. Li and Creehan.
3. The Economic Times, "Can the new RBI framework on NBFCs stop DHFL, IL&FS type failures?", November 15, 2021, https://bfsi.economictimes.indiatimes.com/news/nbfc/can-the-new-rbi-framework-on-nbfcs-stop-dhfl-ilfs-type-failures/87711805.
4. Adrian Jimenea, John Wu and Harry Terris, "The world's largest bank by assets, 2024, Standard and Poor's, April 30, 2024, https://www.spglobal.com/marketintelligence/en/news-insights/research/the-worlds-largest-banks-by-assets-2024.
5. Asian Development Bank, "Asia Bond Monitor: June 2023," http://dx.doi.org/10.22617/SPR210452-2.

6. Fitch Ratings, "Industrial and Commercial Bank of China Limited," Rating Report, December 9, 2021, https://www.fitchratings.com/research/banks/industrial-commercial-bank-of-china-limited-09-12-2021.
7. Maxwell Sutton, "The Indian Banking System," Reserve Bank of Australia, December 9, 2021, https://www.rba.gov.au/publications/bulletin/2021/dec/the-indian-banking-system.html.
8. Ministry of State-Owned Enterprise, "Ongoing quest for advancing state-owned enterprises," CISION PR Newswire, Jakarta, Indonesia, February 27, 2022, https://www.prnewswire.com/news-releases/ongoing-quest-for-advancing-state-owned-enterprises-301491181.html.
9. McDowell Ramintas, Zia Khan, and Rehan Ahmad, "Indonesia banks may attract more foreign investment as capital deadline looms," S&P Global Market Intelligence, February 16, 2022, https://www.spglobal.com/marketintelligence/en/news-insights/latest-news-headlines/indonesia-banks-may-attract-more-foreign-investment-as-capital-deadline-looms-68624982.
10. The World Bank & International Monetary Fund, "Financial Sector Assessment: A Handbook," September 2005 https://www.imf.org/en/Publications/Manuals-Guides/Issues/2017/01/01/Financial-Sector-Assessment-A-Handbook-18600
11. Corporate Finance Institute (CFI) Team, "Top banks in Poland," CFI, August 27, 2021, https://corporatefinanceinstitute.com/resources/careers/companies/top-banks-in-poland/.
12. Antony Sguazzin and Moses Mozart Dzawu, "Development Bank Ghana, has 5-year, $4 billion capital target," Bloomberg US Edition, June 13, 2022, https://www.bloomberg.com/news/articles/2022-06-14/development-bank-ghana-seeks-fivefold-lending-leap-in-5-years?sref=9BZJXmVl.
13. Grameen Research, Inc., "History of Grameen Bank," http://grameenresearch.org/history-of-grameen-bank/#:~:text=The%20origin%20of%20Grameen%20Bank,targeted%20at%20the%20rural%20poor.
14. Ira W. Lieberman, Paul diLeo, Todd A. Watkins, and Anna Kanze, eds., "The Future of Microfinance," Brookings Institution Press, June 30, 2020, https://www.brookings.edu/book/the-future-of-microfinance/.
15. Grameen Bank, grameenbank.org.

16. Grameen Bank.
17. Lieberman, et al., "The Future of Microfinance."
18. Claudio Gonzalez Vega, "The Regulation of Microfinance," BBVA, June 29, 2018, https://www.bbva.com/en/the-regulation-of-microfinance/.
19. Robert Cul and Jonathan Morduch, "Microfinance and Economic Development," Policy Research Working Paper, No. 8252, World Bank, Washington, D.C., 2017, http://hdl.handle.net/10986/28913.
20. Lieberman, et al., "The Future of Microfinance."
21. Dimitri Vittas, "Pension Funds and Capital Markets: Investment Regulation, Financial Innovation, and Governance," Viewpoint, World Bank, Washington, D.C., 1996, https://openknowledge.worldbank.org/handle/10986/11632.
22. Willis Towers Watson (WTW), "Top pension fund assets rise strongly despite pandemic uncertainty," September 7, 2022, https://www.wtwco.com/en-US/News/2021/09/top-pension-fund-assets-rise-strongly-despite-pandemic-uncertainty.
23. Sovereign Wealth Fund Institute (SWFI), "Top 100 largest insurance rankings by total assets," accessed September 9, 2022, https://www.swfinstitute.org/fund-rankings/insurance.
24. Twinkle Zhou, "Ping An focusing on property, A-shares, Reits for 2021," Asian Investor, December 1, 2020, https://www.asianinvestor.net/article/ping-an-focusing-on-property-a-shares-reits-for-2021/465262.
25. Twinkle Zhou, "China Life eyeing more government bonds, equities," Asian Investor, March 25, 2021, https://www.asianinvestor.net/article/china-life-eyeing-more-government-bonds-equities/468588.
26. Reuters, "In milestone move, China launches private pension scheme," April 21, 2022, https://www.reuters.com/world/china/china-unveils-private-pension-plan-ageing-population-2022-04-21/.
27. Mercer CFA Institute, "Global Pension Index 2021: India's pension system needs impetus to ensure adequate retirement income," Mercer Consulting, October 19, 2021, https://www.mercer.co.in/newsroom/global-pension-index-2021-india.html.
28. Ashish Rukhaiyar, "This is how LIC invests its money to generate returns," BusinessToday.IN, February 14, 2022, https://www.businesstoday.in/latest/corporate/story/this-is-how-lic-invests-its-money-to-generate-returns-322487-2022-02-14.
29. Ashutosh Joshi, "Why LIC's $128 billion stock portfolio can withstand global shift toward higher rates," ThePrint, February

15, 2022, https://theprint.in/economy/why-lics-128-billion-stock-portfolio-can-withstand-global-shift-toward-higher-rates/832603/.

30. Nupur Acharya, Ashutosh Joshi, and Filipe Pacheco, "Insurer LIC joins year's worst debutants after record India IPO," Bloomberg US Edition, May 17, 2022, https://www.bloomberg.com/news/articles/2022-05-17/insurer-lic-slumps-in-debut-after-record-2-7-billion-india-ipo?sref=9BZJXmVl.
31. Funds Society, "Chilean Pension Funds Remain 17% Below their Pre-Withdrawal Levels, September 10, 2024, https://www.fundssociety.com/en/news/pensions/chilean-pension-funds-remain-17-below-their-pre-withdrawal-levels/.
32. Andres Schipani and Bryan Harris, "Can Brazil's pension reform kick-start the economy?", Financial Times, October 22, 2019, https://www.ft.com/content/c32a93f2-f1d6-11e9-ad1e-4367d8281195.
33. Barbara E. Kritzer, "Chile's Next Generation Pension Reform," Social Security Bulletin, Vol. 68, No. 2, 2008, https://www.ssa.gov/policy/docs/ssb/v68n2/v68n2p69.html.
34. Matias Eguiguren, "Pockets of Opportunity in Latin America's Evolving Pension Fund Picture," Preqin, November 12, 2021, https://www.preqin.com/insights/research/blogs/pockets-of-opportunity-in-latin-americas-evolving-pension-fund-picture.
35. Heryadi Indrakusuma, "The Indonesian Mutual Fund Industry: Challenges and Opportunities," Nomura Journal of Asian Capital Markets, Spring 2020 Vol. 4/No. 2, https://www.nomurafoundation.or.jp/en/wordpress/wp-content/uploads/2020/04/NJACM4-2SP20-03.pdf.
36. Yue Yue and Tang Ziyi, "Inside China's plans to overhaul its $3.7tn mutual fund industry," Caixin, Nikkei Asia, May 28, 2022, https://asia.nikkei.com/Spotlight/Caixin/Inside-China-s-plans-to-overhaul-its-3.7tn-mutual-fund-industry#:~:text=China's%20securities%20regulator%20is%20plowing,to%20get%20into%20the%20sector.
37. S. Birruntha, "Malaysia's top five funds managers account for over half of total RM975.48 billion AUM, Business Times, March 25, 2024, https://www.nst.com.my/business/corporate/2024/03/1030097/malaysias-top-five-fund-managers-account-over-half-total#google_vignette.
38. Birruntha.

39. https://www.outlookindia.com/business/retail-investors-contribute-over-half-of-mf-industry-s-rs-40-trillion-assets-under-management-amfi-news-284267.
40. The Hindu Business Line PTI, "Mutual funds add over 3 cr folios in FY22 on sharp rally in equity market, digitisation," New Delhi, April 17, 2022, https://www.thehindubusinessline.com/money-and-banking/mutual-funds-add-over-3-cr-folios-in-fy22-on-sharp-rally-in-equity-market-digitisation/article65328908.ece.
41. Fitch Ratings, "Fitch Ratings 2022 Outlook: IMQ Ratings for Brazilian Asset Managers," December 9, 2021, https://www.fitchratings.com/research/fund-asset-managers/fitch-ratings-2022-outlook-imq-ratings-for-brazilian-asset-managers-09-12-2021.
42. Susannah Hammond, "The ESG potential of Islamic finance," Thomson Reuters, June 14, 2022, https://www.thomsonreuters.com/en-us/posts/news-and-media/islamic-finance-esg/.
43. Chloe Domat, "Islamic Finance: Just For Muslim-Majority Nations?," Global Finance, August 1, 2024, https://gfmag.com/banking/islamic-finance-just-muslim-majority-nations/.
44. Franklin Templeton, "Global sukuk market on the rise," June 26, 2024, https://www.franklintempleton.lu/articles/2024/western-asset/global-sukuk-market-on-the-rise.
45. International Monetary Fund (IMF), "Financial Sector Assessment: A Handbook," IMF, September 29, 2005, https://www.imf.org/en/Publications/Manuals-Guides/Issues/2017/01/01/Financial-Sector-Assessment-A-Handbook-18600.
46. Redaccion Opportimes, "The balance of the APAB of Mexico at the end of 2021," June 16, 2022, https://www.opportimes.com/the-balance-of-the-ipab-of-mexico-at-the-end-of-2021/
47. Kenya Vision 2030, https://vision2030.go.ke/.
48. Duncan Miriri, "Kenya's first green bond starts trading on the bourse," Reuters, Nairobi, Kenya, January 16, 2020, https://www.reuters.com/article/us-kenya-bonds-green-idUSKBN1ZF1WH.
49. Reuters, "Climate change to displace tens of millions of East Africans by 2050—World Bank," Nairobi, Kenya, October 27, 2021, https://www.reuters.com/business/cop/climate-change-displace-tens-millions-east-africans-by-2050-world-bank-2021-10-27/.

50. GuarantCo, Guarantees of Development, https://guarantco.com/about-guarantco/.
51. Elizabeth Kivuva, "NSE index to measure firms' climate action," Business Daily Africa, March 9, 2022, https://www.businessdailyafrica.com/bd/economy/nse-to-introduce-climate-change-index-to-measure-listed-firms-3741380.
52. Nasi Haki, "First gender bond to be listed on a stock exchange in Africa," ESI Africa, May 3, 2022, https://www.esi-africa.com/industry-sectors/business-and-markets/first-gender-bond-to-be-listed-on-a-stock-exchange-in-africa/#:~:text=The%20NMB%20Jasiri%20gender%20bond,bonds%20with%20a%20gender%20focus.

5

Capital Markets and Private Equity

Public capital markets are at the heart of the asset class, with performance measured through domestic and foreign stock and bond benchmarks and indices that evolved from the late 1980s. They also include currency and derivative credit default swap subsets. The relevance of international credit ratings for investors and casual followers is a core theme, along with the establishment and implementation of corporate and sovereign workout and insolvency laws when borrowers run into trouble, with often gaping divides between written laws and actual practice. Retail and institutional investor activity are separate development tracks culminating in the rise and dominance of Exchange Traded Funds (ETFs). Private equity-venture capital has grown dramatically, aided by early World Bank IFC arm sponsorship and a separate trade association, Global Private Capital Association. The industry has shifted concentration from infrastructure and consumer staples to e-commerce and fintech, with proven techniques for valuation and exit from investments in the absence of standard indices.

Capital Markets: Measures of Development

As explored in the first chapter, emerging stock markets became "fashionable" in the late 1980s, and international and local debt markets took off after the introduction of Brady bonds and IMF structural reform programs in Latin America at about the same time. For more than a decade bilateral and multilateral donors poured millions of dollars into developing local stock

B. Morrissey and G. Kleiman, *Emerging Economies and Financial Markets*,
https://doi.org/10.1007/978-3-031-85669-3_5

and bond markets across the world, especially in the transitioning countries in Central Europe and Central Asia after the fall of the Berlin Wall. Virtually every country across the emerging market universe clamored for a startup or functioning stock market, with the same enthusiasm and patriotic embrace as a national airline. Frequently in countries where we provided technical advice and assistance in developing capital markets to lure foreign investors, the macro-economic environment and broader financial sector were stumbling blocks. In the mid-1990s we provided regular training for Central Asian market participants, but most representatives still had state-dominated banking sectors and nascent privatization programs that stifled progress and diverted policymaker attention.

This experience is a reminder for the "top-down" macro-economic and policy view to pass inspection—including solid GDP growth, low inflation, direct-portfolio investment access—before taking the next step to scrutinize the market. For equities, the size of the market and number of listings are typically the first stage of assessment. A solid 20–30% range saving/investment rate as a portion of GDP is an auspicious base but does not necessarily translate into banking and securities takeoff. Market capitalization/GDP is key, with advanced economies typically over 100 percent. In sub-Saharan Africa, for example, in 2023 the continent's biggest economy, Nigeria had a ratio of only 19.3 percent, while the second largest economy, South Africa, had market capitalization/GDP at 289.1 percent.[1] Nigeria's 172 company stock exchange compares with South Africa's total of 224.[2] South Africa has long had a market-determined exchange rate and adequate hard currency reserves for investors repatriating proceeds and cutting-edge sophisticated banks and institutional investors. In contrast, Nigeria only adopted a floating exchange rate in 2023.

Assessing local debt market development is focused on the corporate-official composition of bond issuers and the length of the yield curve. Typically, in the early stage of market development the only offerings are government securities—short-term Treasury bills and government bonds with maturities out to 2–3 years—generally tax-free. They are often popular for offering double-digit yields on short-term paper, but outsized borrowing by the government crowds out the private sector's access to debt financing. Initially the market is illiquid as local banks are obligated to buy and hold government securities for capital adequacy and prudential purposes, with scant secondary trading. As financial markets begin to mature, banks are generally the first non-government private issuers, while early corporate entrants often seek backup bank guarantees for their bonds, so the risk is shared between the bond buyers and the guarantor. A local debt market is deemed advanced when corporate bonds with maturities of 3 years are actively traded by domestic and foreign institutional investors, and not just by local banks.

Bond market development, particularly the corporate segment, substantially lagged stock market building in emerging economies worldwide, with the exception of China. In Asia, the Asian Development Bank and ten countries launched a dedicated effort to develop bond markets in the 2000s, after the 1997–98 Asian Financial Crisis revealed the absence of local currency financing alternatives. Today China accounts for three-quarters of the emerging market bonds in the region and has spurted to nearly $20 trillion size, globally second only to the US in terms of the amount outstanding, with a two-thirds/one-third government-corporate split. In Thailand, the overall market in 2024 was 93% of GDP, but the corporate segment was only 2 percent of GDP [3] (Fig. 5.1).

Another key measurement of capital market development is market liquidity, the ability of participants to undertake securities transactions without triggering large price changes.[4] Low bid-ask spreads and high transaction volumes suggest good liquidity. The turnover ratio is a common read as the total number of shares traded divided by the average number outstanding during a set period. By region, during the 2020 Covid-19 pandemic emerging Asian markets, with turnover at 25.7 percent, were more active than in the Middle East/North Africa which came in at 23.3 percent.[5] Free float is also a reflection of market sophistication with analysts focused on the percent of shares available in listed companies. Even large

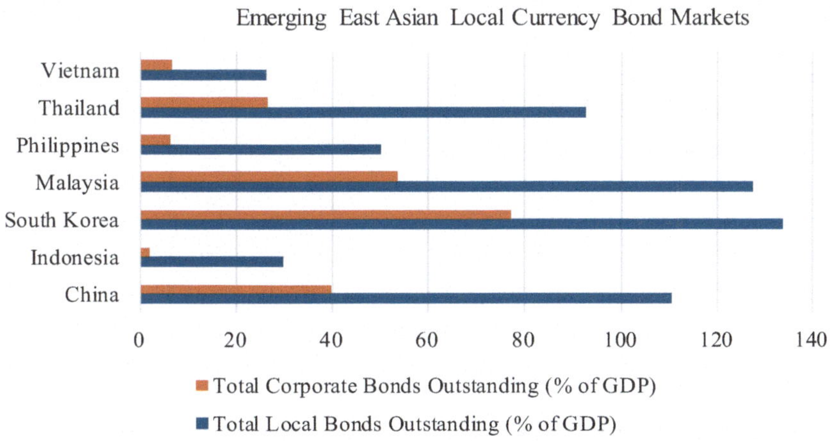

Fig. 5.1 Emerging East Asian Local Currency Bond Markets (*Source* asianbondsonline.adb.org/documents/abm_sep_2024.pdf)

pioneer markets, like South Korea, were notable laggards on this front, as major chaebol conglomerates were still closely held by company owners and management, with limited shares offered for public trading. Today free float is still considered lagging in China and the Gulf Cooperation Council countries where governments retains a firm hold on a significant portion of listed state company shares.

Investors also measure market development by assessing ease of entry and costs as taxes and entry curbs can proliferate. Foreign shareholders often face ceilings on individual and aggregate shareholding despite direct access in principle, not only in the early stages of market opening and development but also sometimes in sectors a government deems "strategic" like financial services or infrastructure. Taxes across all investment categories, such as capital gains and withholding interest income, should be roughly equalized so as not to unduly favor one class over another. Levy removal and reduction registers a government's "seal of approval" in promoting local capital markets. New levies or a hike—such as Brazil which regularly imposes and alters a charge on foreign exchange transactions—are deterrents. Sudden and unexpected imposition of new levies gives investors pause not only due to the added cost of investment, but also more broadly as such moves often indicate a broader economic problem such as a widening fiscal deficit that needs to be plugged. Both bond and stock investors see the presence of market makers and primary dealers which function as auction participants and underwriters, respectively, as a sign of maturity. They are generally banks or brokers which create liquid markets by quoting both buy and sell prices.

Establishment of a transparent legal and regulatory system with examples of verified rule enforcement is also critical to market development and necessary to attract foreign inflows and protect investors more broadly. An independent securities commission with a mandate for transparency and enforcement is presumed. Beyond power in law and responsibility, the agency must use tools at its disposal such as forcing a company to de-list when it fails to report earnings. Disclosure rules mandating timely and adequate release of all market-related information are key and investors expect enforcement. Internationally accepted accounting and auditing standards and periodically updated financial statements are the reporting routine. Investors shun markets with delays in quarterly or annual reporting, or with sharp stock or bond sell-offs before a company reports bad news which indicates insider trading.

Similarly, corporate governance rules are paramount. Investors seek markets that have adopted the G20/OECD Principles that were last updated in 2015.[6] Surveillance that listed companies are compliant is a frontline duty of the securities regulator and/or the stock exchange, and also falls to institutional investors as fiduciaries protecting their investors' interest. While most countries have national laws or regulations, they may not be compulsory. Despite years of technical assistance from donors like the World Bank, particularly in the post-Soviet economies, standard application is often lax. For example, adoption of the Czech Corporate Governance Code is voluntary for companies listed on the USD 37 billion Prague Stock Exchange.[7] The only provisions are included in its Act on Corporations but companies reference OECD and other best practice in reports and compliance statements. The dozen or so Czech companies listed on other EU exchanges have adopted European Union standards.

Broadly, corporate governance standards are enshrined in either company or securities law and are designed to protect and facilitate shareholders' rights and ensure equitable treatment.[8] Issues include annual meeting notification and voting eligibility results. The principles also cover the roles and responsibilities of the corporate board of directors and the existence of an independent external auditor. The OECD found in the 50 jurisdictions it follows that as of end-2020 three-fifths had requirements to report the gender composition of boards.[9]

Also included in legal and regulatory assessment are bankruptcy and insolvency laws, with many markets experiencing repeat instances of a law on paper that is not applied or takes years to settle beyond stipulated guidelines (see case study: India). When considering allocation, the framework can offer comfort, but actual enforcement can diverge and also reveal wide treatment disparity between domestic and foreign investors. In the initial phase of China's property developer debt crisis that began in 2021, onshore obligations were paid with offshore ones in default. Sovereign insolvencies are addressed in the final chapter.

Case Study: Bankruptcy/Insolvency Laws: Theory versus Track Record

Prior to 2016 it took an average of 4.3 years to deal with insolvency in India, according to the World Bank in its longstanding Doing Business report discontinued after data discrepancies. That year parliament passed a new bankruptcy law, at the time a flagship reform under the two-year-old Modi government. The code aimed to streamline the process and reduce court resolution to 180 days and allowed assets to be sold to repay creditors absent at final workout. The law reflected the urgency of dealing with bad debt at state-owned banks that dominate the system which stood at 14.3 percent of total loans, in contrast with less than 5 percent for private lenders. The bankruptcy rules were also expected to create a market for restructured debt that could attract so-called distressed high yield or "vulture" investors.

The new law looked great on paper as it drew from global best practice, but reality was the opposite. Soon after passage the "fast track" timeline was extended to 270 days and then to 330 days. In an immediate test of the law the Reserve Bank of India, the central bank, directed state banks to put a "distressed dozen" large corporate debtors which owed billions to the state-owned banks into bankruptcy. On referral of the giant cases to the new bankruptcy tribunals, the central bank was hoping to rid the banking system of one-quarter of bad loans in a decisive endgame.[10]

Essar Steel, which owed more than USD 7 billion to mostly state banks, was one of the original dozen. Instead of 270 or 330 days, the case dragged on for nearly two-and-a-half years. Under the original terms of the law the company should have been liquidated but the bankruptcy tribunal's decision was appealed to the Supreme Court, which finally allowed the sale of the company to global giant ArcelorMittal. It ended up paying the banks 90 percent of their claims.[11]

For legal protection bond investors look to so-called covenants in prospectuses that spell out safeguards for investments in detailed contract and financial ratio terms. The clauses include issues such as conditions for completing corporate dividend payments and maximum allowed debt-equity leverage ratios. The war in Ukraine made investors again realize the importance of the "fine print" in documents. Several of Russia's state and private companies that had issued bonds in dollars or euros had provision for payment in rubles in their covenants that longtime emerging markets had basically ignored absent any precedent. In the weeks after the invasion, the Russian central bank ruled the ruble was no longer convertible and instituted capital controls.

In capital market development futures, options, and other derivatives are a last stage of market development, and are common in Europe, Asia, and Latin America and now spreading to the Middle East and Africa. Creation is often spurred by foreign investor interest or technical assistance from donors. The first products are typically created for hedging currency and interest rate risk and stock indices. A recent example is Kenya's derivatives market, dubbed "NEXT," launched in 2019 after years of discussion and debate among the investment community, stock exchange, and regulators. The first instruments created and traded were single stock and equity index futures.[12] In the bigger emerging markets stock, bond, and currency derivatives have been widely embraced. The National Stock Exchange of India is ranked among the largest derivatives exchange in the world, along with by Brazil's B3 (Brasil, Bolsa, Balcao)—previously the BM&FBovespa—which is the combined stock and derivatives market in Sao Paulo. Both are now bigger than the former world giant CME, the Chicago Mercantile Exchange.[13]

The efficiency and safety of post-trade clearing and settlement is another critical factor to determine market engagement. Today it is now almost universally automated with a central depository, as a function of readily available technology. As outlined in Chapter 1, in the early days of development, these processes were conducted manually and could take weeks instead of the few days standard currently. Investors arranged their own paper securities safekeeping with friendly banks with no formal custody capacity. Now most markets have modern electronic trading and post-trade systems which can be purchased "off-the-shelf." The automated facilities protect investors from fraud and settlement delays and generally meet international settlement standards (see case study: Ghana).

Case Study: Ghana's Post-Trade Plumbing Clog

The Ghana Stock Exchange was officially launched in January 1991. At the time all trading and post-trade clearing and settlement was completed manually and on paper. In the early days we knew foreign investors who rented safety deposit boxes at the popular Labadi Beach Hotel to hold their paper shares between trips. By the exchange's second decade a formal securities depository had been established and was housed at the central bank.

The World Bank assisted the Ghana Stock Exchange with automation at a cost of USD 1.8 million[14] Electronic trading and a clearing and settlement system were launched, with the latter managed by a separate subsidiary of the exchange in line with international standards. Instead of reinventing the wheel or creating a whole new electronic system with the latest bells and whistles from scratch, hardware and software were purchased from the Lahore Stock Exchange and installed by the same Pakistani company that performed the work for Lahore. Systems vendors, including Nasdaq in the US, have pan-emerging market franchises as winning bidders, but technically these globally available systems may be incompatible with local broadband capacity and should fit with the larger infrastructure of the bank payments network.

Capital Markets: Risk and Performance Benchmarks

Stock, bond, and currency investors have different styles and selection criteria against a common background. Currency traders with no specific instrument screening start with "top-down" national account indicators to determine the likely exchange rate direction against the US dollar or Euro. The data they assess include GDP growth and inflation data, interest rates, external debt, and central bank reserves as measured by the number of months of imports they cover, with 3 months as the critical cut-off. In the wake of repeated emerging market crises, the current account balance, remittances, and goods and services trade became critical decision-making factors for investors, with policymakers and ratings agencies also assessing these data points as part of broader vulnerability analyses.

More than a decade ago during the so-called "taper tantrum" when the US Federal Reserve hinted at marginal monetary tightening which sent investors fleeing emerging markets, a "little known research analyst" at Morgan Stanley identified a group of emerging economies as "the fragile 5."[15] The group included Turkey, Brazil, South Africa, India, and Indonesia, economies that had financed massive current account deficits on "fickle" portfolio inflows in the capital account.[16] The Fed's retrench preview wracked currencies as investors dumped local stocks and bonds and retreated to the safe haven US dollar (see case study).

Case Study: Emerging Market Turmoil: 2013 Taper Tantrum and 2008 Global Financial Crisis[17]

In the first six weeks after the US Federal Reserve Chair Bernanke initially revealed in May 2013 that the amount of cheap money being pumped into the US economy would ease as growth and employment picked up, turmoil mounted in emerging markets as investors dumped local stocks and bonds which pressured currencies and central bank reserves. Countries with worrisome current account deficits were the hardest hit by currency drops as foreign investors fled to the US safe haven dollar. Turkey's lira lost 7.4 percent against the US dollar—compounded by rising domestic social unrest and political uncertainty at the time—while South Africa's rand was off nearly 12 percent, and the Indian rupee was down over 9 percent.

For fund flows tracked on a weekly basis by EPFR—the Boston-based company that reports on global institutional and retail mutual fund flows and fund manager allocations—the sell-off for the six weeks through mid-June 2013 was more severe than for the six weeks following the collapse of US investment bank Lehman Brothers in September 2008 that was a spark for the Global Financial Crisis (Fig. 5.2).

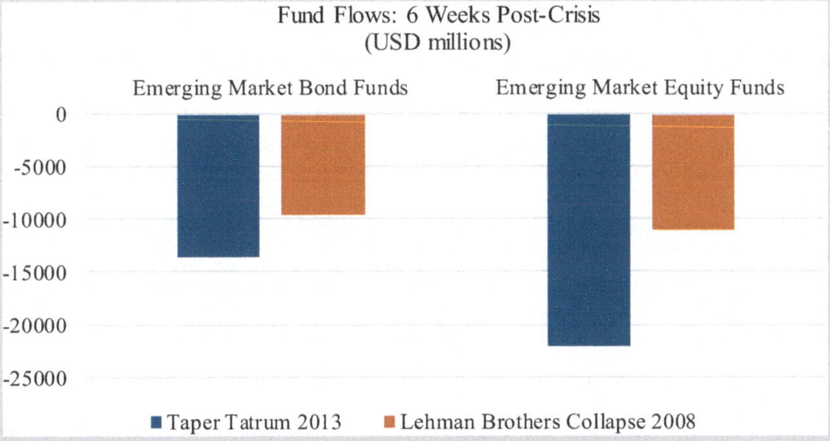

Fig. 5.2 Fund flows: 6 weeks Post-Crisis (USD millions) (*Source* EPFR)

Key commodity producers experienced significantly higher outflows, including Indonesian equities which had redemptions of USD 404.5 million vs. USD 112 million in the 2008 period. In South Africa where the USD 181 million outflows from bonds were nearly four-times higher, while equity fund outflows were USD 421.8 million against USD 56.8 million in the 2008 period.

On the equity side, the four original BRIC markets—Brazil, Russia, India, and China –experienced the heaviest selling pressure in the six weeks, with USD 4.3 billion redeemed from China, USD 2.9 bn from Brazil, USD 1.3 billion from India, and USD 755 million from Russia. ETF selling accounted for 77 percent of the sell-off from Brazil, 71 percent from China, 57 percent from India, and 30 percent from Russia as retail investors fled from risker assets. In stark contrast, in the immediate post-Lehman period in 2008, Chinese ETFs attracted over USD 2 billion, Russian USD 795 million, Brazilian USD 546 million, and Indian USD 282 million. Overall redemptions from tracked equity funds were USD 2 billion for Brazilian equities, USD 1.2 billion for Indian, USD 994 million for Russian, and USD 302 million for Chinese funds as some investors sought safety in diversification as global markets sank.

During the taper tantrum in 2013, Brazil had the largest bond redemptions (USD 951 million), followed by Russia (USD 274 million), Mexico (USD 258.3 million), and Indonesia (USD 229.5 million). ETFs accounted for only 10 percent of the outflows from Brazil, but ETF selling accounted for 38 percent for Russia, 29 percent for Mexico, and 25 percent for Indonesia. In the six weeks following the fall of Lehman, these countries experienced even greater outflows, with redemptions from Brazil at USD 960.7 million, Mexico at USD 617.5 million, Russia at USD 603 million, and Indonesia at USD 394 million. Selling by ETFs accounted for less than one percent for these markets in 2008, with the exception of Indonesia which accounted for 2.5 percent, as there were few emerging market bond ETFs then.

In response to the turmoil in 2013, policymakers responded rapidly across the emerging market universe to contain the damage from the selloffs. Indonesia and Brazil—which each battled currency appreciation prior to the market meltdown—took the most aggressive action. In Brazil, in addition to regular swap auctions—derivatives contracts designed to strengthen the currency—that totaled USD 6.7 billion from early May through mid-June, the Central Bank hiked its benchmark Selic interest rate by 50 basis points to 8 percent, sold on the spot market—as much as USD 3 billion in one day alone—and removed the 6 percent tax on fixed income inflows and the one percent levy on derivatives in an effort to attract inflows. The Brazilian Treasury conducted extraordinary auctions to buy back debt. Indonesia responded similarly. Bank of Indonesia surprised the markets by raising the rate it pays for overnight deposits by 25 basis points to 4.25 percent and then hiking its benchmark rate by the same amount to 6 percent. In addition, the Ministry of Finance and central bank bought bonds on the secondary market—as foreign investors pulled USD 1.7 billion out in just three weeks—and the Bank of Indonesia regularly sold dollars in an effort to buoy the ailing currency.

A similar wholesale sell-off across all emerging markets occurred in 2022 as developed market inflation levels soared to multi-decade highs and the Federal Reserve outright began a series of rate hikes. In the nearly ten years after the 2013 "taper tantrum," most of the original "fragile 5" built up foreign reserve war chests to avoid a repeat scenario. India accumulated USD 600 billion it also used for regular rupee intervention and was able to offer swap lines and loans to neighboring Sri Lanka, which ultimately suspended foreign debt payments and sought IMF assistance in its own current-capital account crash.

South Africa is a good example of policy shifts after the "fragile 5" sell-off. It was included in 2013 due to its current account deficit of 5.4 percent of GDP, but in 2021 reported a surplus of 3.7%, the highest since 1987. It was boosted by commodities exports, with the value of gold sales abroad the most in more than sixty years, according to the Reserve Bank. Despite its own domestic economic troubles due to ongoing power shortages, the war in Ukraine benefitted the country's trade balance as Russia had been a major global supplier of both precious and industrial metals which are top exports from South Africa. The rally in commodity prices globally boosted the South African rand at the beginning of the war as a long-established overall emerging markets proxy. The currency appreciated 6.7 percent against the USD in 2021 and through the first quarter of 2022 was up with the same gain, only one of six major emerging markets currencies to appreciate in that period as investors anticipated a series of sharp US Federal Reserve rate hikes to rein in inflation, which traditionally sends emerging markets investors fleeing to safe USD assets. The unit is often one of the worst hit currencies in times of global selloffs because the local market is deep and liquid and has large domestic institutional investors, so foreign investors can disengage quickly.

Despite no longer being a "fragile 5" country, South Africa's economic growth has been low in recent years due to regular power cuts from highly indebted state power company Eskom which slowed manufacturing and hurt corporate profits. Eskom, which supplies almost the entire country's electricity, 80% from coal, has USD 26 billion in outstanding debt, most explicitly government guaranteed. Major western governments pledged USD 8.5 billion at the COP26 climate summit in Glasgow in 2021 to help the company reduce its emissions, and the African Development Bank later announced a further USD 450 million as part of a broader USD 2.8 billion 5-year financing commitment. Despite the power cuts, President Cyril Ramaphosa was re-elected in May 2024 although his African National Congress party lost the parliamentary majority it had held since the end of apartheid.

Investors in emerging market stocks fit broadly into three categories: active stock pickers, passive index investors, and hybrid combination of these styles. For more than 30 years at Templeton—now Franklin Templeton—Mark Mobius was perhaps the most renowned bottom-up value-theme individual stock picker among emerging markets investors. He did not focus on whether the economy was in recession or where the currency was headed. Instead, his preference was to travel on-site to "kick the tires," meeting with company management, touring factories, and asking management hard questions. In contrast passive portfolios are purely based on existing stock indices (see below). The investor often sets the country weight of a portfolio against an international or local index, and stock purchases will replicate those included in the index. Positions in countries undergoing political or economic crises remain unchanged until the index provider revises their weights in the index which can lead to sharp losses if investor confidence shifts abruptly.

Index investing has come under scrutiny for ESG factor bypass, particularly after the Russian invasion of Ukraine. Russia's weight in the popular MSCI Emerging Markets index had fallen steadily after the 2008 global financial crisis when it was 10 percent. It dropped further after Moscow annexed Crimea in 2014 with select economic sanctions from the US and EU. At the start of 2022, its portion was under 4 percent.[18] Just a week after the war started, MSCI removed it altogether as blanket uninvestable due to sanctions from the West and capital controls in Moscow. Investors knew that there were political and governance risks in Russia, but the attraction of large blue chip commodity producers outweighed concerns.

The third group of emerging stock market investors is a hybrid, with broad index tracking mixed with proprietary stock selection. Often stock choices include not only local listings, but also companies that have offerings in overseas markets through global depository receipts which are priced in dollars or euros. Some buy shares of advanced economy-based multinational banks and companies with large exposure to emerging markets, such as Unilever. For example, the year before the pandemic the corporate giant reported that its sales in emerging markets, up 5.3 percent, were critical to its overall global sales growth of 2.9 percent.[19] Spanish banking giant BBVA is in this definition as well since its large operations in Turkey and Mexico traditionally accounted for the bulk of profits with slow home recovery in the wake of the 2013 Eurozone crisis and then the global pandemic followed by inflation and interest rate pressures. For example, for the first six months of 2024 BBVA reported that its profits were up 28.8 percent on an annual basis, with just over 50 percent of the increase from its Mexico operations.[20]

Bond investors can similarly be grouped into three broad categories. They may specialize in a cross-section of locally listed instruments denominated in the countries' currencies—including government, municipal, and corporate—or hard currency-denominated sovereign or corporate bonds. Like their equity counterparts, some follow global indices and others have an absolute return strategy. The most conservative funds and public pension plans by law depend heavily on the issuers' credit rating from the major agencies: Standard & Poor's, Moody's, and Fitch. Many emerging markets have their own home-grown ratings, with also high professional standards and credibility that local issuers must tap for approved placement. Some emerging markets-based raters were started as joint ventures with the international majors, while others are purely home grown. For example, CRISIL in India was established by several of the country's biggest financial institutions and it is now a subsidiary of Standard & Poor's. China has eleven domestic raters and has also allowed Standard & Poor's and Fitch to rate local issues. In 2021 as part of its bond market opening and as a series of property developers started to default, Beijing tightened governance and operating rules for ratings agencies (see case study: China).

Case Study: China's Long March Equity Experiment

A multi-volume book is in order to do justice to the history and paramount role of China's capital market, but milestones can be briefly traced from the "wild west" unregulated beginning, in a culturally awkward reference that regularly features. They draw on a chronology formally prepared by the China Securities Regulatory Commission in 2008 and from original client analyses over the past three decades.[21]

Unusually for emerging economies, China's markets started with bonds, not stocks. In the early 1980s state-owned enterprises began issuing debt, and by 1986 nearly USD 3 billion was outstanding. No regulation applied beyond the 1987 State Council mandate that the central bank had to approve sales. Along with the Ministry of Finance and State Planning Commission, it set quantitative limits based on pure discretion. A full decade later the PBOC established the interbank bond market for organized transactions, where institutional investors traded government and enterprise bonds through the China Government Securities Depository Trust & Clearing platform.

Initially central bank advance approval was required to trade, but by 2000 it was pro forma registration and the market was opened to individuals. It was dominated by central government bonds with large state-owned policy bank instruments also available. By end-2004 the total size was 42 percent of GDP, but the corporate market was only 0.75 percent. More than 70 percent were Treasury and central bank bills, with financial bonds from policy banks one-quarter and all activity concentrated in Shanghai.

The corporate segment lagged due to a series of defaults in the 1990s and lack of credit ratings agencies and non-bank institutional investors. In 2005 the IFC and Asian Development Bank issued RMB-denominated 10-year bonds as a benchmark for corporate issuers and domestic and joint venture ratings agencies were established. Standard & Poor's was an early presence and later established a wholly owned local unit.

Fast-forward to today, and China's bond market is the second largest in the world after the US with the amount outstanding over USD 20 trillion.[22] Central and local government issues together account for 45 percent of the market, financial institutions 35 percent, non-financial institutions 19 percent, and private companies only one percent as of 2024.[23] The domestic and offshore corporate market experienced a wave of defaults starting in 2019 from over-leveraged property developers. Treasury and policy bank bonds were added to international indices at the same time, attracting vast inflows with opening and juicy real yields before the US interest rate spikes in 2022. The Fed ratchet marked the first time in two decades that nominal returns on China's bonds were lower than comparable US Treasuries.

On the equity side, the government permitted Shanghai and Shenzhen to establish stock exchanges in late 1990 and a year later the former had 8 listed stocks and the latter 6. By mid-1991 both had composite indices, which existed alongside informal, unregulated markets all over the country largely trading internal company shares owned by employees.

In early 1992 reformer Deng Xiaoping called the stock exchanges an "experiment." In a speech in Shenzhen the CSRC history reports his ambiguity: "Securities, stock markets, are they good or evil? Let's try for one or two years; if it goes well, we can relax controls; if it goes badly, we can correct or close it." Later that year the Securities Committee and China Securities Regulatory Commission (CSRC) were established to draft definitive rules and regulations. The CSRC as a technical body reported to a Committee made up of various heads of ministries, with no hint of independence. In 1998 the two were merged and an insurance supervisor was carved out under a separate overseer. By then the combined market capitalization topped USD 200 billion, of which only USD 62 billion was tradable due to closely held state enterprise shares.

With tight capital controls and limited FX reserves in the early 1990s, China devised a series of schemes to attract foreign investors.

- "B shares:" domestically listed, denominated in RMB but sold and traded in USD or HKD by overseas investors
- "H shares:" shares of Mainland companies listed and traded in Hong Kong in HKD or another foreign currency
- "Red Chips:" shares of Mainland companies incorporated in Hong Kong and traded in HKD

Initially popular despite the registration hoops, the attractiveness of "B" shares plummeted as more companies either domiciled in or listed on the larger, more liquid, well-regulated Hong Kong market which still follows UK standards from its colonial history.

As China headed toward World Trade Organization accession in 2001, it enacted the first comprehensive Securities Law in 1999. It enshrined stock exchanges as here for the duration, no longer a pilot that could be closed down. Markets were recognized in statute for their economic function, as a funding outlet for both private and state-owned enterprises. The CSRC finally developed true enforcement power through the 2000s, with a sanctions committee and law enforcement task force for investor protection, despite chronic short staffing. It held listed companies to tighter accounting and reporting standards, although far from the accepted international benchmarks Chinese companies faced when selling stakes overseas. Retail investors have always been the main actors, and insider trading was overlooked except in the most egregious instances.

Despite stricter oversight and new IPO rules, the early 2000s saw market turmoil, with years of index correction and offering backlog. The State Council undertook another round of reforms, including professionalizing securities firms and promoting mutual and insurance funds. To draw in underserved business, the Shenzhen Stock Exchange set up a Small and Medium-sized Enterprises Board which attracted more than 200 companies lacking access to traditional bank capital in just 18 months.

In 2002 the Qualified Foreign Institutional Investor program was launched to allow high quality institutional investors to directly buy and sell mainstay "A" shares. An offshoot Renminbi Qualified Foreign Institutional Investors followed, which imposed even fewer restrictions and total assets under management conditions. These schemes had multi-billion-dollar quotas progressively raised until they were finally eliminated in 2019.

Further liberalization came through the 2014 dedicated "Stock Connect" link between Shanghai and Hong Kong, extended two years later to the

Shenzhen exchange, as a seamless cross-trading conduit between the centers. Chinese investors can take the "southbound" route and purchase Hong Kong and Chinese companies in the offshore hub. Bond Connect was next in 2017, offering cross-border fixed income market access.

As of September 2024, the total capitalization of Chinese stocks was about USD 10 trillion and accounted for 28 percent of the MSCI Emerging Markets Index, down from about one-third several years earlier as India's market grew and outperformed its bigger Asian counterpart to converge in investable size. Its outsized weighting, as well as government moves to crack down on some sectors and escalating geo-political tensions, had a growing number of fund managers calling for China's separation from the rest of the universe. In 2017 MSCI introduced its Emerging Markets-ex-China Index. By the end of the third quarter of 2024 so-called some 70 "ex-China" funds increased assets under management by more than 75 percent through the year to more than USD 26 billion, according to Morningstar, while "ex-China" equity funds had received USD 10 billion in new inflows, according to JPMorgan data.[24]

Credit Ratings

For sovereigns, the credit ratings agencies' grades are designed to serve as a forward-looking estimate of default probability and assess the government's ability and willingness to service debt. Ecuador illustrated potential divergence in the last two concepts when it defaulted on external bonds in 2008 during the global financial crisis, despite having adequate international reserves and a relatively low debt/GDP level. While the sovereign's credit rating from international agencies was solidly below investment grade, it was not in the "near default" range despite earlier bouts of non-payments and bond restructurings. (see case study) The sovereign simply said it was unwilling to pay bondholders for several outstanding obligations, claiming they were an "illegitimate" burden taken on by previous administrations.[25]

Case Study: Ecuador's Ability versus Willingness to Pay

In 2006 the left-wing candidate for President, Rafael Correa, promised voters that if elected he would again renege on the country's external bond obligations, just six years after restructuring from a previous default. Following his win, Correa formed a public debt audit commission which found that some of the country's bonds were "illegitimate" and claimed they gave unfair gains to private investors under "oppressive" contract terms."[26]

In 2008 Ecuador had international reserves of USD 4.47 billion and a low debt/GDP ratio of 33 percent.[27] Nonetheless, late that year President Correa declared two of its external bonds "illegitimate," called bondholders "real monsters," and defaulted without keeping up even minimal repayment. The raw macro-economic data cited by rating agencies underscored ability to pay, although it was rated far below "investment grade" prior to the payment stoppage. After the USD 3.2 billion default, the country began to repurchase the bonds as prices dropped in a secretive secondary market operation that further antagonized investors. Within six months a formal offer at 35 cents-on-the-dollar was conducted, with over 90 percent of bondholders eventually accepting. The oil-rich country kept current on a separate bond that matured in 2015, it considered straightforward and "legitimate," presumably to smooth eventual market re-access after the buyback.

Just five and half years later, Ecuador was back in the international market. In the interim, the country relied on China and multilateral loans to close gaping budget and balance of payments deficits. Low global interest rates and the search for yield attracted investors, even if they had held the defaulted paper earlier. They flocked to the USD 2 billion, 10-year bond priced to yield 7.95 percent.[28] Like Argentina in serial trouble, oil price collapse during Covid later forced another bond swap, this time on "friendly terms" with little outright interest-principal reduction due entirely to inability to pay.

The sovereign ratings are based on a series of qualitative and quantitative building blocks, explained on public websites that communicate methodology. The former include the effectiveness, stability and predictability of policymaking, and the transparency and reliability of statistical information. Quantitative measures include macro-economic data such as growth prospects, income levels, external indebtedness, international reserves, and fiscal performance. The components and sub-components have different weightings, and ESG rankings from official and private sources offer supplemental input. As a rule of thumb, local currency is presumed to be rated higher than FX debt, since governments can always print money to cover internal obligations even if it faces challenges with external ones. Often currency depreciation makes foreign currency payments difficult and until the pandemic-era debt sovereign defaults were generally on foreign debt, but more recently domestic and foreign local currency bond holders have also faced defaults and restructurings.

Similarly, sovereigns are generally assessed as more creditworthy than corporates, but the distinction can disappear with state-owned banks and enterprises borrowing with implicit or explicit government guarantees. The global ratings giants have a comparable scale where BBB is prime quality and below that level speculative. They also offer a separate outlook that is not letter based, but positive, negative, or stable. The outlook indicates the direction the rating is most likely to take over time.

Over the years the raters' reputations have suffered as a snapshot in time regulatory box to tick. With changes in fast-moving crises, they are often seen as "behind the curve." Since the business model is issuer pay, suspicion is also cast on a conflict of interest between revenue streams and harsh judgment. For example, at the onset of the global pandemic in early 2020, Suriname, was below investment grade but rated "B" by Standard and Poor's before the collapse in oil prices and exports resulted in two defaults. In July that year it completed a distressed exchange and then several months later a new government proposed a total standstill on foreign currency debt service payments.[29] Other sovereign defaulters at the time were rated lower—including Zambia and serial non-payer Argentina—and Suriname's blowup was cushioned by its small creditor base as a rare issuer in the market.

In early 2021, we began to anticipate a default by Sri Lanka, resulting not only from Covid but from years of economic mismanagement as cited in two blog posts.[30] After Standard & Poor's downgraded the sovereign twice in 2020, by early 2021 it had graded it CCC+ , with a stable outlook. A CCC+ is in the bottom tier, in the "danger" range for non-payment. By August it adjusted the outlook to negative, and then in January 2022 followed through with a further cut to CCC. The agencies again lagged evolving market consensus. It was clear to most analysts for almost 18 months that the monetary and fiscal policies of the government, along with the repercussions on the tourism-reliant economy from Covid, would result in a formal debt payment moratorium which was finally announced in April 2022. As with Argentina in the 1990s and its latest restructure, the end game was grasped before the Big 3 ratings agencies could catch up, in an acknowledgment of the process limitations (see case study) (Fig. 5.3).

Case Study: China Tears for Teardrop Island Sri Lanka

In early 2021 worry about debt sustainability in Sri Lanka surged as investors eyed a first "post-Covid" sovereign default. News from the Central Bank that gross official reserves continued to slide in January to USD 4.8 billion from USD 5.2 billion a month earlier further pressured bond prices and the rupee (LKR). After losing 7% against the USD in 2021—and 17% vs. EUR—the LKR came under increasing pressure. Foreign currency repayment obligations for 2021 totaled USD 5.7 billion. The fall in reserves came as the central bank settled a USD 400 million currency swap facility from the Reserve Bank of India. Originally granted in the summer of 2020 for pandemic-related spending, it was rolled over until February. Further extension by the RBI was contingent on Sri Lanka reaching at least a staff-level agreement for an IMF program. The government, however, insisted an IMF deal was not necessary and held out for further assistance from long-time bilateral funder China, focused on a USD 1.5 billion swap facility.

Fig. 5.3 Sri Lanka's Debt Crisis (*Source* Sri Lanka development update, "Bridge to recovery," The World Bank, April 2024; *2023 Data is preliminary)

With some of its external sovereign bonds trading 40 percent below face value, the debt office also had massively undersubscribed Treasury Bill sales with 2021 auctions routinely seeing only one-third of offers taken up by banks and investors. At the same time, US dollar-denominated auctions for Sri Lanka Development Bank bonds were similarly undersubscribed despite hefty yields.

Foreign portfolio investment had fallen off a cliff. Foreign investors sold net USD 25 million of shares in January 2021 after dumping USD 273 million the year before, according to Bloomberg data. However, local investors had poured into the Colombo Stock Exchange as they fled fixed-income offerings. Stock trading volumes in January 2021 exceeded annual volumes from 2016–2019.

In April 2022 Sri Lanka suspended its foreign debt payments for the first time in its history, and two months later the government collapsed. Nearly a year later, in March 2023, the new government finally sealed a three-year USD 3 billion IMF bailout loan. A deal with foreign bondholders to restructure some USD 12.5 billion in debt, including a 27 percent "haircut—loss for investors—was finally agreed in September 2024.

Indices

Stock indices measuring the price performance of a market were the first to appear as country funds and a database rolled out under World Bank auspices as described in Chapter 1. The MSCI Emerging Markets Index is the mainstay as the longest, with an industry of Exchange Traded Funds (ETFs) tracking it. It was launched in 1988 covering 10 countries, and today it tracks 27 countries and 26 percent of global market capitalization.[31] The perennial disconnect between emerging and developed markets, with around a 25% gap between share of the global economy and market size, is a compelling long-term argument for expansion. Markets like South Africa are converging with advanced economies, where capitalization is a multiple of GDP. The industry-sector composition of the index changed dramatically over time from the original "beer-cement-banks" mix. In the early days of emerging market investing, these sectors were top picks as investors bet on both rapidly growing economies, driving cement stocks higher on infrastructure development, and an expanding middle class that would have better access to finance and buy more non-essential products like beer. In 2009 tech stocks made up 11 percent and just over a decade later accounted for one-fifth.[32]

When Russia was removed from the index after it invaded Ukraine China accounted for 30 percent, followed by Taiwan (16 percent), India (13 percent), and South Korea (12.5 percent) for over two-thirds Asia domination. All but one of the ten biggest companies in the 1399 index are in Asia, and they make up nearly one-quarter of the total USD 7.3 trillion capitalization.[33] In addition to the main index, the MSCI suite offers investors MSCI Emerging Markets-ex-China, regional and stand-alone options. India is the largest weight in the MSCI Emerging Markets Index-ex-China at 27.4 percent, followed by Taiwan (24.3 percent), and South Korea (14.4 percent). MSCI also has a Frontiers Market Index for smaller less liquid markets with the same rough 25 count, and also offers an ESG index for these markets (Fig. 5.4).

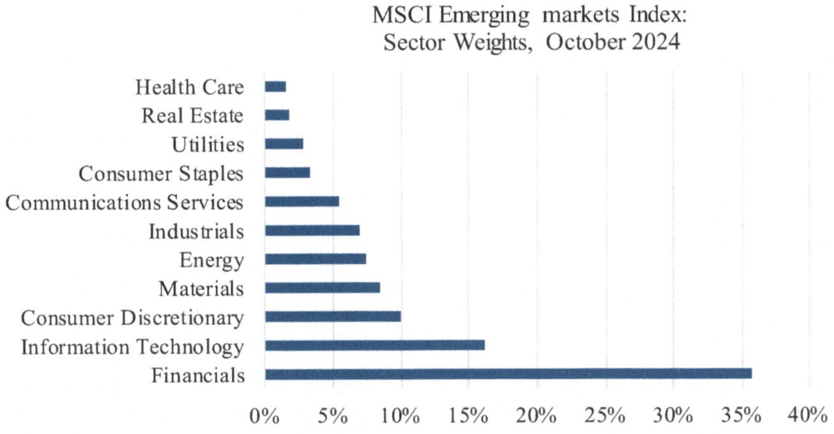

Fig. 5.4 MSCI Emerging markets Index: Sector Weights, October 2024 (*Source* MSCI)

MSCI is not the only game in town. The Dow Jones Emerging Markets Index covers 3952 companies with China, Taiwan, and India as the largest constituents as in its rival. South Korea is included in MSCI as an emerging market but is categorized as developed by Dow Jones, while Pakistan is in the latter as full status emerging but ranked as Frontier in the former after it was removed from emerging markets status due to a decline in its size and liquidity. (see case study: South Korea) The FTSE Russell Emerging Index covers 23 markets and 1907 companies of which 1059 are in China.[34] Nasdaq's Emerging Markets Index was launched in 2012 and also covers 1907 stocks, with nearly one-third in the technology and telecommunication sectors and financial sector share about 25 percent.[35] All of the indices are market capitalization-weighted and adjusted for the amount of "free float," shares that are actually investable. These gauges have noticeably lagged the US S&P 500 for over a decade, and value hunters and dedicated emerging markets investors often cite historically low price/earnings ratio just above 10, and discount to developed markets to justify allocation. The 2020–23 sell-offs in emerging market stocks driven by the pandemic, war, and US Federal reserve rate hikes left stocks massively discounted both historically as well as when compared to US counterparts.

Case Study: Korea's Index Identity Conundrum

The index providers use a variety of criteria to classify a market as developed, emerging, or frontier. South Korea, with a market capitalization/GDP of over 130 percent, has been classified as developed since 2001 by S&P Dow Jones due to its high level of per capita income, economic development, market size and liquidity, and absence of significant foreign investor restrictions including on short-selling.[36] [37] FTSE has it in the same category since 2009, and cites its independent external committee of practitioners and market professionals for the decision.

MSCI is the exception as it still classifies the country as emerging. In South Korea's 2022 presidential race both candidates had an upgrade from emerging to developed market status demand in their campaign platforms. MSCI acknowledges that the South Korean stock market has met broad standards based on wealth and turnover but cites lingering market access administrative and technical issues. Foreign investors must register with the Financial Supervisory Service and cannot participate in the interbank foreign exchange market which has limited trading hours for investors based in European and North American time zones. Reflecting sensitivity since it had to turn to the IMF after the Asian financial crisis, the won is not fully traded offshore, but only in the non-deliverable forwards market which is an over-the-counter cash agreement settled between two counterparties. South Korean authorities have for several years promised liberalization, especially as central bank currency intervention practice to maintain an export competitive rate has also been regularly criticized in US Treasury reports. They have been accused of backtracking on short sales as well with a longtime suspension early in the Covid pandemic, which spurred a one-way online retail investor boom.

The index options for bond investors are narrower, and J.P. Morgan dominates this space. It launched the first Emerging Market Bond Index (EMBI) in the early 1990s after Brady bonds were created to track sovereign bonds issued in hard currencies. As domestic bond markets developed, the New York-based firm, building on early World Bank work, added the Government Bond Index-Emerging Markets (GBI-EM) for local currency instruments. Local currency bond markets have grown and broadened. In 2000 the amount of government bonds issued in local currency by emerging markets was only 39 percent of the total debt sold, and it now tops 90 percent. Local currency government bond markets have grown 290 percent since the 2008–9 Global Financial Crisis to USD 12.8 trillion, making them the largest component of emerging bond markets, and in the same period access for international investors has more than doubled from 24, largely on openings in "frontier markets." Assets under management benchmarked to JP Morgan's Global Bond Index-EM totaled USD 238 billion in 2022, while for hard currency sovereign debt the total benchmarked was USD 382 billion.[38]

In addition to indices tracking hard and local currency government debt markets, J.P. Morgan offers the Corporate Emerging Markets Bond Index which tracks hard-currency denominated bonds from state-owned quasi-sovereign, and private banks and firms. Assets under management benchmarked to this index totaled USD 134 billion in 2022.[39]

FTSE Russell has its own Emerging Markets Government Bond Index (EMGBI) for local currency bonds from 16 countries. It covers more than 425 issues with a total market value of more than USD 4.5 trillion as of 2024. FTSE's Emerging Markets Broad Bond Index covers US dollar-denominated debt from governments, regional agencies, state-owned enterprises, and corporations in some 60 emerging markets, while its Emerging Markets US Dollar Government Index includes 50 countries.

Bloomberg offers an Emerging Markets USD Aggregate Bond Index which tracks US dollar-denominated debt issued by sovereigns, quasi-sovereigns, and corporates. The company reviews inclusion annually based on World Bank income group classifications of low- and middle-income countries.

By index size J.P. Morgan's sovereign EMBI is roughly USD 1 trillion but dwarfed by local currency and corporates twice as large. The asset class maintained a winning streak to surpass US Treasury returns over the same period equities were in the doldrums in the pandemic, war, and US rate hike period, withstanding cycles of ratings downgrades and mutual fund outflows without lasting damage. A separate CDX index has appeared for derivative credit default swaps, a tool to hedge against state and company non-payment when a "credit event"—a non-payment or default—is declared under industry rules and a payout auction is held by the International Swaps and Derivatives Association (ISDA) governing body.

In addition to being the most widely followed emerging market equity index, MSCI is also the favored currency index, tracking two dozen units relative to the dollar to complement the stock foundation. The index mirrors the currency exposure in the MSCI EM equity indices.[40] In 2017, the Bloomberg ING Global Emerging Markets FX Indices were launched for a dozen of the most liquid currencies. For money markets the main tool is the JP Morgan Emerging Local Markets Index Plus created in 2012, which tracks the total returns for local currency in two dozen countries with at least USD 10 billion of external trade. In 2021 Deutsche Bank introduced a version for 21 emerging market currencies, noting the massive increase in foreign holdings of local currency government bonds which more than doubled in the 15 years prior to the global pandemic. The indices track both spot—exchanged for immediate delivery—and carry trade performance where a low-cost currency funds a trade with a high yield one and the investor collects the difference. Brazil's real has long been a popular play as the interest rate differential between it and the US dollar or Japanese yen is traditionally wide. This strategy unwound abruptly in mid-2024 when Japan's central bank finally raised interest rates to marginally positive from sub-zero under longtime quantitative easing.

Institutional investors employ the indices described above but retail investment in emerging markets has boomed since the turn of the century as Exchange Traded Funds (ETFs) offer inexpensive ways for individual investors to have exposure. The iShares Emerging Markets ETF (EEM) was the first US-listed emerging market ETF in 2003, followed two years later by the Vanguard FTSE Emerging Markets (VWO).[41] By 2024 there were 229 emerging markets ETFs traded in the US, with total assets under management of USD 340 billion and an average expense ratio of 0.58 percent.[42] The two largest equity ETFs remain VWO and EMM, topping USD 85 billion, while the largest fixed-income fund, iShares JP Morgan USD Emerging Markets Bond ETF, has USD 15.4 billion.[43]Emerging market equity ETFs dominate the exchange traded fund space, with global, single country, and sector-specific offerings. In late 2024 ETFs accounted for 44 percent of the total net assets of all emerging market equity funds tracked by EPFR.

Private Equity

Just as it spurred emerging markets index creation in the 1980s, the World Bank's private sector arm, IFC, fostered development of private equity investment through financing and organization. IFC co-invested with private funds in the 1990s in early dedicated vehicles and assisted in founding the industry association Emerging Market Private Equity Association, now the Global Private Capital Association. In 2000 the IFC created a separate department to manage its venture capital investment noting that returns from the 1990s were disappointing due to lack of "proper deal flow."[44] It found that in 2000 the only countries with enough critical mass for country-specific funds were Brazil, Russia, India, China, and South Africa (the original BRICS).

Private equity (PE) investments are directed to illiquid, unlisted private sector companies, and investors commit to a long holding period that includes turning around and/or building companies, generally over a 3–7-year time frame. In contrast, investors in listed equities can buy and sell daily if they choose. PE investing is a hands-on management skill set working with entrepreneurs, and big managers known as general partners target double-digit internal rates of return. PE investors employ the same "top-down" macro-economic screening as do investors in publicly listed equities but also undertake intensive individual company screening. Owners must be willing to give up control in return for equity finance and solid personal and board relationships are assumed.

The private equity funds we have advised with long time horizons conduct due diligence by mapping the direction of the economy, currency, and policy-making through the next five years. Assessing the outlook requires knowledge of the country's recent economic performance and policies, as well as potential policy changes at times of government transition. This "crystal ball gazing" meets a checklist but has immediate on the ground application where policies affect the deal sector and broader startup eco-system. Venture capital is under 0.5 percent of GDP as a tiny portion of the financial sector in most emerging markets, and often the legal and tax regime is nascent. Transactions are subject to negotiating discretion, with the government's reputation for respecting contractual rights and middle-class economic growth historic consistency between administrations both decisive factors.

Private equity investment in emerging markets peaked in 2021 at USD 249.3 billion, with three-quarters of it directed to emerging Asia.[45] Within Asia, China accounted for 57 percent of the total while India took in 30 percent. Investment in 2021 was particularly active as much of the money was "dry powder," funds that had been raised in late 2019 through 2020 that

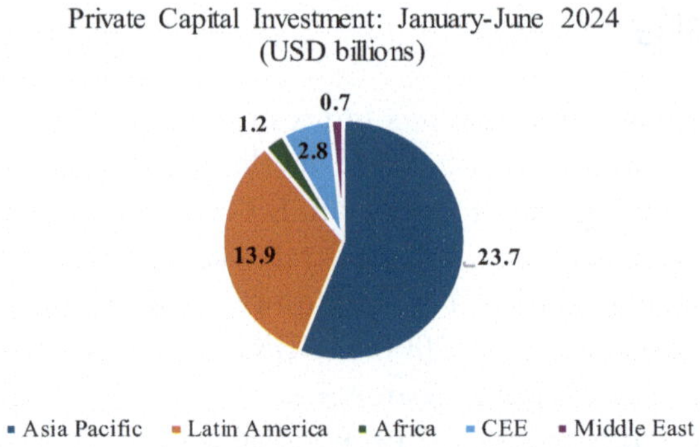

Fig. 5.5 Private Capital Investment: January–June 2024 (USD billions) (*Source* GPCA, Global Private Capital Association, https://www.globalprivatecapital.org/research/; *Excludes Japan, South Korea, Australia and New Zealand)

had not been invested due to the global pandemic. A year later investment in emerging market PE dropped 25 percent as the US Federal Reserve moved to tighten monetary policy and in 2023 fell to USD 96.3 billion. Through the first half of 2024 investment continue to drop with 55 percent of investment directed to Asia while flows to Latin America accounted for 32 percent of the total [46] (Fig. 5.5).

Following the global pandemic, healthcare has attracted significant interest, with PE investors committing USD 7 billion of the total USD 49 billion in the January-June 2023 period to the sector, while 70 percent of flows were directed to infrastructure in the first half of 2024. Digital infrastructure and telecommunication accounted for just over 22 percent of flows, with 5 percent directed to renewable energy in the January-June period of 2024.[47] In recent years PE funds have shifted their focus from formerly popular areas such as ride sharing and consumer goods.

Private and public equity interrelate as desired cash-out can be through a public offering on the stock exchange that can be a stand-alone or combined with a direct sale. Through the first three quarters of 2024, ten Indian start-ups came to market raising over USD 1.9 billion.[48] Other exit strategies include a merger and acquisition deal with a domestic or international company, or the fund can sell its stake back to the original owner or employees. General partners have started to branch out into private credit as another business line, where high-risk loans and debt are structured for a complete package. This dual capability is tapped for infrastructure projects, but also can fill a void where export credit is scarce such as in Africa.

This reach mirrors the multi-asset diversification model increasingly embraced by large public market fund houses, and also derives from a private equity industry reinvention phase after the notorious Abraaj scandal in Dubai in 2018. The acclaimed manager claimed $10 billion in assets as the field's largest at its peak, with clients/limited partners from the Gates Foundation to the World Bank. The founder of Abraaj and his team were prosecuted for massive fraud and stripped of their licenses. Professional association members have since pledged to improve back-office procedures and disclosure, including creation of an indicative index as an outside check on internal reported returns. Large PE houses have been motivated to feature best practices as they begin to offer portfolio participation to retail investors in their own public funds. The asset class has been under rare scrutiny in the emerging markets panoply during Israel's war in Gaza/Lebanon from 2023–24, as the so-called "startup nation" has a top ranking global high-tech scene. At the outbreak foreign and local sponsors pulled back by half, but by mid-2024 multi-billion dollar commitments had rebounded.

Key Takeaways

- After a market is analyzed from a "top-down" perspective—with growth, inflation, fiscal and monetary policy, and structural reform in the mix—a deeper dive into stock or bond market carries distinct quantitative and qualitative dimensions. Investors have currency exposure in local markets and international stocks and bonds.
- Equity and debt investors look at headline size and liquidity in a first cut. Local bond markets are scrutinized for the range of government and corporate offerings, length of maturities, and yield curve. Stock exchange assessments will turn to "microstructure" aspects like turnover and P/E ratios, market makers, and free float. Investors also weigh background factors including ease of entry, taxes, the legal/regulatory environment, and corporate governance.
- Stock investor styles are active pickers, passive index, and a hybrid combination. Bond investors may specialize in a cross section of local instruments including government, municipal and corporate or focus on hard currency-denominated sovereign or corporate bonds. Numerous indices track stock, bond, and currency performance, the best known are from MSCI and JP Morgan. Global and domestic ratings agencies provide guidance for bond creditworthiness as a standard reference that sophisticated institutions are typically legally bound to apply in overall examination. They answer the basic question of capacity and willingness to pay, but at times of crisis they are often behind the curve in lowering ratings.
- Private equity investments are directed to illiquid, unlisted on exchange companies, and investors commit to a long holding period, generally

3–7 years. Exit strategies can include a public offering, a mergers and acquisition deal with a domestic or international company or the fund can sell its stake back to the original owner or employees. Public equity fund managers have diversified into the strategy, and private debt is a burgeoning asset class. In the modern era, the World Bank's IFC also jump started the field with stakes in pioneer funds and professional body formation.

Notes

1. The World Bank, "Market capitalization of listed domestic companies (% of GDP)," World Federation of Exchanges database, 1975–2020, https://data.worldbank.org/indicator/CM.MKT.LCAP.GD.ZS.
2. 2023 Annual Statistics Guide, World Federation of Exchanges, June 19. 2024, https://www.world-exchanges.org/our-work/articles/2023-annual-statistics-guide
3. ThaiBMA, "The Thai Domestic Bond Market," https://www.thaibma.or.th/EN/Education/ThaiBondMarket.aspx.
4. European Central Bank, Eurosystem, "Financial Stability Review," June 2007, https://www.ecb.europa.eu/pub/pdf/other/financialstabilityreview200706en.pdf, pp. 81–83.
5. The World Bank, "Stocks traded, turnover ratio of domestic shares (%)," World Federation of Exchanges database, 1975–2020, https://data.worldbank.org/indicator/CM.MKT.TRNR.
6. OECD, "OECD Corporate Governance Factbook 2021," 2021, https://www.oecd.org/corporate/OECD-Corporate-Governance-Factbook.pdf, p. 13.
7. OECD, "OECD Corporate Governance Factbook 2021," p. 47.
8. OECD, "OECD Corporate Governance Factbook 2021," p. 13.
9. OECD, "OECD Corporate Governance Factbook 2021," p. 15.
10. Andy Mukherjee, "Common sense wins in India bankruptcy case," Bloomberg, US Edition, November 17, 2019, https://www.bloomberg.com/opinion/articles/2019-11-18/india-s-bankruptcy-ruling-showed-common-sense-in-essar-steel-case?sref=9BZJXmVl.
11. Mukherjee.
12. Nairobi Securities Exchange, "About NEXT," https://www.nse.co.ke/derivatives/about-next/.
13. Annabel Smith, "Brazil's B3 overtakes CME Group in rankings for largest derivatives exchange," The Trade, January 22, 2021, https://www.thetradenews.com/brazils-b3-overtakes-cme-group-in-rankings-for-largest-derivatives-exchange/.

14. Emily Aggrey, "World Bank automates Ghana Stock Exchange," Networkworld, December 19, 2008, https://www.networkworld.com/article/2271071/world-bank-automates-ghana-stock-exchange.html#:~:text=A%20World%20Bank%2Dassisted%20project,a%20crippling%20global%20financial%20market.
15. Landon Thomas, Jr., "'Fragile Five' is the latest club of emerging nations in turmoil," *The New York Times*, January 28, 2014, https://www.nytimes.com/2014/01/29/business/international/fragile-five-is-the-latest-club-of-emerging-nations-in-turmoil.html.
16. Thomas.
17. Excerpted from a Kleiman International proprietary client analysis submitted June 23, 2013.
18. Peter Zangari, "From crisis to crisis: Russia's diminished role in emerging markets," MSCI, March 3, 2022, https://www.msci.com/research-and-insights/russia-ukraine-war/russias-diminished-role-in-emerging-markets.
19. Unilever, "Full-year growth led by emerging markets and home care," January 29, 2020, https://www.unilever.com/news/press-and-media/press-releases/2020/full-year-growth-led-by-emerging-markets-and-home-care/.
20. "BBVA Mexico obtained a profit of about US$ 2.8 billion in first half of 2024," El Economista Mexico, July 31, 2024, https://www.americaeconomia.com/en/node/288002.
21. China Securities Regulatory Commission, "China Capital Markets Development Report," World Bank, https://openknowledge.worldbank.org/bitstream/handle/10986/12643/712710ESW0P0990602802 0120Box370067B.pdf?sequence=1&isAllowed=y.
22. Asian Development Bank, "Asia Bond Monitor: March 2024," https://www.adb.org/sites/default/files/publication/783036/asia-bond-monitor-march-2024.pdf.
23. Louis Kuijs, Charles Change, and Lei Yi, "China Bond Market Reforms Key to Growing with Less Debt," S&P Global, June 2024, https://www.spglobal.com/en/research-insights/special-reports/china-bond-market-reforms-key-to-growing-with-less-debt.
24. Emma Dunkley, Alan Livsey and Joseph Cotterill, "Global investors pile into EM funds that cut out China," *Financial Times*,

October 23, 2024, https://www.ft.com/content/d0631629-568e-4fe6-adb2-b7b8395c91f4.

25. Barbara Kotschwar, "Does Ecuador's default foreshadow the next Latin American debt crisis?" Peterson Institute for International Economics (PIIE), December 18, 2008, https://www.piie.com/blogs/realtime-economic-issues-watch/does-ecuadors-default-foreshadow-next-latin-american-debt.
26. Adam Feibelman, "Ecuador's 2008–2009 Debt Restructuring: A Special Case?" Chapter. In *Sovereign Debt Crises: What Have We Learned*," edited by Juan Pablo Bohoslavsky and Kunibert Raffer, 48–64. Cambridge: Cambridge University Press, 2017. https://10.0.3.249/9781108227001.004.
27. The World Bank, "Total reserves (includes gold, current US$)—Ecuador," International Monetary Fund, International Financial Statistics, and data files, 1960–2021, https://data.worldbank.org/indicator/FI.RES.TOTL.CD?locations=EC.
28. Enda Curran, Liz McDormick, and Anchalee Worrachate, "End of easy money brings a $410 billion global financial shock," Bloomberg, US Edition, May 1, 2022, https://www.bloomberg.com/news/articles/2022-05-01/global-economy-faces-410b-financial-shock-as-central-banks-pull-back?sref=9BZJXmVl.
29. S&P Global Ratings, "Default, transition, and recovery: 2020 annual sovereign default and rating transition study," April 12, 2021, https://www.spglobal.com/ratings/en/research/articles/210412-default-transition-and-recovery-2020-annual-sovereign-default-and-rating-transition-study-11888070.
30. Kleiman International Consultants, Inc., "Sri Lanka currency line no predicament swap," March 13, 2021, https://kleimaninternational.com/2021/03/sri-lanka-currency-line-no-predicament-swap/.
31. Morgan Stanley Investment Management, "Emerging Market Allocations: How much to own?" 2021, https://www.morganstanley.com/im/publication/insights/articles/article_howmuchtoown_us.pdf.
32. Gabriela Santos, "Why are Emerging Market equities underperforming during this year of recovery?" JPMorgan Asset Management, June 2, 2021, https://am.jpmorgan.com/us/en/asset-management/adv/insights/market-insights/market-updates/on-the-minds-of-investors/why-are-emerging-market-equities-underperforming-during-this-year-of-the-recovery/.

33. MSCI, "MSCI Emerging Markets Index (USD)," August 2022, https://www.msci.com/documents/10199/c0db0a48-01f2-4ba9-ad01-226fd5678111.
34. FTSE Russell, "FTSE Emerging Index (USD)," https://www.ftserussell.com/products/indices/awallen.
35. Nasdaq, "Nasdaq Emerging Markets Index," June 30, 2022, https://indexes.nasdaqomx.com/docs/FS_NQEMT.pdf.
36. The World Bank, "Market capitalization of listed domestic companies (% of GDP)," World Federation of Exchange database, 1975–2020, https://data.worldbank.org/indicator/CM.MKT.LCAP.GD.ZS.
37. John Welling, "Is South Korea crowding your emerging markets allocation?" S&P Global, November 24, 2020, https://www.spglobal.com/en/research-insights/articles/is-south-korea-crowding-your-emerging-markets-allocation.
38. Jonny Goulden, "EM Local Markets Guide," Emerging Markets Research, 13th Edition, J.P. Morgan Securities, September 2022, https://markets.jpmorgan.com/research/email/b251vo1e/SlnPnoJJYWgoQWqbimCPpQ/GPS-4215295-0.
39. Goulden.
40. MSCI, "MSCI Global Currency Indices: July 2008", https://www.msci.com/documents/10199/0b995d45-15ef-4570-9aa0-ef28baa89083.
41. Sumit Roy, "EEM's ETF first mover advantage," ETF.com, September 1, 2021, https://www.etf.com/sections/features-and-news/eems-etf-first-mover-advantage?nopaging=1.
42. https://www.etf.com/topics/emerging-markets.
43. ETF.com.
44. Darek Klonowski, ed., Private Equity in Emerging Markets: The New Frontiers of International Finance, Chapter 5, "Emerging Market Private Equity, It's Recent Growth and Differences with Private Equity in Developed Markets," Palgrave McMillan, 2012, https://www.ifc.org/wps/wcm/connect/75c95444-9f5e-492d-9619-66f33ad422a4/PE+in+EM+The+New+Frontiers+of+International+Finance.pdf?MOD=AJPERES&CVID=jG9YrOi.
45. Global Private Capital Association, "Mid-Year 2023 Industry Data & Analysis," August 28, 2023, https://www.globalprivatecapital.org/research/gpca-mid-year-2023-industry-data-analysis/.
46. Global Private Capital Association, Mid-Year 2024 Industry Data & Analysis, August 2024, https://www.globalprivatecapital.org/research/mid-year-2024-industry-data-analysis/.

47. Global Private Capital Association, Mid-Year 2024 Industry Data & Analysis, August 2024, https://www.globalprivatecapital.org/research/mid-year-2024-industry-data-analysis/.
48. Ink 42, "Indian Startup IPO Tracker 2024," October 15, 2024, https://inc42.com/features/indian-startup-ipo-tracker-2024/.

6

Emerging Markets and the Global Economy/ Financial Landscape

Historical and current foreign direct and portfolio flows offer lasting patterns and are prone to sudden shocks which often emanate from the developed world and are not emerging markets own fault. New official bilateral and multilateral financing has come on to the scene over the past 15 years, with actors including China's Belt and Road Initiative, the Asian Infrastructure Development Bank, and the BRICS New Development Bank. The private sector policy and funding role is now as important as that of the public sector in crisis management with Sovereign Wealth Funds from Asia and the Gulf wielding multi-trillion-dollar portfolios as a prominent force.

Foreign Direct/Portfolio Investment Nexus

As emerging and frontier markets liberalized economies and opened previously closed financial and real sectors to private competition, foreign direct investment (FDI) flows preceded portfolio ones as banks followed developed country-based clients into new markets. FDI as long-term outlays for plants and factories is an economic growth staple. Foreign bank entry has been found to inject know-how and technology, while the record on whether they lower borrowing costs is mixed. The two categories of investors—direct and portfolio—do not move in tandem in terms of engagement and tend to offset each other. In 2021, for example, even as China began its crackdown on the private sector and foreign stock market investors dumped shares, FDI directed to the country hit a record high of USD 334 billion. Covid took less of a toll on China than other countries that year, and investors

B. Morrissey and G. Kleiman, *Emerging Economies and Financial Markets*, https://doi.org/10.1007/978-3-031-85669-3_6

engaged as Beijing overhauled inbound investment rules to extend a pattern of reducing the number of so-called "negative list" sectors.[1] In 2022 China's National Development and Reform Commission and Ministry of Commerce cut restricted industries from 33 to 31, with controls on foreign investment remaining in agriculture, utilities, and other fields including mining for rare earth elements critical for green energy production.[2]

Basic decision-making criteria for foreign direct investors mirror those of portfolio investors with political-economic and legal-regulatory stability at the top of the list. Sector and operation-specific determinants can veer heavily into the weeds depending on a company's needs, with adequate infrastructure a paramount factor for export-oriented manufacturing. Electricity, roads and ports, and acceptable tariffs and customs procedures are preconditions for FDI investors. Flexible labor markets and a skilled work force, and intellectual protection for patents and technology also are boxes to tick.

While global sources exist with internationally accepted definitions of FDI—the IMF's Balance of Payments Manual and the OECD's Benchmark Definition—individual country reporting of investment suffers from differences in methodology, lack of standardization, and reporting lags. China has long practiced "round-tripping:" mainland funds leave the country and return as foreign investment to take advantage of tax and other incentives which distorts reported FDI data. For years Indonesia published foreign investment approvals that never translated into actual flows. Now it tallies on the ground follow-through but excludes the "sensitive" banking and oil and gas sectors.[3]

Global events often tank FDI, as they do for portfolio flows to emerging markets. In the wake of the collapse of the technology market in 2000 and after the September 11th attacks on the US a year later, risk aversion soared, and it battered both emerging and developed markets. According to UNCTAD data, global mergers and acquisition activity almost halved in 2001, and would have even been worse without a landmark Mexico transaction. In Latin America that year Mexico surpassed Brazil as the favored country but half of reported volume was Citibank's purchase of Banamex, before it turned around two decades later with a plan to divest it after poor earnings.

The onset of the Covid-19 pandemic was shattering to foreign direct investment in 2020 when much of the world "locked down." Investors were unable to travel internationally to start or complete deals and Zoom calls were an inadequate replacement for in-person meetings with counterparts and host country officials. FDI fell 42 percent in 2020 and more than 30 percent more in absolute terms than after the 2008–09 global financial crisis.[4] Direct investment in emerging markets dropped only 12 percent due to a

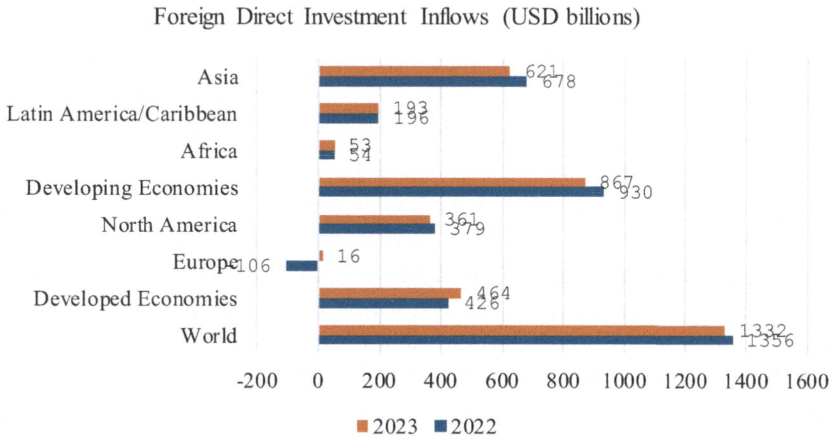

Fig. 6.1 Foreign Direct Investment Inflows (USD billions) (*Source* UNCTAD, World Investment Report, 2024)

few large deals and accounted for a record 72 percent of the global total of USD 859 billion.[5] However, greenfield investment—when a company starts new operations in a country—sank 46 percent on the more limited fiscal support available to jump-start the economies including through tax incentives. Global FDI rebounded by 77 percent in 2021, surpassing the pre-Covid level as investors re-engaged and began to travel again.[6]However, FDI in emerging markets rose only 30 percent that year with data distortions that routinely factor. India dropped 26 percent as several large deals were recorded in 2020 and not repeated. In contrast India recorded USD 3.8 billion in equity inflows in 2021, despite USD 3.9 billion in outflows in the second half, as the stock market advanced 25 percent in dollar terms on the MSCI Index with foreign buyers attracted to a wave of tech-related initial public offerings, many ready when Covid hit a year earlier.[7] The dollar figure for FDI in South Africa surged from USD 3 billion in 2020 to USD 41 billion a year later, mainly on a financial engineering share swap between South Africa's global consumer internet giant Naspers and its Dutch-listed investment arm. In contrast, portfolio outflows reached nearly USD 30 billion in 2021, according to the South African central bank (Fig. 6.1).

Portfolio "Fast Movers"

Unlike foreign direct investment literally stuck in the ground for multi-year time horizons, portfolio flows are often swift in comparison and are described under the loaded term "hot money" which seems to describe funds moving on a whim. However, the "hot money" description fails to account for illiquidity which sometimes traps investment, or deliberate decisions to keep bond and stock allocations over 3–5-year periods to match the cycle of long-term contractual savings pools like pension funds and life insurance companies. These long-term strategies can unravel in times of global geopolitical or market surprise, or US Federal Reserve rate hikes which makes the dollar more attractive, as funds traditionally flee every segment of the emerging market asset class for "safe havens." This recourse would include the few remaining AAA-rated advanced economy bonds, as well as currencies like the Japanese yen and the Swiss franc. A highlights list of major incidents in the past few decades with unrelenting capital outflows from emerging markets features:

- Surprise US Federal Reserve tightening, 1994–95;
- Asian financial crisis, 1997;
- Russia's default and Long-Term Capital Management's collapse, 1998;
- Attacks on the US on September 11th and Argentina's default on USD 93 billion in external debt just months later, 2001;
- Global Financial Crisis, 2007–2008;
- "Taper tantrum," 2013;
- Outbreak of the global Covid-19 pandemic, 2020;
- Ukraine war, global inflation surge and US Federal Reserve hikes, 2022.
- Israel-Gaza war first days, 2023

During these crises emerging market assets were dumped indiscriminately in a wholesale rush to "safety," and mutual fund managers had little choice but to sell since they had to raise cash to cover customer redemptions or plug losses. In August 1998's serial meltdown when Russia defaulted on its debt and devalued the ruble, and US-based giant hedge fund Long-Term Capital Management collapsed, emerging market bond asset value sank 34 percent in a month. Following the air attacks on the Pentagon and World Trade Center and closure of the New York Stock Exchange in September 2001, investors followed the same pattern. Of the USD 10.8 billion under management at the time, monthly sales totaled more than USD 800 million over the next three months, 7.5 percent of the total.[8]

More recently, in the spring of 2022, Russia's war on Ukraine, soaring global inflation, and the onset of US Federal Reserve rate hikes triggered months of retreat from stocks, bonds, and currencies. The Institute for International Finance, which tallies a smaller group of the largest, most liquid markets forgoing frontier representation in its universe, reported that debt and equity outflows in March were a record USD 7.8 billion followed by USD 4 billion in April.[9] For the full year global fund tracker EPFR's data had bond outflows of USD 90 billion while equity funds recorded modest outflows of USD 4.1 billion after a strong pre-war start in January.[10]

In 2022 the MSCI Emerging Markets Index was down more than 22 percent, and the average yield on dollar-denominated sovereign debt hit 6.3 percent.[11] The bond sell-off was driven by more than US rate hikes, a strengthening dollar, and global inflation. The shock also included a weeks long shut down of major Chinese cities due to the "Covid-19-zero" policy. The main manufacturing index there fell to the 30's where 50 is a neutral reading, as demand dried up and ports were shut, compounding two years of pandemic-related global supply chain bottlenecks. In this episode Beijing aggravated the exodus, unlike in 2008's financial crash when it pumped out hundreds of billions of dollars in stimulus to offset the global economic ripples from the US prime mortgage debacle. China's economy expanded only 3 percent in 2022—far below the average 7 percent GDP expansion recorded from 2010–2020—on its "home-grown" slowdown from property market correction and full disease isolation abandoned by all other public health authorities, and never considered as viable throughout the developing world with outsize informal economies (Fig. 6.2).

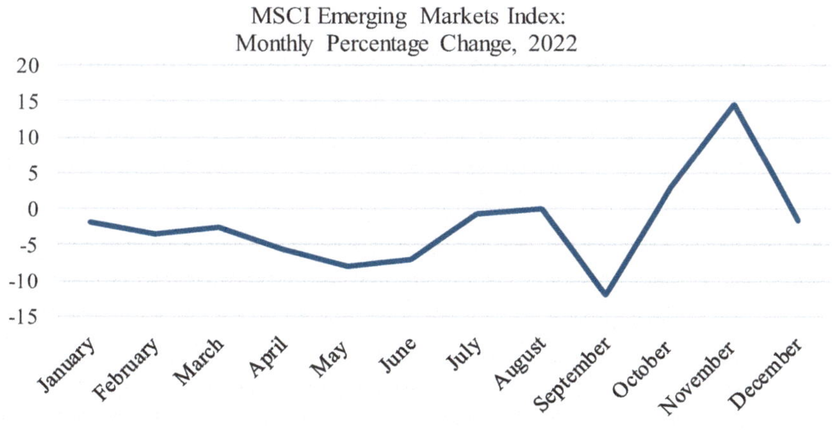

Fig. 6.2 MSCI Emerging Markets Index: Monthly Percentage Change, 2022 (*Source* MSCI)

Bilateral/Multilateral Finance Fresh Crowd

The so-called Bretton Woods institutions and their cohort can trace their history to the post-World War II era as the oldest. They include the World Bank and regional counterparts like the Asian Development Bank, Africa Development Bank, European Bank for Reconstruction and Development which was launched in the 1990s, and Inter-American Development Bank. They provide loans and grants to governments and have a singular arsenal of technical assistance often provided by outside consultants with direct industry expertise. This guidance and training is designed for example to bring the central bank regulatory and supervisory regimes up to international standards.

(See case study on technical assistance) The multilateral lenders also have private sector arms which support projects through equity investments and loans and guarantees on more of a commercial than policy basis.[12] The World Bank's IFC stands out and along with the better-known regional peers as arms of the regional development banks. The Islamic Development Bank (IsDB) also has this mandate. The IsDB is based in Saudi Arabia and provides infrastructure finance using Sharia, Islamic finance compliant principles where a guaranteed return replaces interest in mutual risk-sharing endorsed by religious scholars.

Case Study: Multilateral Technical Assistance Through the Years

The Kleiman International partners have undertaken dozens, if not hundreds, of technical assistance projects in every emerging market region. Early ones in the 1990s included a two-week, on the ground, review of the Algerian economy and financial sector as part of a team of World Bank staff and consultants. We provided recommendations for multilateral assistance in both the broad financial sector, and specific capital market reform and development programs. The giant state-owned oil company, Sonatrach, was identified for a pilot and it was one of the first listings on the Algerian Stock Exchange when it was launched in 1999.

Also in sub-Saharan Africa, we developed and taught a three-day workshop on "Raising Debt via the Private Sector" in Zimbabwe and Kenya for the United Nations Institute for Training and Research. UNITAR subsequently engaged us to review other training programs which at the time focused solely on the public sector and international debt markets. Our recommendations were for total revision of the program's focus to instead concentrate on domestic bond market development and include a wide range of private sector participants in training programs.

In Latin America and the Caribbean World Bank projects completed included critiquing Dominican Republic's draft capital markets law and analyzing the impact of Panama's Brady Plan/commercial debt restructuring. The latter effort entailed wide-ranging on-the-ground interviews with the local financial community to determine the impact on sovereign creditworthiness and domestic financial sector deepening, with recommendations focused on the need to promote new instruments on the local market.

The technical assistance we provided was often through creating and offering training programs for capital market development for public and private sector market participants, including regulators, stock market staff, and local bankers and brokers. For instance, we developed and organized a "Central African Securities Market Development" workshop in Cameroon for the World Bank and BEAC, the central bank that oversees the six-country Economic and Monetary Community of Central Africa. Similarly, we planned a series of workshops and presented papers on financial sector reform for Central European and Central Asian officials for the World Bank and Organization for Economic Cooperation and Development. Workshop topics included sequencing in securities market development, banking and non-bank financial institutions risks, and securities market development for market regulators.

Our unique contribution to these technical assistance and training programs was to offer the "real world" views of the international private sector based on our work with bankers and brokers rather than simply providing a laundry list of "how to" develop capital markets. For example, as noted earlier, we focused on sequencing market development. Rather than urging local market participants to buy and install expensive state-of-the-art trading and settlement systems, we focused on issues like developing domestic institutional investors like mutual funds to be counterparts to foreign investors and the need to build regulatory capacity to enforce rules rather than just passing laws that looked internationally acceptable on paper but could be easily sidestepped.

Official public sector finance for emerging markets in recent years has been dominated by bilateral sources which account for more than 70 percent.[13] These national lenders and aid agencies are concentrated in wealthier OECD countries and are usually independent with a core mission to support private sector development. In 2023 total overseas development assistance reached a record high of USD 223.7 billion, up 1.8 percent over a year earlier, 99 percent in the form of grants, loans, debt relief, and contributions to multilateral institutions on a grant-equivalent basis.[14] Assistance to Ukraine was up 9 percent while aid to the West Bank and Gaze rose 12 percent. Official development assistance has surged 34 percent from before the global pandemic. In US dollar terms, the largest donors were the US, Germany, Japan, France, and the United Kingdom.

In the past decade, the multilateral assistance cohort has been upended with new entrants. In 2013 China's President Xi Jinping announced the creation of One Belt One Road, renamed the Belt and Road Initiative (BRI) in 2016. The BRI was established as a plan to develop two new trade routes connecting China with the rest of the world. The "Belt" was designed to resurrect the ancient Silk Route connecting Asia and Europe, while the "Road" was to re-establish the old Marco Polo Sea trade route to connect China, Southeast Asia, Africa, and Europe. It morphed beyond original infrastructure and natural resources exploits to embrace far flung cultural, diplomatic, and sports engagement. An implicit purpose was always to recycle capital abroad from the large trade surplus and offer Chinese workers, typically paid higher than counterparts in the countries where projects are undertaken, more positions than are available domestically. It has been geopolitically and economically contentious since launch with ESG factors discounted by Western formulas, and charges that bank project lending on quasi-commercial terms fostered a "debt trap," as in the case of a Sri Lanka port takeover with default. Combined with slowdown at home from breakneck 8 percent growth, the trillion-dollar initial scope has dramatically dwindled (see case study).

Case Study: China's BRI Political/Debt Tug

Launched in 2013 with great fanfare as "One Belt One Road," China's renamed Belt and Road Initiative (BRI) envisioned a land-based "Silk Road Economic Belt" for Central and South Asia, the Middle East and Europe, and a sea-based "twenty-first century Maritime Silk Road" into Africa and Latin America.[15] The project was focused on building high-profile physical infrastructure to boost bilateral trade, investment, and economic integration with the member countries, as a central tenet of President Xi Jinping's foreign policy. Initially just ten countries in Central, South, and Southeast Asia signed cooperation agreements with Beijing but by 2023 150 countries had joined. While originally emerging economies were the priority, particularly those more politically in "China's orbit" than aligned with the US, 33 high-income countries entered, including Italy, Greece, and the United Arab Emirates, although Italy later pulled out.[16]

From the start the BRI's geopolitics mixed with loan/development policy for a contentious brew. The US, most of the EU, and Japan saw it as a raw Beijing commercial and diplomatic power play, but domestic demand limits in China were an important driver. During the Global Financial Crisis years Beijing spent more than half a trillion dollars on infrastructure stimulus at home to bolster growth. When the domestic spending spree wound down, the BRI provided an outlet for Beijing's state-owned companies to continue their money-making fixed asset investment push elsewhere and keep Chinese workers employed.[17]

Project lending and investment peaked just 3 years after launch, and direct central government budget support was withdrawn in 2017. Funding comes through China's policy and "Big 4" state-owned commercial banks, with the China Development Bank and Export–Import Bank the main conduits. Despite steady decline in annual financing over the past decade, ten years after launch cumulative investment topped USD 1 trillion, with about 60 percent in construction contracts and the rest in non-financial investments. Future investments are expected to be in manufacturing new technologies, renewable energy, trade-enabling infrastructure like roads and pipelines, and resource-backed deals like mining[18] (Fig. 6.3).

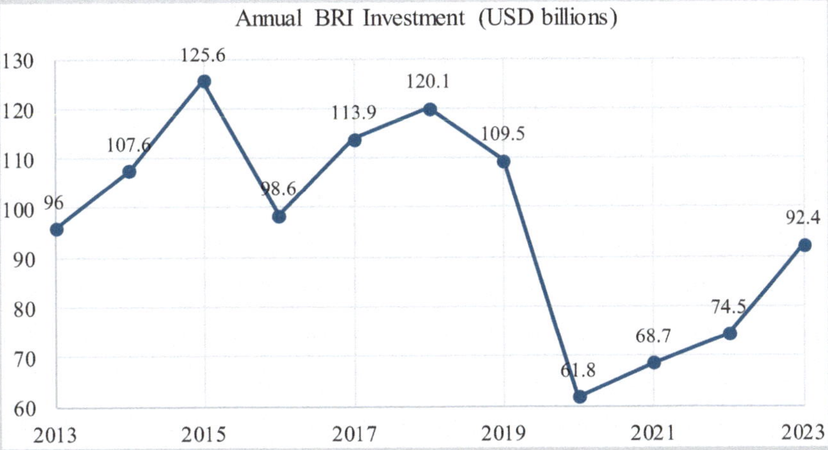

Fig. 6.3 Annual BRI Investment (USD billions) (*Source* China Belt and Road Initiative (BRI) Investment Report 2023, Griffith University and Fudan University)

Loan terms have been confidential, with even host country parliaments unable to access government agreements as in a long-running battle over Kenya's USD 3 billion railway. The massive sums are on quasi-commercial rather than concessional rates, with dedicated escrow accounts set up for collateral. They have been excluded from official debt statistics such as the World Bank's annual database, with common criticism of "debt diplomacy" creating a trap for unwary borrowers. Sri Lanka's Hambantota Port is the standout case for this argument. Expansion was not China's idea, but part of the government's broader plan to rebuild the southern part of the country after the 2004 tsunami. While one foreign engineering firm undertook a feasibility study and found the rationale lacking, another was optimistic, and Colombo pushed ahead. China was willing to lend at a rate of 6.3 percent, versus 3 percent or less had the money been sourced from traditional multilateral development banks like the World Bank or Asian Development Bank. When a new government was elected in 2015 and determined that more than 90 percent of its revenue was directed to debt servicing, construction was halted. With default looming, negotiations resulted in the island nation handing over 70 percent of the port's equity and giving Beijing a 99-year lease.[19]

Beijing was also criticized for loose environmental standards from the early buildup of a giant fossil-fuel portfolio but has since scaled back financing of "dirty" energy with a specific coal phase-out timetable. While part of the pullback came from debt crises in BRI countries, China has a next decade zero carbon emissions pledge accelerating the shift at home and abroad to green energy.[20]

In 2022, Sri Lanka was again in trouble and declared an outright debt moratorium, including for Chinese obligations which Kleiman International predicted more than 14 months in advance (See Case Study in Chapter 4). At the same time neighboring Pakistan, with net negative international reserves, sought financial assistance from Beijing as it attempted to restart an IMF aid package after the prime minister was removed in a no-confidence vote. A "flagship" BRI project, launched in 2015, was the China-Pakistan Economic Corridor as an outline 15-year, USD 62 billion vision. The bilateral relationships were opaque, including the tariff regime with dozens of Chinese independent power producers in the zone owed billions of dollars. In early 2022, the IMF found that Pakistan's debt to China was USD 18.4 billion, 20 percent of the external total, a combination of CPEC and direct loans and central bank currency swap lines.[21] Two years later China, along with Saudi Arabia and the UAE, agreed to reschedule Pakistan's debt, which allowed the country to seal a new USD 7 billion loan from the IMF to avoid default.

Africa earlier fell into distress when Zambia was the first emerging-frontier market to default on its external debt during the height of the pandemic. Following the election of a new government in 2021, Lusaka began negotiations with the IMF for a bailout and restructuring help. When Zambia's debt total was revealed after a comprehensive internal audit, China's exposure at about USD 6 billion was double the amount owed to international bondholders and nearly half the USD 15 billion outstanding. Although it is not a member of the Western official creditors Paris Club, for the first time China agreed to co-chair the negotiations group with France. After almost four years, Zambia completed its debt restructuring, the first country to use the Group of 20's Common Framework for debt restructuring agreed at the height of the global pandemic in 2020. The new mechanism brings together the traditional Paris Club of official lenders with new ones like China and Saudi Arabia. The framework was designed so that after a country in default agreed with the IMF to reduce its debt to a sustainable level—one under which it was able to pay its external obligations through tax hikes, etc.—public and private creditors would accept comparable treatment in a restructuring. In the eventual deal creditors took a 21.6 percent "haircut," or loss expressed in net present value terms on their holdings, and Zambia issued two new Eurobonds worth USD 3 billion. However, it took another three months for the country to reach a deal to restructure USD 1.5 billion of debt owed to the China Development Bank and Industrial and Commercial Bank of China.

With China's economic slowdown, BRI vanguard banks have again turned inward to boost domestic growth, and the resolution of non-performing loans with Sri Lanka, Zambia, and other test cases will shape more cautious outward lending as a clear pattern post-pandemic. While Western governments may welcome consolidation from a geopolitical perspective as denting China's influence, low-income countries with outsize bilateral exposures and debt/ GDP above 50 percent, will face a reckoning as alternative official-commercial sources for large-scale infrastructure bets fail to materialize.

Another official lender emerged after the creation of the BRICS. In 2000 the acronym "BRIC" was coined by Jim O'Neill, first an analyst and later chief economist at Goldman Sachs. The underlying thesis of his research paper was that the large economies of Brazil, Russia, India, and China would continue to grow at the same rapid pace they had through the 1990s and that the group's heft should be represented in global financial institutions where they were minor shareholders. South Africa was added as an "S" a decade later. Previously big emerging markets were grouped under forgettable acronyms like BEMS and not linked as an asset class proposition with long-term research scenarios.

Investment house competitors criticized the BRICS term as a marketing stunt but embraced the concept and launched dozens of funds for the original four countries. The original reasoning had broad political overtones, particularly on representation at the Bretton Woods institutions. Goldman's thesis argued that extrapolating the same strong growth as in the 1990s, they collectively deserved a bigger voice in global governance.[22] It offered concrete suggestions for consolidating the big European powers—France, Germany, and Italy—into a single seat at the G7, IMF and World Bank, paving the way for these entrants to have a seat at the table and greater shareholding.[23]

The 2008 financial crisis finally opened the doors for the original BRIC members to participate in a core global economic decision-making forum. The US government under President George W. Bush convened a new grouping, the Group of 20 (G-20), to include them and it has since met annually for summits. After years of negotiation IMF quotas were also recalculated to grant marginally larger individual shares for these big emerging markets during the Obama administration, and Chinese nationals in particular were appointed to senior posts.

In 2009 South Africa was invited to join the group and they went on to create the BRICS Bank, officially named the New Development Bank, the newest multilateral lender. The five held regular summits and within a decade had more than doubled their contribution to global output to 19 percent of the total.[24] Their economies held up in the aftermath of the 2008–9 US mortgage originated debacle, partially due to China's massive USD 580 billion stimulus, but sputtered the following decade.

While China outperformed, largely due to infrastructure project borrowing it is still unwinding today, the other four encountered turbulence to pause their high-flyer streak. The group's longstanding lure to emerging market investors was open capital accounts, which resulted in major outflows during the US Federal Reserve so-called 2013 Taper Tantrum previewing phase-out of the bond-buying program. Three of them—Brazil, India, and South Africa—were lumped into Morgan Stanley's "fragile 5" classification, with reliance on "hot money" portfolio inflows to bridge gaping current account deficits. Two years later it was China's turn as spoiler when it surprised markets by devaluing the rough peg to the dollar about 3 percent, and then imposing harsh capital controls to stem erosion of its multi-trillion-dollar foreign exchange reserves.

Between 2010 and 2019 China and India turned in still strong growth averaging 7.6 percent and 6.5 percent, respectively, albeit lower than a decade earlier. In contrast, Brazil's average rate for the period was 1.46 percent and Russia's not much better at 2 percent. China began the decade with annual GDP expanding at 10.6 percent but by 2019 it was 5.9 percent on debt run-up in previous years, particularly in the property sector with onset of an offshore bond default wave. Brazil and Russia were turning in 7.5 percent annual growth before the former entered outright recession in 2015–16, reducing its average to 1.4 percent. Russia's clip dropped to 2 percent in the 2010s on economic policy and oil price swings, banking and corporate debt buildup, and sanctions imposed in 2014 after its takeover of Crimea[25] (Fig. 6.4).

Post Covid-19 and Ukraine war, the BRICS outlook is uneven, with Brazil and South Africa potential trade winners due to their critical commodity exports which overlap with those traditionally sold by Ukraine and Russia. Russia as a pariah will likely suffer from Western isolation and materials shortages for years. China has reverted to the fixed asset playbook to reboot earlier growth with consumption in the doldrums, but is on track for subdued 4–5 percent medium-term GDP advance weighed down by debt and property market collapse. India is the growth champion at 7 percent spurred by domestic demand by the world's largest population base but has run up public debt/GDP over 80 percent as a binding constraint. Brazil as an agricultural export powerhouse benefits from replacing Russian and Ukrainian commodities but high inflation and interest rates are chronic bottlenecks.

The 2023 BRICS summit increased the group's membership and indicated it could be further enlarged. Energy producers Iran and the United

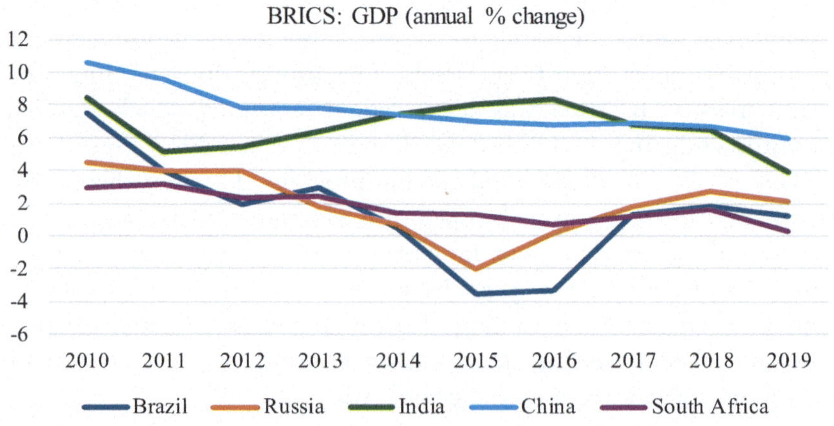

Fig. 6.4 BRICS: GDP (annual % change) (*Source* Data.worldbank.org)

Arab Emirates were added, as were heavily indebted Argentina, Ethiopia, and Egypt. When the new members officially joined in 2024 the expanded BRICS grouping represent an estimated 46 percent of the world's population and 35 percent of total global output. However, due to rocky relations between some members—notably China and India and Egypt and Ethiopia—the overall economic and political impact will likely be more symbolic than a major shift in the world economy. In 2024, the BRICS summit was held in Kazan, Russia. It was the first multilateral meeting convened since the outbreak of war in Ukraine and the imposition of Western sanctions. Thirteen new "partner countries" linked with the BRICS group, including Bolivia and Cuba, as well as NATO member Turkey. Spearheaded by Russia, China, and India settling a hefty portion of bilateral trade in local currency, affiliated countries have joined the bandwagon in a noticeable erosion of USD-EUR exclusive purview. The future financial markets agenda that will change the calculus at the margin has central banks holding international reserves in each other's domestic assets, forming a cross-border digital payments network SWIFT alternative, and creating a common securities depository and insurer/reinsurer platform.

As a distinct emerging market asset class subtype, BRICS has faded from the scene. Goldman Sachs shuttered its pioneer BRIC fund in 2015 and peers followed, not least due to under-performance. Other monikers caught on after its initial popularity, such as the Next 11 for frontier markets with a range from Iran to Nigeria. They met the same fate, abandoned as a dedicated product, and then folded into more scalable generic retail and wholesale funds although the composite indices remain.

A concrete outcome of the creation of the BRICS was the 2014 launch of a new multilateral lender. After two years of consideration and analyses by member finance ministers, the "BRICS Bank"—officially the New Development Bank (NDB)—was created. According to the bank's website the institution's mandate is to mobilize resources for infrastructure and sustainable development projects in the founding and other emerging economies.[26] Members agreed to initial capital of USD 100 billion, shared equally. Additional funding has come from bond issuance, largely in US dollars and in RMB. "Green" and "sustainable" bonds, including a special Covid one, were placed.

The bank is headquartered in Shanghai and leadership rotates among the members. The NDB is rated generally AA+ by the major global agencies while domestic ones in China and Japan awarded it an AAA grade. Following the Russian invasion of Ukraine, Fitch Ratings revised the outlook on its AA+ rating to "negative" and then in 2023 it shifted the outlook to "stable."

It initially noted that Russia is a large shareholder—19 percent as of end-2021—and NDB's country exposure was 13 percent of loans, 70 percent to the sovereign.[27] In March 2022, new Russian projects were placed on hold with the war and sanctions, even though members did not back the West's blockade.

In 2021 the bank started to extend its partnerships beyond the original members and by 2024 Bangladesh, UAE, Uruguay, and Egypt had been admitted. Growing the membership beyond the original core will allow it to expand global outreach as a strategic goal.[28] Unlike the traditional international financial institutions where the US and Europe have prohibitive stakes, NBD's bylaws state that every member country has equal voting shares and none veto power.[29] As of the third quarter of 2024, it had approved USD 35 billion in loans for 105 projects, and in its 2022–2026 strategy it has planned 40 percent of its USD 30 billion financing plan for green initiatives, with climate mitigation the focus.[30] In South Africa and China it has migrated into local currency lending, with the Bank CEO, ex-Brazil President Dilma Rousseff, envisioning the majority of the portfolio in member units by end-decade.

The third new multilateral player on the scene is the Asian Infrastructure Investment Bank (AIIB), launched in 2016 with 57 founding members, 20 outside of Asia. By 2024 membership had climbed to nearly 100 members, 48 regional and 50 from other emerging and developed economies. Its website boasts that that is enables clients to build "Infrastructure for Tomorrow (i4t)," focusing on green versions with "sustainability, innovation, and connectivity at its core."[31] Based in Beijing, it has an AAA rating from the main agencies. The largest shareholders are China and India.

At first the AIIB was seen as a direct challenge to the G-7 dominated Asian Development Bank and World Bank for the yearly trillion of dollars infrastructure prize in Asia. The World Bank is always headed by an American and Japan has always appointed the ADB president. It was also viewed as a captive conduit to boost China's BRI program, and the US stayed away from the outset on governance reservations. However, 14 founding members were European Union states and 21 came from the rich-country OECD. China as creator only holds a 26.5 percent stake without veto power, while India is the second largest shareholder. The AIIB has gone out of its way to recruit veteran development bank hands for senior staff and advisory bodies, and actively pursues joint operations where counterpart ESG standards are more rigorous. It has an international board of directors and an "Accountability Framework," which includes an oversight mechanism.[32] Like the other new multilateral players, the AIIB suspended all activity with Russia (and Belarus) within a week of Russia's invasion into Ukraine.

As of end-2023, the AIIB had approved 286 projects and invested some USD 55 billion. From 2016 through 2023 the Covid Crisis Recovery Facility has topped projects by sector at 27 percent, followed by energy (21 percent) and transport (17 percent). The AIIB co-financed USD 250 million in budget support with the Asian Development Bank for Bangladesh during Covid-19.[33] In 2023 it released a Climate Action Plan to measure them to 2030. The plan aligns with the Paris Agreement and targets at least 50 percent of all financing approvals are consistent with low-carbon and climate mitigation. In 2023 climate financing topped USD 3.4 billion, 60 percent of total approved regular financing.[34]

Today there are more than forty regional and global multilateral development banks in the mix, a crowded space but collectively positive for the enormity of the development tasks.[35] The Asian Development Bank says that developing Asia and the Pacific need USD 1.7 trillion annually through 2030 for growth, poverty, and climate change, an elusive target.[36] Less than a decade old, the new trio—BRI, AIIB, and NDB—from the outset have incorporated ESG and the United Nation's seventeen Sustainable Development Goals into project consideration.[37] For example, China's BRI has halted all coal lending in contrast with its early fossil fuel binge, while the AIIB has a keen focus on clean energy projects.

Multilateral lenders are supplemented in closing massive financing gaps by another sudden power, sovereign wealth funds. China, Singapore, Saudi Arabia, and the UAE have in-house fund size and professional teams to rival global investment giants. Their mandate is to invest for commercial as well as geopolitical reasons, and although an international association exists the biggest participants fall short on disclosure and governance. Together with other state-owned investors including public pension funds and central banks they manage over USD 50 trillion, with public pension funds managing 46 percent, central banks 30 percent, and Sovereign Wealth Funds 22 percent.[38] In 2022 emerging markets attracted 20 percent of the USD 261 billion deployed by state-owned investors, now screening also through an ESG lens[39] (see case study).

Case Study: Sovereign Wealth Funds Transparency Trample

The 2022 Sovereign Wealth Funds Report, a regular industry reference, found that total assets under management at these mostly secretive government run pools worldwide topped more than USD 10 trillion. It noted their combined size as equivalent to GDP would make them the third largest country in the world after the US and China.[40] While oil producer Norway boasts the largest one globally, China Investment Corporation is the second biggest, with more than USD 1.2 trillion in assets.[41] It manages and invests portions of the country's USD 3 billion-plus foreign exchange reserves, with scant self-reporting on allocation and performance after time lags. Like most leading SWFs it is a member of a decades old global forum dedicated to following the so-called Santiago principles breaking down activity and governance, but the organization scorecard is poor for the main Asian and Gulf giants.

Sovereign wealth funds (SWFs) are typically established using balance of payments surpluses, proceeds of privatizations, government transfer payments, fiscal surpluses, and/or proceeds from resource exports.[42] The majority rely on one or two basic commodities for income. Kuwait, the third largest globally with USD 738 billion under management, has the oldest SWF which was established in 1953, to invest its oil proceeds. Abu Dhabi, Qatar, and Saudi Arabia similarly have large pots of money that can be tapped short-term to protect against volatility in key exports but are enshrined with the broader purpose of future generation and strategic policy goal investment along with earning commercial returns.

These organizations deploy both their own experienced and global elite fund managers, but are accountable only to government overlords, with finance ministers and other senior officials typically on oversight boards if they exist. High profile forays have been major news like in 2010 when Qatar's SWF bought London's famous Harrod's department store. Portfolio choice is weighted toward listed equities and real estate, but in recent years has added private equity, venture capital, and hedge funds to the mix.

Unlike most SWFs, China's mandate from the start was both domestic and overseas, but during the pandemic the vast swathe turned to internal support at emergency behest. In the Middle East, the absorptive capacity for massive capital infusion had been a natural limit, but the calculus has changed as players like Saudi Arabia Public Investment Fund with a USD 500 million assets goal underwrite showcase projects such as the proposed Neom artificial city. In Africa, oil rich Gabon, with nearly USD 2 billion under management, has similarly directed investments locally, largely into green-friendly infrastructure development.[43] Established a decade ago, it has small portfolio stakes in Nigeria, Cote d'Ivoire, and Togo but has announced diversification from oil reliance to forestry as part of climate change strategy.[44]

Energy producer Russia has a USD 10 billion SWF, The Russian Direct Investment Fund (RDIF), created to modernize the economy and facilitate foreign private equity partnership. It was launched in 2011 but a decade later the vehicle and its Chief Executive Officer were among the first to be targeted by US sanctions after Russia invaded Ukraine.[45] After the earlier Crimea episode in 2014, RDIF lost key advisors including US prominent name tycoons who were attracted by the dangled prospect of 50–50 deal match, which never happened.[46] According to its now offline website, less than 10 percent of the money was invested in joint projects with international counterparts.[47] The US Treasury Department has described the RDIF as "a slush fund for President Vladimir Putin and is emblematic of Russia's broader kleptocracy," although it was instrumental in funding Russia's own Covid vaccine development.[48]

Turkey inaugurated a hybrid version TVF in 2016, a month after a failed coup attempt, as the government acted to bolster its reputation against the background of perennial current account deficits. The fund's mission is "strategic mega projects," that could boost annual GDP growth by 1.5 percent annually for ten years.[49] President Erdogan is chair, and the head of an opposition party has called it "a highly dangerous parallel Treasury that should be abolished."[50] Public assets in its portfolio have been pledged as collateral for sovereign borrowing, and TDV has tapped global bond markets separately.

It was formed by transferring assets from the Privatization Administration and the Treasury, giving it control over high profile industrial and land holdings worth nearly USD 40 billion.[51] Instead of mega-project pursuit, it has been mobilized to bail out state-owned companies, inject capital into banks and essentially renationalize the fixed line telecom operator. This irregular SWF in action is also exempt from public auditing and accountability in critic views.[52]

The global SWF Association was created to address diplomatic and political controversy as these actors gained prominence in the 2000s before the global financial crisis. They were accused of sinister hidden agendas but have since made at least nominal strides toward openness in presenting their role as another institutional investor variety for deliberate patient capital. In big emerging market destinations, several have banded together as anchor investors in initial public offerings, particularly of tech companies, with a long-term view. In 2021 four SWFs from the Middle East participated in the share increase of India's e-commerce giant Flipkart, valued at USD 38 billion. Total direct transactions in 2023 for the universe were USD 124.7 billion in 324 deals.[53] They continue to proliferate in even far-flung locations like Guyana and Namibia, as they become a natural base for securities demand and economic vision in future institution-building.

Even with their vast capital, the record has been mixed on decades of forming public–private partnerships (PPPs) and the distance persists to meet the infrastructure-living standards in the UN's Sustainable Development Goals by 2030. PPPs are again in vogue after a decade in the shadows after payment streams and debt-equity structures were modernized to reflect institutional investor preference. The basic driver is greater cost handling and return than traditional government procurement, as the private sector partner has documented risk management skills and stays with projects from initiation to completion. However, they have a long history of mutual recrimination with delivery failure accusations and sudden contract change demands. Projected cash flow for repayment is often guesswork with first-time facilities and at the start balance sheet assets may not be available to use as collateral.[54] Over the course of transactions, state sponsors in joint ventures have often found themselves on the hook for unexpected large contingent liabilities that spill over into the sovereign balance sheet.

Key Takeaways

- Foreign direct, portfolio, and private equity investors have different investment timelines, but all begin analysis the same way with political-economic and legal-and regulatory stability. Major global/geopolitical events—and US Federal Reserve Monetary tightening—result in often rapid portfolio investment outflows in contrast with direct and private equity long-term commitments, but crisis episodes deter future investment regardless of type.
- The original Bretton Woods institutions—The IMF/World Bank and regional multilateral development banks like the Asia Development Bank—have been joined in by a new range of actors coinciding with emerging market takeoff including the Asian Infrastructure Development Bank, "BRICS Bank," and China's Belt and Road Initiative. Of the more than 40 multilateral lenders many have private sector arms which support projects through equity investments and loans and guarantees on a more commercial basis. Official public sector financing has been dominated by bilateral sources tracked by the OECD, and bigger emerging economies now have their own aid programs.
- The global pandemic and its aftermath resulted in a series of sovereign external debt defaults, beginning with Zambia in 2021. China's exposure was more than double that owed to bondholders and for the first time China agreed to co-chair the negotiating group under the G-20's "Common Framework." Full resolution took four years with low-income economies now heavy private borrowers, and blurred distinctions and conflicting interests between commercial and official creditors.
- Sovereign Wealth Funds are another large component in the emerging market investment community although the full extent of their activities is not known due to lack of transparency despite an internationally agreed voluntary code. Pools in Asia and the Gulf control trillions of dollars in assets and are active across real and financial classes at home and abroad and allocate for straight return as well as political/ geo-strategic purpose.

Notes

1. Tianlei Huang and Nicholas R. Lardy, "Foreign corporates investing in China surged in 2021," Peterson Institute for International Economics

(PIIE), March 29, 2022, https://www.piie.com/blogs/realtime-economic-issues-watch/foreign-corporates-investing-china-surged-2021.

2. China Briefing, "China's negative list for foreign investment access (new edition): English version available," China Briefing, December 28, 2021, https://www.china-briefing.com/news/chinas-foreign-investment-negative-list-2021-edition-english-version/.
3. Bernadette Christina and Gayatri Suroyo, "Indonesia targets 33% jump in 2022 investment by tapping resource processing," Reuters, January 27, 2022, https://www.reuters.com/markets/commodities/indonesia-targets-33-jump-2022-investment-by-tapping-resource-processing-2022-01-27/.
4. United Nations Conference on Trade and Development (UNCTAD), "Global foreign direct investment fell by 42% in 2020, outlook remains weak," January 24, 2021, https://unctad.org/news/global-foreign-direct-investment-fell-42-2020-outlook-remains-weak.
5. UNCTAD, "Global foreign direct investment."
6. United Nations Conference on Trade and Development (UNCTAD), "Global foreign direct investment rebounded strongly in 2021, but the recovery is highly uneven," January 19, 2022, https://unctad.org/news/global-foreign-direct-investment-rebounded-strongly-2021-recovery-highly-uneven.
7. Ruchit Purohit, "FPI equity inflows drop to $3.8 billion in 2021," Financial Express, December 30, 2021, https://www.financialexpress.com/market/fpi-equity-inflows-drop-to-3-8-billion-in-2021/2393672/.
8. Data provided to authors on request from historical database of EmergingPortfolio.com, 1995–2002.
9. Rodrigo Campos, "Foreigners pull money out of EM portfolios for second month—IIF," Yahoo Finance, May 10, 2022, https://uk.finance.yahoo.com/news/foreigners-pull-money-em-portfolios-101906313.html.
10. Cameron Brandt, "EPFR—Global Navigator," July 1, 2022, https://financialintelligence.informa.com/epfr
11. Selcuk Gokoluk, "Emerging market debt sales plunge amid Ukraine war, rising rates," Bloomberg, May 3, 2022, https://www.bloomberg.com/news/articles/2022-05-03/emerging-market-debt-sales-plunge-amid-ukraine-war-rising-rates?srnd=premium&sref=9BZJXmVl.

12. Organization for Economic Co-operation and Development (OECD), "ODA to Developing Countries, Development finance data, https://www.oecd.org/dac/financing-sustainable-development/development-finance-data/
13. OECD, "Press Release: International aid rises with increased support to Ukraine and humanitarian needs," Paris, April 11, 2024, https://www.oecd.org/en/about/news/press-releases/2024/04/international-aid-rises-in-2023-with-increased-support-to-ukraine-and-humanitarian-needs.html.
14. OECD.
15. David Sacks, "Countries in China's belt and road initiative: who's in and who's out," Council on Foreign Relations, March 24, 2021, https://www.cfr.org/blog/countries-chinas-belt-and-road-initiative-whos-and-whos-out.
16. Sacks.
17. Dr. Yu Jie and Jon Wallace, "What is China's belt and road initiative (BRI)?," Chatham House, September 13, 2021, https://www.chathamhouse.org/2021/09/what-chinas-belt-and-road-initiative-bri.
18. Christoph Nedopil Wang, "Brief: China belt and road initiative (BRI) investment report 2023, " Green Finance and Development Center, February 2, 2022, https://greenfdc.org/brief-china-belt-and-road-initiative-bri-investment-report-2021/.
19. Center for Strategic and International Studies (CSIS), "Game of loans: how China bought Hambantota," CSIS, April 2, 2018, https://www.csis.org/analysis/game-loans-how-china-bought-hambantota.
20. Bloomberg Markets, "China belt and road banks halted overseas energy loans last year," Bloomberg, March 15, 2022, https://www.bloomberg.com/news/articles/2022-03-15/china-belt-and-road-banks-halted-overseas-energy-loans-last-year?srnd=premium&sref=9BZJXmVl.
21. FM Shakil, "Debt-ridden Pakistan begs China for a bailout," Asia Times, February 10, 2022, https://asiatimes.com/2022/02/debt-ridden-pakistan-begs-china-for-a-bailout/.
22. Jim O'Neill, "Twenty years on, the Brics have disappointed," Financial Times, November 29, 2021, https://www.ft.com/content/034ba0e7-7518-437e-854c-7c0dd5d74e34.
23. O'Neill.
24. Enda Curran, Ben Bartenstein and Lizzy Burden, "How Goldman's BRICs flew then faded in two decades," Bloomberg, November 16, 2021, https://www.bloomberg.com/features/brics-emerging-markets-jim-o-neill-2021/?sref=9BZJXmVl.

25. The World Bank: Data, "GDP growth (annual %)—Brazil, China, India Russian Federation," The World Bank, https://data.worldbank.org/indicator/NY.GDP.MKTP.KD.ZG?locations=BR-CN-IN-RU
26. New Development Bank, https://www.ndb.int/.
27. Fitch Ratings, "Fitch revises outlook on new development bank to negative; affirms at 'AA + ,' March 17, 2022, https://www.fitchratings.com/research/sovereigns/fitch-revises-outlook-on-new-development-bank-to-negative-affirms-at-aa-17-03-2022.
28. New Development Bank, Press Releases, "NDB admits Egypt as new member," New Development Bank, December 29, 2021, https://www.ndb.int/press_release/ndb-admits-egypt-as-new-member/
29. Amin Mohseni-Cheraghlou, "Economic and financial multilateralism in disarray," Atlantic Council, April 12, 2022, https://www.atlanticcouncil.org/blogs/econographics/economic-and-financial-multilateralism-in-disarray/.
30. Anna Siampani, "NDB's Role in Driving Growth and Sustainability in Emerging Markets," CEOWORLD Magazine, October 32, 2024, https://ceoworld.biz/2024/10/23/ndbs-role-in-driving-growth-and-sustainability-in-emerging-markets/
31. AIIB, aiib.org/en
32. AIIB.
33. Humayan Kabir, "AIIB emerging as one of BD's major dev financiers," The Financial Express, October 9, 2022, https://today.thefinancialexpress.com.bd/print/aiib-emerges-as-one-of-bds-major-dev-financiers-1665246438
34. 2023 AIIB Annual Report, Asian Infrastructure Development Bank, Beijing, China, 2024 https://www.aiib.org/en/news-events/annual-report/overview/index.html
35. Mohseni-Cheraghlou, "Economic and financial multilateralism.".
36. Nicholas Nhede, "ADB move to address infrastructure financing gap in Asia," Smart Energy International, September 22, 2020, https://www.smart-energy.com/finance-investment/adb-move-to-help-address-sustainable-infrastructure-financing-gap-in-asia/.
37. United Nations, Division for Sustainable Development Goals, https://sdgs.un.org/.
38. Global SWF, "2024 Annual Report.".
39. Global SWF, "2024 Annual Report.".

40. Javier Capape Aguilar, “Sovereign wealth funds take to the stage,” ieUniversity, March 11, 2022. https://www.ie.edu/insights/articles/sovereign-wealth-funds-take-to-the-stage/#:~:text=Sovereign%20wealth%20funds%20are%20often,are%20invisible%20to%20most%20people.
41. Sovereign Wealth Fund Institute, “Top 100 largest sovereign wealth fund rankings by total assets,” https://www.swfinstitute.org/fund-rankings/sovereign-wealth-fund.
42. Sovereign Wealth Fund Institute, https://www.swfinstitute.org/.
43. Leanne de Bassompierre, “Wealth fund with climate focus in its DNA looks beyond Gabon,” Bloomberg, US Edition, September 22, 2021, https://www.bloomberg.com/news/articles/2021-09-22/wealth-fund-with-climate-focus-in-its-dna-looks-beyond-gabon?sref=9BZJXmVl.
44. Bassompierre.
45. John Hyatt, “How Putin used Russia’s sovereign wealth fund to create a ‘state-sponsored oligarchy,’” March 8, 2022, https://www.forbes.com/sites/johnhyatt/2022/03/08/sanctions-on-russian-fund-show-dashed-hope-of-moscows-cooperation-with-democracies/?sh=4e189724a431.
46. Hyatt.
47. Hyatt.
48. Hyatt.
49. Sovereign Wealth Fund, “Turkey’s sovereign fund switches from high ambitions to crisis management and nationalization,” March 10, 2022, https://globalswf.com/news/turkey-s-sovereign-fund-switches-from-high-ambitions-to-crisis-management-and-nationalization.
50. Mustafa Sonmez, “Turkey’s ‘wealthless’ wealth fund a tangle of problems,” Al-Monitor, January 13, 2021, https://www.al-monitor.com/originals/2021/01/turkey-economy-wealthless-wealth-fund-a-tangle-of-problems.html
51. Sovereign Wealth Fund, “Turkey’s sovereign fund switches.”.
52. Sonmez, “Turkey’s ‘wealthless’ wealth fund.”
53. Global SWF, “2023 Annual Report: State-Owned Investors in a Multipolar World,” https://globalswf.com/reports/2023annual
54. Frank Beckers and Uwe Stegemann, “A smarter way to think about public–private partnerships,” McKinsey, September 10, 2021, https://www.mckinsey.com/business-functions/risk-and-resilience/our-insights/a-smarter-way-to-think-about-public-private-partnerships#print.

7

A Changed World: ESG/Sustainable/New Tech Investment Trends

Despite political push-back in some developed countries, ESG and sustainable investment will continue to expand and deepen in emerging economies where the impacts of climate change and poverty are the most severe. Investment in energy transition will continue to be a key priority. At the same time, the development of new technologies, particularly artificial intelligence (AI) and innovative fintech, will drive fresh investment into emerging and frontier markets to further hasten economic development.

During 2020 and 2021 multilateral and bilateral assistance veered almost exclusively to funding for health care, social protection, and vaccines. At the same time, flagship events—ranging from the Black Lives Matter movement in the US to the COP26 United Nations Climate Conference in Glasgow—spotlighted ESG and sustainable investment beyond their decades of niche following. New emerging markets investment products embraced the broad United Nations Sustainable Development Goals (SDGs) envisioned by 2030.[1] The first three of the 17 SDGs—end poverty, zero hunger, and good health and well-being—were singled out by investors and donors at the height of the pandemic.

Public and Private Sector Response to "Polycrisis"

The impact of the global Covid-19 pandemic, Russian war in Ukraine, and monetary tightening in response to inflation compounded global emerging market challenges. In 2023 the World Economic Forum embraced a new

B. Morrissey and G. Kleiman, *Emerging Economies and Financial Markets*,
https://doi.org/10.1007/978-3-031-85669-3_7

term when it warned of a "polycrisis," a series of connected and interrelated risks. From the outbreak of the global pandemic through the end of its fiscal year in April 2023 the IMF lent USD 272 billion to 94 of its 190 member countries.[2] At the direction of the IMF, low and middle-income countries spent heavily during the pandemic to meet health care expenditures, provide support for vulnerable citizens and grant tax relief for businesses. As economies began to recover in 2021 inflation took hold globally on renewed demand and ongoing supply chain issues, many related to China's extended Covid-related lockdown measures.

The Russian invasion of Ukraine on February 24, 2022 sparked global economic turmoil. Foreign portfolio investors fled to "safe havens"—the US dollar—compounding capital outflows that started pre-war on the US dollar rally in late 2021. Measured against the greenback currencies tumbled, with some losing half their value, which raised dollar costs for key imports and debt servicing. Global supply chains still not recovered from the pandemic seized, and key commodity prices soared. As the US and its Western allies moved quickly to impose sanctions on Russia and Belarus, including for critical exports like grain, oil and fertilizer, cost and scarcity intensified. Shortages ensued despite the Black Sea grain deal agreed by Russia, Ukraine, Turkey, and the United Nations.

While the impact was felt globally, emerging, frontier and low-income countries, already facing high debt and deficit levels and low international reserves as pandemic recovery continued, were most exposed without a safety net. Food insecurity became pronounced, particularly in the Middle East, Africa, South Asia, and low-income island nations already suffering from the impact of climate change with historic droughts, flooding, and rising sea waters. These countries saw trade and current account deficits balloon and international reserves tumble, leaving them unable to import basic necessities.

The multilateral development institutions rallied to provide financial assistance, but program access was unequal and coordination improvised. In order to tap emergency or traditional IMF and other multilateral and bilateral funding countries had to undergo an exhaustive debt sustainability analysis gauging whether they had the capacity to repay. At the same time, rising inflation in advanced economies resulted in punishing interest rate hikes, making commercial access unaffordable for poor country borrowers. Non-traditional bilateral lenders—including China, Saudi Arabia, and the United Arab Emirates—provided currency swap lines and non-conditional lending which helped buoy international reserves for many countries during the pandemic and early days of the war.

The IMF estimates that additional funding needs for low-income countries to address the legacy of Covid-19 and rebuild external buffers in the wake of the war in Ukraine will be in the range of USD 440 billion through 2026. At the same time, both the pandemic and war derailed progress emerging, frontier and vulnerable countries had made in working toward achieving the United Nation's Sustainable Development goals by 2030 as poverty, hunger, and climate catastrophe worsened. The war's reverberations through the emerging markets served as a wake-up call that trade, investment, and financial flows remain volatile and can only indirectly foster basic social and physical provisions.

While Zambia was the first to default on its external debt obligations in the wake of the Covid-19 outbreak, debt levels there and in other countries had been building steadily through the 2010s. For over a decade, frontier markets new to commercial borrowing had, in the wake of historically low global interest rates, been issuing hard-currency denominated debt. From 2012–2022 African sovereigns alone borrowed USD 30 billion in bonds. At the same time, non-Paris Club bilateral lending, especially by China and the Gulf states, also surged.

Emerging economies had seen current account deficits shrink during 2020 on the combination of lockdowns and supply chain bottlenecks curbing import demand, but global openings sharply reversed the trend in 2022. Supply chain issues due to congestion and blockages in the production and distribution systems, which hit advanced economies particularly in electronics and cars from semiconductor chip shortages, resulted in a squeeze in basic goods like medicine and household products in emerging markets.

The pandemic also severely affected countries which rely on tourism revenues. For example, in Sri Lanka they accounted for 5.6 percent of GDP in 2018 but in 2020 only 0.8 percent.[3] Elsewhere, Grenada and Macao, which recorded very few Covid-19 cases and no pandemic-related deaths in 2020, saw GDP collapse by 13 percent and 56 percent, respectively.[4] The downturn added to unemployment and increased poverty. Remittances, however, held up during 2020 better than originally expected. Just months after lockdowns began, the World Bank had estimated that foreign worker transfers to low- and middle-income countries would collapse by 20 percent. Instead, they fell only 1.6 percent to USD 540 billion from a year earlier and accounted for more than foreign direct investment and overseas development assistance together which totaled USD 438 billion.[5] Remittances were buoyed by fiscal stimulus in host countries which encouraged migrants to continue to send money home.

Low-income countries—of which over 50 percent of the 60 are fragile/conflict states—were particularly hard hit during the global pandemic. By the end of 2021 almost 60 percent were assessed at high risk of, or already in, debt distress, up from 30 percent in 2015.[6] The global economic recovery that began in 2021 sent food and commodity prices soaring, with staple grains up 21.1 percent in 2021, according to the United Nations Food and Agriculture Organization. The World Bank's energy price index surged 81 percent during 2021, while its non-energy commodity benchmark was up 32 percent.

Prior to the global pandemic and war in Ukraine, much of sub-Saharan Africa was already suffering from food insecurity due to climate change, with droughts and flooding devastating crops. Nearly three-quarters of the population of the region live in rural areas largely dependent on agriculture, which accounts for more than 25 percent of the continent's output.[7] The outbreak of the war compounded the problem. In low-income countries food accounts for over 40 percent of consumer spending and prices soared. Disruptions to fertilizer exports from Russia and Belarus and restrictions on some food exports from other countries compounded the rising crisis caused by climate change. The African Development Bank puts continental imports of cereals at over 100 million metric tons at an annual cost of USD 75 billion. The lender states that Russia's invasion of Ukraine triggered a shortage of at least 30 million tons of food across the continent, especially wheat, maize, and soybeans. The war resulted in wheat price increases of more than 40 percent in some countries while fertilizer costs rose nearly four-times from the 2020 level.[8]

In Kenya, for example, food accounts for one-third of the consumer price index and agriculture accounts for an estimated 20 percent of GDP. Prior to the war, it imported 44 percent of its wheat from Russia and Ukraine and after the war prices doubled. In an effort to offset the impact, the government distributed fertilizer subsidies to farmers and set aside cash for food relief. However, with fuel prices at record highs in the country, ordinary citizens turned to climate harming charcoal for cooking and heating. A World Agroforestry Report found that more than half of the 50 million Kenyans had been using charcoal even though Kenya had banned illegal logging five years earlier.[9] The research shows that 8 percent and 15 percent of the charcoal sold in Nairobi and Mombasa, respectively, comes from the Democratic Republic of Congo, Uganda, and South Sudan. Climate analysts warn that the area's war is threatening the existence of the Congo Rainforest, the second largest in the world.

Inflation in Kenya at year-end 2022 hit 9.1 percent even after the Central Bank tightened 175 basis points in an attempt to rein it in. At the same time, the constitutionally mandated public debt ceiling of 64 percent of GDP was breached and closed at 67 percent, up from 62.4 percent at end-2019. Annual debt service reached 54 percent of domestic revenue, up from 40 percent in 2020. The government had planned to issue a Eurobond but market conditions and loss of investor appetite for emerging market sovereign debt prevented access and instead the also expensive syndicated loan market was tapped. While Kenya's overall debt level is high, its external obligations are low compared to neighbors at only 33 percent of GDP. However, it faced a USD 2 billion Eurobond payment in June 2024. The current account deficit soared to 5.7 percent of GDP while foreign exchange reserves slipped to only 3 months of imports on higher food and fuel prices, with part of the fall also attributed to foreign portfolio outflows as investors fled emerging markets more generally. Retreat was spurred by the rapidly depreciating shilling and dollar shortages in Kenya.

In addition to inflation driven by drought and the war in Ukraine, Ethiopia faced even more dire challenges. In a report the World Bank stated, "Multiple conflicts combined with historic drought and other shocks have severely impacted millions of Ethiopians, jeopardizing the economic and social development progress the country has achieved in recent years." The country's natural disaster combined with the Tigray war compounded food insecurity. Ethiopia's debt/GDP level at just under 60 percent is quite low compared with neighbors. It was one of very few countries to take advantage of the G-20's Covid-related Debt Service Suspension Initiative (DSSI). Most countries in the region that qualified for DSSI did not sign on fearing extended loss of private market access and sovereign ratings downgrades. When DSSI was replaced with the G-20 Common Framework—which in theory gathers all official creditors together to resolve unsustainable debt—Ethiopia applied in September of 2021.

At the same time, the rise in food and fuel import prices sent Ethiopia's current account deficit over 5 percent of GDP in 2022 with further pressure due also to poor coffee exports from drought. Fitch Ratings downgraded the sovereign's ratings to CCC- noting the lack of ability to meet its external financing gaps. It finally secured a fresh IMF arrangement in mid-2024 after gaining a debt service pause from bilateral creditors and defaulting on a $20 million coupon for its only $1 billion sovereign bond to be redeemed in December the same year.

To the south, Zambia was the first sovereign to default on its external debt during Covid as its debt/GDP ratio topped 130 percent. Like Ethiopia the sovereign struggled to finish a much-delayed restructuring of its debt under the Common Framework process, complicated by the fact that China was

Zambia's largest creditor. Of its total external obligations, 46 percent was owed to private lenders, 22 percent to China, 8 percent to other governments, and 18 percent to multilateral institutions.[10]

The country has suffered from severe drought almost continuously since 2015. Power cuts are regular occurrences due to record low water levels at the Kariba dam, the world's largest human-made reservoir. Like Zambia, Zimbabwe, already an international pariah due to unpaid bills to multilaterals and unable to access Western financing, is similarly suffering the effects of catastrophic drought. Annual inflation there was in triple digits, driven by food and energy shortages as well as overall economic mismanagement and severe hard currency scarcity.

In the Middle East/North Africa (MENA), fragile and conflict states account for more than one-third of the region's countries. Consumer price inflation in these countries topped 30 percent in 2022. The Gulf countries are perhaps the only sub-region globally to have been beneficiaries of the war on high global oil and gas prices, as well as an influx of wealthy Russians, particularly to Dubai. In 2022 sales of residential property there surged 60 percent despite rising interest rates and prices were up 11 percent on an annual basis. Eighteen out of 22 Arab countries are deemed "scarce water countries," and food production, particularly cereals, is tiny. The combination of climate change and urbanization challenges have been compounded by Russia's war.

Egypt was hit particularly badly at the onset of the war. In recent years, the country had become increasingly dependent on "hot money" inflows to balance the books as the Egyptian pound did not float freely and local Treasury bills offered high real yields. When the war broke out, emerging and frontier market portfolio investors fled to safe havens and dumped some USD 20 billion in local Treasury bills and bonds. Less than a year after the start of the war, the Egyptian pound had lost half its value against the USD as the government also ran through its foreign reserves as the costs of imports, notably wheat, soared pushing inflation over 21 percent by end-2022. The country lacked foreign exchange and imports were held in ports for lack of cash to pay for them, aggravating goods shortages.

Before the pandemic and war, Egypt had just exited an IMF program, but had not floated the currency or reduced debt through structural reforms like privatization and better tax collection as outlined in the Fund program. After the war started, Cairo was forced to go to the IMF for the third time in seven years. Even before it secured a new USD 3 billion loan in October 2022, it was already the fund's second biggest debtor after Argentina.

Also in North Africa, Tunisia is in worse shape not only due to Covid-19 and the war, but because of three years of drought and political chaos. Following a landslide win in 2019, President Kais Saied disbanded parliament and held sham elections with only about 10 percent of the population voting. Consumer prices topped the double-digit mark in 2022 for the first time since 1984 as authorities limited water supplies to farms to ensure adequate drinking water, which sent food prices soaring. The country's food insecurity became so dire that grocery store shelves were half empty and Libya's Tripoli-based National Unity Government donated some 100-truck loads of essentials in early 2023. The state was unable to pay for imports and a preliminary agreement on a USD 1.9 billion IMF loan in late 2022—which called for gradual lifting of food and fuel subsidies—stalled on lack of reform and the president's rejection of "Western edicts."

While portfolio investors fled during Covid-19, after the war started even long-time foreign direct investors pulled out of Tunisia because they were not being paid. Royal Dutch Shell, which operated gas fields that accounted for almost half of domestic production, left in 2022 and multinational pharmaceutical manufacturers exited because they were stiffed by the bankrupt state drug distributor.

The food crisis in Jordan was even worse as the arid country, host to millions of Syrian and Palestinian refugees, imported 98 percent of its wheat and 78 percent of barley from Russia and Ukraine before the war. The OPEC Fund for International Development provided a loan to the Kingdom for additional grain imports and storage. There were demonstrations against the cost of living as truck drivers and other transport workers protested rising fuel prices.

Jordan's public debt stands at some USD 47 billion, 112 percent of GDP, the highest level in the country's history. The World Bank noted that public debt service in 2022 rose to 7.9 percent of GDP as compared with 6.6 percent a year before. However, Jordan repaid in full a USD 1 billion Eurobond in June 2022. To meet external obligations, it issued USD 650 million in new paper at 7.75 percent for 5.5 years in the international market, with the offer three-times oversubscribed. The Kingdom raised the rest through US dollar denominated bonds on the local market, which is dominated by banks obligated to also hold the paper for backup reserves.

Lebanon has been in economic and political crisis for years and Covid, the explosion at the Port of Beirut in 2020, and the war worsened the situation which the World Bank has noted in published reports is "among the most severe crises globally since the mid-nineteenth century." The currency lost 95 percent of its value against the USD since 2019, and the banking system is insolvent. Already expensive food and fuel soared in price after Russia's invasion, and the country ran out of dollars to pay for imports. In 2020 the World Bank estimated that over half of the population was below the poverty line, and the situation worsened following the total removal of subsidies on food and fuel due to the state's inability to fund them. In June 2021, the dysfunctional Lebanese parliament approved a ration card law for a USD 556 million program to support vulnerable households affected by the lifting of subsidies, but as of end-2022 the program was still nascent due to lack of funding. Pre-war, Lebanon sourced 80 percent of its wheat imports from Ukraine and 15 percent from Russia.[11]

Prior to the global pandemic, "China would deliver 34 percent, 35 percent, 40 percent of global growth. It is not doing it anymore. It is actually quite stressful for the Asian economies," stated the IMF's Managing Director on the popular US talk show "Face the Nation" on January 1, 2023. Covid, China lockdowns, climate change, and the war were ruinous economically for the small countries in South Asia. In the large East Asian countries, the overall fallout was more manageable despite China's extended Covid lockdown which dampened trade and disrupted regional supply chains. India and China imported Russian oil at reduced rates. When India's inflation rate exceeded the Reserve Bank's target, it tightened monetary policy in 2022. Food and energy account for 55 percent of the CPI basket, with food alone at 46 percent. The rise in commodity prices also pressured India's perennial current account deficit. After the war broke out, India tapped its near record high foreign exchange reserves to provide assistance to neighboring debt-ridden Sri Lanka. In addition to the spike in commodity costs, foreign portfolio investors dumped more than USD 21 billion of local stocks and bonds from October 2021 when the US Federal Reserve first indicated it would begin tightening through year-end 2022, and the rupee lost 12 percent against the US dollar. India was the fastest growing economy in Asia and in Fiscal Year 2023–24 it expanded 8.2 percent.

India's small South Asian neighbors were dramatically roiled by the war. After decades of economic mismanagement and mounting debt in recent years with funding for vanity projects prior to the pandemic, the war was the breaking point for Sri Lanka. The country defaulted on its sovereign debt in April 2022 as it ran out of funds for needed food, fuel, fertilizer, and medicine. The long-ruling Rajapaksa family was forced from power and the new government finalized a USD 2.9 billion IMF loan a year later. Debt/GDP reached 120 percent, and the fiscal deficit was in double-digits as a percentage of output from 2020 through 2022. The economy contracted 7 percent in 2022, and annual inflation stood at just under 60 percent at year-end 2022 after the rupee depreciated 45 percent.

Also in South Asia, the war compounded Pakistan's long running economic and political chaos. Months after the onset, amid suspension of IMF funding due to lack of promised reforms, the country was devastated by summer floods which the World Bank estimated caused USD 40 billion in damages. The natural disaster was attributed to climate change from melting glaciers combined with heavier than usual annual monsoon rains and killed nearly two thousand people and displaced an estimated 8 million. Infrastructure, buildings, and crops were destroyed. A donor conference in Geneva in January 2023 resulted in USD 9 billion in bilateral and multilateral aid pledges.

Even South Asian neighbor Bangladesh, which lent Sri Lanka USD 200 million in 2021 prior to its default and had a low debt/GDP ratio of just under 40 percent, turned to the IMF in the wake of the war. The finance ministry sought the loan to tackle a severe foreign currency shortage which was slowing energy and food imports. The Fund loan was quickly negotiated after the government hiked fuel prices by 50 percent since it could no longer afford the subsidies and let the currency float in 2022. The taka lost 22 percent against the dollar in 2022, almost double the depreciation of next-door India's 12 percent drop. The current account deficit soared to 4 percent of GDP, and the central bank injected USD 7.8 billion into the financial system in the final half of 2022 to help banks finance imports. Total reserves, excluding a recently formed USD 7 billion export development fund which the IMF does not consider eligible in the count, dropped USD 16.3 billion in 2022 from a record high of USD 48.6 billion in August 2021.[12]

To the east, small indebted Laos and Cambodia and island nations like Papua New Guinea suffered singularly from the triple whammy Covid/war/rate hike crisis. Small states are particularly vulnerable due to their reliance on external trade and financing, limited economic diversification, elevated debt, and susceptibility to natural disasters, according to the IMF. In Laos inflation soared to 40 percent in 2022, and the currency fell nearly 40 percent against the US dollar. The country's debt/GDP was estimated at 95 percent by end-2022, but private researchers believe that "hidden debt," exposure to China not included in official data, adds another 35.4 percent of GDP.[13] Nearly 90 percent of the debt is in foreign currencies.

In Latin America, the economies had limited fiscal space to address the cost of the war in the post-pandemic environment, although the region was a first mover in monetary tightening as global prices started to rise in 2021. Brazil was the first to start hiking rates from a record low of 2 percent in March 2021 as inflation started rising on economic re-opening. It tightened 1075 basis points to battle inflation, which reached 12.5 percent, the highest since 1999. Peru and Chile started rate hikes in July 2021, while Mexico, where the monetary authority generally closely tracks the US Federal reserve, started raising rates in June 2021.

Early in the war there was discussion that the region's agricultural production, especially wheat, could help replace global supplies. However, ambition was misplaced as even major producer Brazil had to import the grain to meet domestic demand. In addition, the region had long depended on imported fertilizer from Russia, and the lack of access contributed to lower output and higher food prices.

High inflation contributed to the rise of "anti-establishment" administrations across the region which pressured fiscal deficits as governments increased spending. Colombia elected a leftist former guerrilla, Gustavo Petro, in August 2022 who promised to end oil and gas exploration and reform the healthcare and pension systems. Citing double-digit inflation and inequality, the minimum wage was hiked by 16 percent. Significant tax reform was passed late in 2022, which was expected to increase revenue by 1.3 percent of GDP. However, Petro promised the government would buy up land and give parcels to rural communities as part of his promised agricultural reform. The cost of half a million hectares—only a quarter of what the president pledged—is estimated at more than USD 2 billion, about half of what the new tax reform was expected to take in.

In Brazil, left-wing Liuz Inacio Lula da Silva, commonly known as Lula, narrowly defeated conservative President Jair Bolsonaro in late 2022. Despite the outgoing president's last-ditch fiscal stimulus packages to win votes which slashed taxes and expanded welfare for the poor, the economy grew only 2.8 percent on an annual basis in 2022. Just under half of growth came from the services sector, which accounts for about 70 percent of GDP, while the drag was from a 0.9 percent contraction in agriculture attributed to climate change and insufficient fertilizer due to the war.

The Caribbean and Central American economies were particularly hurt by the global pandemic as tourism revenues dried up on lockdowns and border closures. These small open economies, which rank among the world's most indebted economies, are—except for oil producers Trinidad and Tobago and Guyana—net food and fuel importers and inflation spiked. While the Caribbean Development Bank reported that its member countries grew 10.3 percent in 2022, the growth was largely due to increased energy production in Guyana and Trinidad on higher international oil prices. Guyana's economy grew more than 57 percent on new oil output. Tighter monetary policy in the US and Europe put downward pressure on foreign direct investment and critical remittances. These smaller economies have seen rising food insecurity which has boosted already high debt levels as governments across the region provide support for the most vulnerable. At the same time many of these economies have currency pegs with the US dollar, preventing monetary flexibility to address the impact of price shocks.

Finally in Europe, in 2022 energy prices in the European Union spiked by 25.5 percent and food by 13.8 percent, driving Hungarian inflation to 24.5 percent, the highest in the region. Prices soared after the government ended support schemes to ease energy-related bills. The price caps had resulted in shortages as importers and retailers refused to sell products below cost, but food price ones were regularly extended on "staples" including sugar and flour. Food and power prices were up nearly 50 percent for the year on a weakening currency. According to the World Bank, food prices were up 44 percent, the tenth highest in the world. Hungary's budget deficit soared to 5.3 percent of GDP, more than double the EU average, on heavy spending.

Similarly in next door Poland, which welcomed 1.5 million Ukrainian refugees, inflation spiked and growth slowed. In response to rising food and energy prices, the government introduced an "energy deal" to cap electricity and gas prices at a cost estimated at 1 percent of GDP, which nearly doubled the original 2022 fiscal deficit target to 3 percent of GDP. The rising cost of imports pushed the current account deficit to just under 4 percent of GDP in 2022.

Further east, Kazakhstan saw inflation soar to 20 percent in 2022, the highest level since 1996, despite six rate hikes which brought the benchmark rate to 16.7 percent. Food price inflation was 25.3 percent, with prices on some goods like sugar nearly doubling. Supply chain disruptions and a "migration shock" also pressured prices. In just a week in September 2022 more than 100,000 Russians arrived after Putin announced the partial military mobilization. Rental costs and demand for all goods and services soared. Kazakhstan is heavily dependent on Russian imports which account for an estimated 40 percent of all foreign purchases. While the government opposed most sanctions on its largest trade partner, it sent humanitarian aid to Ukraine and banned weapons exports.

Global multilateral lenders, having put in place rapid responses to financial needs for Covid, acted quickly again to the growing crisis in emerging, frontier, and vulnerable countries following the Russian invasion of Ukraine. Just two months after the war started the major international financial institutions prepared an "Action Plan to Address Food Insecurity."[14]

The IMF, World Bank Group (including IFC and MIGA), the United Nations' International Fund for Agricultural Development, European Bank for Reconstruction and Development, and the African, Asian, and Inter-American Development Banks came together to develop plans to address the "latest global shock." In detailing their joint plan, they noted the war exacerbated the "sharp increase in both acute and chronic food insecurity in recent years driven by conflict, climate change, and economic downturns, such as those associated with the Covid-19 pandemic."

They pledged to leverage existing tools and programs in a "fast-tracked and scaled up manner," and launch specific new initiatives. Six priority goals were identified: supporting vulnerable people; promoting open trade; mitigating fertilizer shortages; supporting food production now; investing in climate resilient agriculture for the future; and coordinating for maximum impact. Each institution's existing and planned programs were detailed, such as the EBRD's Resilience and Livelihood Framework which was approved within weeks of the start of the war.

The IFC pledged to launch a Global Food Security Platform targeting affected countries, including Ukraine, to close the large financing gap for agribusinesses in the food supply chain. The Asian and InterAmerican Development Banks announced they would begin policy discussions within the agriculture sector to encourage countries to increase the efficient use of fertilizer. The International Fund for Agricultural Development pledged to invest USD 3.5 billion in 78 countries to "build the resilience of the world's poorest and most vulnerable rural people," in addition to its post-war Crisis Response Initiative to address short-term food security needs in twenty-two countries primarily in Africa and Asia. The final goal, coordinating for maximum impact while focusing on areas of expertise, included plans for co-financing by the African Development Bank for fertilizer procurement and the United Nations' International Fund for Agricultural Development's outreach to other UN agencies.

Separately each multilateral development agency created new initiatives after the outbreak of the war to meet the needs of emerging, frontier, and conflict economies. For example, IFC launched a USD 6 billion financing facility, Global Food Security Platform, to support vulnerable communities, boost the flow of vital commodities and help reduce food insecurity. The Platform provides emergency financing to farmers, commodity traders, food and feed processors, and other private players facing funding challenges due to cost increases.

In October 2022, the IMF approved a new Food Shock Window under its existing emergency financing instruments created in 2006, the Rapid Credit Facility and the Rapid Financing Instruments. As with all IMF programs, access to the Food Shock Window is subject to debt sustainability and adequate capacity to repay requirements. The IMF identified at least 48 countries that would be eligible for the new facility, including many of the poorest and most vulnerable. Under the program food import prices must be creating a negative balance of payments impact of 0.3 percent of GDP and negative cereal shock of 0.8 percent.[15] Some nations in need, like Zimbabwe shut out from official lending due to non-payment and arrears to official creditors, are unable to access the emergency funding.

Overall, the multilateral development institutions, which have long been viewed by the private sector as slow in decision-making and project implementation, responded with quick concrete initiatives to the debt and food crisis. However, as noted above, access to funding under traditional programs is typically required for tapping new emergency assistance, and countries like Sri Lanka, Ghana, and Pakistan were brought to the brink over debt sustainability and reform issues while mired in hunger and poverty. Global coordination through the covid vaccine common platform proved to have limited reach in poorer regions with miniscule immunization rates as the official lenders also united on that front to adapt their offerings. Universal clean energy is a theme lenders have emphasized at regular climate summits before the Russian invasion, while the prospect of mass starvation in the war aftermath catalyzed a deeper push into improving the entire eco-system which may clash with priority humanitarian agency emphasis on immediate survival provisions, as classic UN appeals in the latter category are chronically underfunded.

ESG/Sustainable Investing

ESG was previously on the asset class fringes, concentrated largely in Europe and the US, with a focus on the "E." "Green investing" dominated discussions and investment offerings, with the social and governance aspects on the back burner, even though the World Bank and advocacy groups had developed detailed rankings for the last two categories. The poverty and income inequalities exposed during the pandemic in divides between skilled and routine jobs, and formal and informal workers, raised the importance of the issues. Ratings agencies, investors, and non-profits continue to scramble for standard quantitative and qualitative measurements across countries and companies. The shared consensus is that coverage must broaden beyond symbolic strides such as headlines around one woman of color on a Board of Directors.

ESG and sustainable investing will accelerate rapidly in both the sovereign and corporate sectors as an integral feature. In 2021 issuance in emerging and frontier markets totaled USD 230 billion, up 227 percent from a year earlier.[16] While worrying about "greenwashing"—proceeds not used for the stated climate purpose—in emerging markets may be larger than in developed country counterparts due to comparative lag in disclosure standards, investors commitment is on a distinct upswing. Through end-2021, emerging markets accounted for only 5 percent of total sustainability-linked sovereign and corporate financing, including loans and bonds.[17] However, the absolute amount was up 327 percent in 2021 over a year earlier.[18] Growth slowed in 2022 and 2023 on geopolitical tensions, slowing economic growth, and high borrowing costs. Globally issuance of sustainable finance products decelerated from USD 1.78 trillion in 2021 to USD 1.53 trillion a year later and dropped to USD 1.44 trillion in 2023[19] (see case study).

Case Study: SDG-ESG Confusion

In the wake of the global pandemic, "ESG" was a catchall investor term embracing health considerations, but awareness of the SDGs outside the UN panels which created them in 2012 barely featured. Corporate or sovereign application of environmental, social, and governance standards was almost entirely skewed toward the first category, focused on climate change adaptation and mitigation in particular, before Covid-19. Rule of law, transparency, and poverty rankings would appear in bond documents as a box-ticking exercise rarely scrutinized to the same degree as macro-economic indicators.

The term ESG originated at the United Nations Environment Program Initiative in 2005. A report author, Paul Clements-Hunt, and colleagues at first thought the acronym should be GES because they believed governance was the most important area. Ultimately, they decided GES was "not so catchy, not so sexy" and that reverse letter order had the best chance of being embraced.[20] Two decades later school age children know the buzzword, hundreds of mutual funds and ETFs come under the umbrella, and government officials insert it both in policies and campaign platforms.

In 2015 later the United Nations unanimously adopted "The 2030 Agenda for Sustainable Development," after an earlier iteration called the Millennium Development Goals. The UN's Department of Economic and Social Affairs describes it as "a shared blueprint for peace and prosperity for people and the planet, now and into the future." The core 17 Sustainable Development Goals (SDGs) are a call for action for developed and developing countries alike.[21] Each one has a series of specific targets and indicators to meet by end decade, covering 231 and 169 items, respectively, for an unwieldy, ambitious agenda.[22] SDG #1 is "End poverty in all its forms everywhere," and Target 1.1 is "By 2030 eradicate extreme poverty for all people everywhere, currently measured as people living on less than USD 1.25 a day."[23] Several replicate ESG definitions: SDG #7 calls for affordable and clean energy and #13 for climate action.

Number 16 mandates peace, justice, and strong institutions, and #5 gender equality.[24]

The Sustainable Development Goals succeeded the United Nation's September 2000 Millennium Declaration, which adopted eight milestones to reduce extreme poverty by 2015. The 2015 SDG agreement was only three months before the Paris one on Climate Change, and world leaders at that summit endorsed declarations with inequality, social justice, and the environment intertwined.

Countries report progress on a voluntary self-determined basis in the far-reaching menu. The earlier MDGs had only 60 indicators and by the 2015 deadline data was available for only 68 percent of the indicators.[25]When the SDGs went operational, 36 percent did not have internationally recognized methodology or standards for measurement. Within three years they had tracking guidelines after the global statistics community weighed in and an Inter-Agency and Expert Group on SDG indicators was convened.[26]

Reporting has been particularly difficult for Goals 5 and 10, gender equality, and reduced inequality. As with assessing economic reform strides in conventional terms, even with new UN tools, they tend to be qualitative rather than quantitative. A World Bank blog noted inadequate SDG data reporting may "not only be a function of statistical capacity but perhaps also of political will," as the domestic voter constituency has yet to surface.[27] It pointed out high income countries are trailing low- and middle-income ones in reporting even though all UN members agreed. Social-sustainable bonds in the absence of comprehensive definitions selectively incorporate specific elements to justify the label. S&G dedicated instruments, with their later start catching up with green ones, improvise criteria from both complexes that can serve as accepted precedents.

Nearly a decade after the European Investment Bank issued the inaugural Green Bond, Fiji and Poland were the first emerging market sovereigns to come to market in 2016. Two years later Seychelles issued the first sovereign "Blue Bond," with proceeds being used for clean maritime projects. Globally in 2023 USD 587.3 billion in green bonds were issued, up 15 percent from a year earlier, while Chile issued five sustainability bonds and Colombia two, totaling USD 59 billion.[28]Mexico was the first with a structure specifically to achieve the UN's SDGs in 2030.[29] The first local currency version came from Colombia in 2021 and was oversubscribed, with the issue upsized by 50 percent. Even then demand was 4.6 times the amount on sale.[30] (Fig. 7.1).

Assessing ESG risk for a sovereign is more complex than for a corporate bond, as cottage industries evolve to screen both, and traditional ratings agencies jump into the mix. Factors include weather swings due to climate change, carbon transition plans/progress, education/labor rights, and rule of law/government stability/corruption. Categories like carbon data and educational access are quantifiable, and index rankings have proliferated for subjective

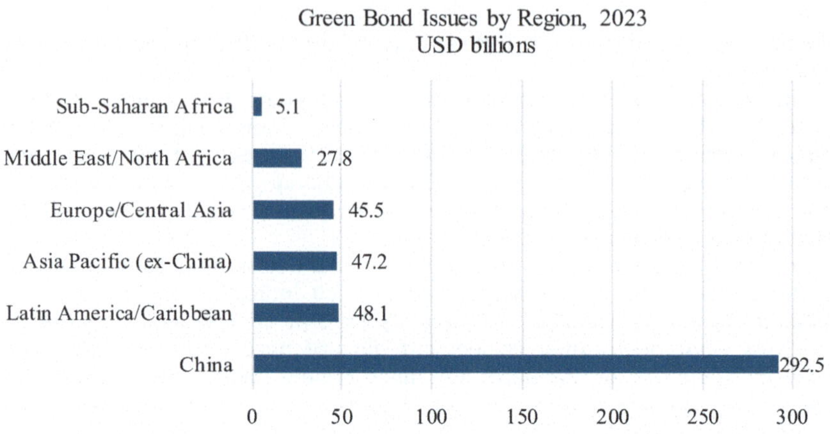

Fig. 7.1 Green Bond Issues by Region, 2023 USD billions (*Source* Statista.com/statistics/1292213/valueof-em-green-bonds-issued-by-region)

judgments using non-profit and official lender data. For example, Transparency International's corruption index is widely cited in the "G" category and was routine in bond prospectuses before the ESG wave as basic macro background. In credit ratings these considerations supplement normal creditworthiness evaluation criteria in their own narrative and scoring sections. Along with ability and willingness to pay, countries get composite scores from the three areas to influence the overall grade. In 2019 the World Bank launched its ESG Sovereign Data Portal which it upgraded significantly with a relaunch in 2022. The database not only covers current country indicators but covers "momentum and improvement as well as a country's position vs. its peers."[31]

Case Study: ESG/SGD Advances in Sub-Saharan Africa

As noted in Chapter 3, the Nairobi Stock Exchange mandated ESG disclosure for listed companies in late 2021. On the continent as a whole, where there are twenty-nine stock exchanges of which two are regional, as of 2024 sixteen have signed onto the United Nation's Sustainable Stock Exchange Initiative (SSE). The SSE was formed to provide a platform for how exchanges—in collaboration with investors, listed companies, regulators, and policymakers—can boost ESG issues and encourage sustainable investing more broadly.

The Johannesburg Stock Exchange (JSE), the continent's largest and deepest market, launched a sustainability segment in 2020 to provide a platform for green, social, and sustainable bond issuance. The JSE and its Egyptian counterpart have both developed indices which feature listed companies adhering to globally recognized ESG criteria. To encourage listings and investment, Zambia has reduced registration fees for green bonds by 50 percent, while Kenya now offers tax exemptions for interest earned on green instruments.

Innovative instruments have been launched across the region. In early 2022 Tanzania's NMB Bank listed the continent's first gender-based bond on the Dar es Salaam Stock Exchange, with proceeds used for lending to women-owned small businesses. The bond was oversubscribed by domestic investors on the USD 7 billion exchange. At the same time Standard Bank and micro-finance developer Urban Ubomi issued social bonds for affordable housing. In June 2022, the African Development Bank launched the first ESG African Frontier Currency Bond. The two-year, 19 billion Uganda shilling paper with a 10.5 percent fixed coupon settled in US dollars with net proceeds directed to lending projects that advance the AfDB's "Feed Africa" strategic priority.

Even as the West argued and retreated from ESG-sustainable commitments as inflation soared and the war in Ukraine raged, countries across Africa continue to accelerate adoption. While many citizens have skipped a generation of technology—from not having access to a telephone at all directly to mobile phones—Africa is home to 4 out of 5 people globally without energy access, according to the African Finance Corporation. The continent is losing 5–15 percent of GDP per capita due to the impact of climate change, according to the African Development Bank, despite only accounting for 4 percent of the world's greenhouse gas emissions. Beyond traditional finance, even some key oil exporters have embraced climate change initiatives, with OPEC member Gabon announcing creation of 187 million carbon credits to protect its section of the Congo Basin, the second largest tropical forest in the world. Funds secured from selling carbon credits will offset reduced oil sales in the years to come. Its sovereign wealth fund with some USD 2 billion of assets under management became the first African SWF to join the Net Zero Asset Owner Alliance, under which it commits to transition its investment portfolio to net zero emissions by 2050.

Consultants and AI-based data houses are increasingly entering the mix, and ESG certification programs are now available through professional bodies like the CFA Institute. The International Sustainability Standards Board and the global disclosure system run by the international not-for-profit CDP, formerly known as the Carbon Disclosure Project, are similarly involved. The European Union has its own detailed reporting directive, and China has formalized stock exchange rules.

Prior to Russia's invasion into Ukraine and despite growing attention, ESG emerging market funds were so focused on yield pick-up that they continued to hold and trade sovereign bonds from countries such as Belarus after its sham election and inhumane crackdown on citizens in 2020. A report by Inclusive Development International found that hundreds have stakes in 33 companies that the United Nations says has provided weapons, communications, and technology to the Myanmar military which overthrew a democratically elected government in 2021. These companies are in MSCI's ESG Screened Index, according to media reports.

As gas prices soared across the globe with rising hunger on wheat prices up nearly 50% after the war in Ukraine started, screening came under the microscope after the euphoria phase. In the immediate aftermath debate centered on military-related companies, which in a "perfect world" would be a red line for ESG funds. Just a year after Sweden's SEB bank's new sustainability policy excluded defense stocks it reversed position. Even the EU has seemingly softened its stance. It raised the pariah bar to companies that outright violate international rules instead of calling all arms and weapons manufacturers harmful. The EU has tightened rules for using the ESG label and in 2024 some of the world's largest investors—including PIMCO and Alliance Bernstein—withdrew from the world's largest climate alliance for investors.[32]

When oil and gas prices spiked, climate change and transition from fossil fuel reliance promises are second-guessed. Despite the "net zero" flurry at the COP26 Climate Summit in 2021 deadlines for carbon reduction were decades away at the earliest. The war distorted the availability and price of clean energy components like nickel. Continued growth of the carbon trading market both through voluntary emissions offsets and regulated markets is not in the forefront of investor attention.

"S" and "G" components are clearer in allocation choice post-war as portfolio and foreign direct investors weave them into "top-down" macroeconomic-political decision-making. For example, when McDonald's closed Russian operations after 30 years, it announced it would continue to pay employees as a labor-management best practice. Even before the outbreak of war—and leaving aside its pre-2023 "unorthodox" monetary policy—investors seized on governance issues in Turkey. The present administration detains political opponents and independent journalists on bogus charges, and President Erdogan has for years ignored a ruling from the European Court of Human Rights to release philanthropist Osman Kavala. Turkey has been threatened with suspension from the Council of Europe democratic club, of which it is a founding member, and the NATO member was viewed as largely neutral about the war in Ukraine. However, the sustainability and governance variables are not new to asset managers. From the early days, macroeconomic analysis has incorporated indicators for poverty, unemployment, and the social safety net, all of which weigh on emerging markets' GDP growth and fiscal balance. Proponents for larger weighting in the allocation process point out that both direct and portfolio investment have been stuck around 1% of GDP for the universe the past decade as the drag from its so-called "misery index" mix may be more pronounced.

Corporate application in stocks and bonds has taken off with the creation of voluntary private sector codes as an implicit seal of approval. Financial institutions have been among the most popular buys after signing the Principles for Responsible Banking launched by the UN in 2019. They pledge to "align with the vision society has set out for its future in the Sustainable Development Goals and the Paris Climate Agreement."[33] More than 345 signatories with nearly than USD 100 trillion in assets represent over half of global banking heft. They are from the largest emerging markets as well as remote destinations like North Macedonia and Paraguay.[34]

Disclosure and transparency are rudimentary and uneven in this field, and often aggravated by underlying norm defects. Post-investment tracking is labor and time-intensive to ensure instrument adherence. For example, as energy costs soared in 2022 due to the war in Ukraine, Chinese and Indian banks were scrutinized for fossil fuel finance backtracking to reinforce domestic capacity.

ESG/sustainable investing is considered "thematic" or "labeled" as a fund product. Hundreds of permutations have already been packaged for emerging market stocks and bonds. Fund tracker EPFR provider data shows that the number of ESG/Sustainable stock and bond funds targeting emerging markets surged more than 100 percent from 2020 through the third quarter of 2024 to 665, of which 80 percent are equity funds, while total assets under management have risen 70 percent (Fig. 7.2).

MSCI offers a suite of thematic indices that capitalize on "opportunities created by macro-economic, geopolitical, and technological trends." It notes four "megatrend categories" shaping the future—environment and

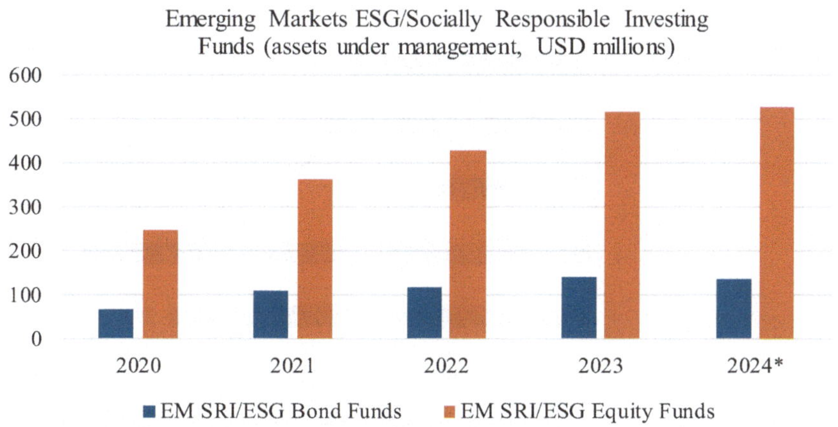

Fig. 7.2 Emerging Markets ESG/Socially Responsible Investing Funds (assets under management, USD millions) (*Source* EPFR)

resources, transformative technologies, health and healthcare, and society and lifestyle.[35] (see case study) Packaging sector and industry categories into custom offerings fuse once separate "socially responsible" and mainstream classification, as the distinction progressively blurs. Single country to diversified geographical exposure in turn is readily available, and only limited by the slice and dice imagination of ETF and traditional fund managers. Securities market innovations will flourish well beyond the green and blue hues of the past decade. Our firm has worked since the 2015 Europe-Syria crisis to promote refugee bond and equity alternatives based on existing foundations. They can raise large scale long-term sums for internal and external displacement, and the unprecedented size of Ukraine's exodus to neighbors at 8 million in just the first months of the war evoked pilot interest from the entire transaction participant spectrum.[36]

Case Study: MSCI Thematic Indices Whirl

Global index provider MSCI describes thematic benchmarks as "forward looking," representing companies associated with long-term structural trends. They include demographic changes, technological disruptions, and changing consumer behavior,[37] and geographically cut across countries and regions to identify companies that will benefit from rapid shifts. The specific themes are geared to retail and institutional investor preference. For example, pension funds and life insurers are interested in companies that will benefit from aging populations,[38] and the demographic plays include pharmaceuticals and retirement/nursing homes (Fig. 7.3).

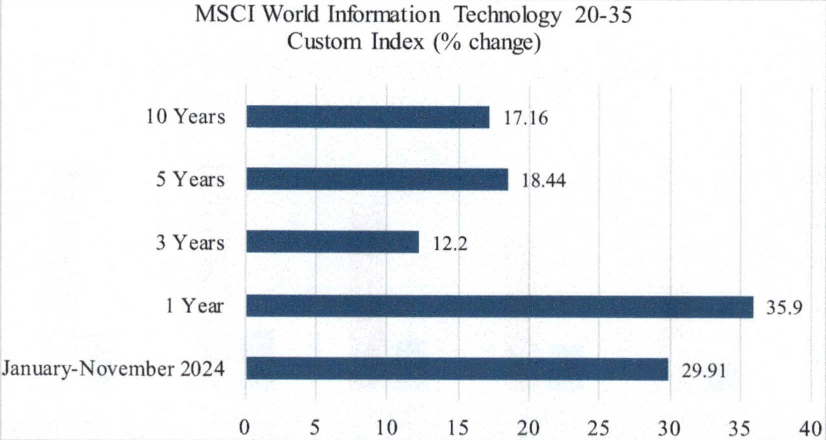

Fig. 7.3 MSCI World Information Technology 20–35 Custom Index (% change) (*Source* MSCI)

Other popular areas include robotics and artificial intelligence, digital economy, and cyber security. MSCI launched nine indices in 2018 from subsets in its All-Country World Index (ACWI). It comprises nearly 3000 mid-cap and large companies in 23 developed markets and 24 emerging markets and encompasses about 85 percent of global investable equities.[39]

While thematic investing has taken off, index composition and "purity" invite doubt.[40] Fund managers argue that investing in a major multinational with numerous business lines dilutes the featured characteristic and may skew weightings. In addition, as technologies evolve, the original components may become obsolete as index inertia preserves the template. Skeptics argue that active managers are better able to scope out market "disruptors" and adjust investments as the theme evolves with the brisk pace of innovation.[41]

Despite criticism, thematic investing as a global geographic and industry hybrid is here to stay, with evidence of superior returns over a medium-term, 5-year period. It is the wave of the future in developed and emerging markets alike. Giants like Blackrock and Fidelity have rolled out a suite of funds, pitted against smaller, specialized players that may have conceptual advantage. VegTech Invest, for example, has a proprietary index and ETF focused on companies worldwide using plants and plant-derived ingredients to create animal free products for sustainable consumption.[42]

Bilateral and multilateral donors will increase aid and technical assistance at the same time. In 2023 the IMF launched a USD 50 billion Climate Resilience Trust to help low and vulnerable middle-income countries build protection to external shocks. The Trust complements its longstanding lending by providing longer-term affordable financing to address challenges including climate change and pandemic preparedness. Bold aspirations may run into their own and borrower resource limits after the Covid-19 pandemic, which resulted in a spike in global debt to USD 315.1 trillion, 332 percent of global GDP by the end of the first quarter of 2024. Total emerging market debt topped USD 105 trillion, nearly doubling in a decade, to reach a new high of 257 percent of their GDP.[43] The war in Ukraine added further pressure to low-income economies, two-thirds classified in debt distress as it broke out to choke agriculture and energy lifelines. A year and a half later Middle East combat leapfrogged from Israel-Hamas to Yemen, Lebanon and Iran as those economies and their tech-commodities export ripples came under the microscope.

Key Takeaways

- The global pandemic, Russia war in Ukraine, and monetary tightening in response to inflation were a three-pronged blow to emerging markets. The World Economic Forum coined a new term, polycrisis, to describe the series of interrelated risks, also compounded by the rising dollar and food insecurity. The multilateral development institutions moved quickly and collaborated to provide assistance as basic commodities scarcity spiked in an all-hands emergency.

- This period heightened interest in ESG and sustainable investment as it exposed poverty and income equality. While investment growth slowed in 2022 and 2023 on geopolitical tensions, slowing economic growth and higher global borrowing costs underlying momentum is intact. Initially climate, "green," bonds were the key focus. The United Nations adopted 17 Sustainable Development Goals in 2015, a decade after the term ESG was coined to pose "a shared blueprint for peace and prosperity for people and the planet, now and into the future."
- ESG/sustainable investing is "thematic" as a fund product sub-type. Hundreds of emerging market stock and bond funds exist as ETFs and standard launches under this description and continue to grow assets under management. Index provider MSCI offers a suite of "forward looking," vehicles representing companies in the frontline of long-term structural trends including demographic changes, technological disruptions, and changing consumer behavior as the next wave of business champions.

Notes

1. United Nations, Sustainable Development Goals, https://sdgs.un.org/.
2. Karmen Naidoo and Nelson Sobrinho, " How Financing Can Boost Low-Income Countries' Resilience to Shocks," IMF Blog, June 14, 2023, https://www.imf.org/en/Blogs/Articles/2023/06/14/how-financing-can-boost-low-income-countries-resilience-to-shocks
3. Sunil Katavia, "Sri Lanka's Economic Crisis Dashes Hopes for post COVID-19 Tourism Recovery," Reuters, April 22, 2022, https://www.reuters.com/world/asia-pacific/sri-lankas-economic-crisis-dashes-hopes-post-covid-19-tourism-recovery-2022-04-22/#:~:text=As%20Sri%20Lanka%20sinks%20deeper,in%202020%20have%20been%20dashed.
4. Gian Maria Milesi-Ferretti, "The Covid-19 travel shock hit tourism-dependent economies hard," Brookings, August 12, 2021, https://www.brookings.edu/articles/the-covid-19-travel-shock-hit-tourism-dependent-economies-hard/#:~:text=The%20COVID%20crisis%20has%20led,120%20million%20direct%20tourism%20jobs.

5. World Bank Press Release, "Defying Predictions Remittance Flows Remain Strong During Covid-19," World Bank, May 12, 2021, https://www.worldbank.org/en/news/press-release/2021/05/12/defying-predictions-remittance-flows-remain-strong-during-covid-19-crisis#:~:text=Remittances%20flows%20to%20Latin%20America,the%20third%20and%20fourth%20quarters.
6. IMF Policy Paper, "Macroeconomic Developments and Prospects in Low Income Countries—2022," International Monetary Fund, December, 2022, file:///C:/Users/Admin/OneDrive/Downloads/PPEA2022054%20(2).pdf.
7. Maureen Teresa Odongo, Roseline Nyakerario Misatu, Anne Wangari Kamau and Kethi Ngoka Kisingu, "Climate Change and Inflation in Eastern and Southern Africa," Central Bank of Kenya, Nairobi, November 9, 2022, https://www.mdpi.com/2071-1050/14/22/14764
8. Katarina Hoije, "Africa Needs up to $65 billion in Loans Every Year to Curb Food Imports," Bloomberg, January 24, 2023, https://www.bloomberg.com/news/articles/2023-01-24/africa-needs-up-to-65-billion-loans-yearly-to-curb-food-imports?sref=9BZJXmVl
9. Geoffrey Ndegwa, Phosiso Sola, Ignatius Siko, et. al., "The Charcoal Value Chain in Kenya: Actors, practices, and trade flows in selected sites," World Agroforestry, Nairobi, 2021, https://apps.worldagroforestry.org/downloads/Publications/PDFS/RP21028.pdf
10. Philiip Inman, "Lenders urged to cancel Zambia debt as country faces economic collapse," The Guardian, September 11, 2022, https://www.theguardian.com/world/2022/sep/16/zambia-debt-lenders-urged-to-cancel
11. Human Rights Watch, "Lebanon: Rising Poverty, Hunger Amid Economic Crisis," December 12, 2022, https://www.hrw.org/news/2022/12/12/lebanon-rising-poverty-hunger-amid-economic-crisis.
12. Staff Correspondent, "Bangladesh's forex reserves fall to $32.9b," New Age, Dhaka, January 29, 2023, https://www.newagebd.net/article/192944/forex-reserves-fall-to-3229b
13. David Hutt, "China Indebted Laos Way more Broke than Advertised," Asia Times, October 14, 2022, https://asiatimes.com/2022/10/china-indebted-laos-way-more-broke-than-advertised/
14. Press Release No.22/158, "Statement by IMF Managing Director Kristalina Georgieva on the publication of the Joint International Financial Institutions Plan to Address Food Insecurity," IMF, May 18, 2022, https://www.imf.org/en/News/Articles/2022/05/17/pr22158-statement-md-on-joint-plan-to-address-food-insecurity.

15. David Lawder, "IMF board approves new food shock financing window to ease war shortages," Reuters, September 30, 2022, https://www.reuters.com/world/imf-board-approves-new-food-shock-financing-window-ease-war-shortages-2022-09-30/
16. Sydney Maki, "Emerging ESG bond boom puts world on path to sell $1.8 trillion," Bloomberg US Edition, February 1, 2022, https://www.bloomberg.com/news/articles/2022-02-01/esg-bond-boom-takes-over-the-world-with-1-8-trillion-in-sight?sref=9BZJXmVl.
17. Raquel de la Orden and Ignacio de Calonje, "Sustainability-linked finance—mobilizing capital for sustainability in Emerging Markets," International Finance Corporation (IFC), Note 110, January 2022, https://www.ifc.org/wps/wcm/connect/306c321d-ea77-448d-85c6-7ce3899136a5/EMCompass_Note+110_Sustainability-Linked+Finance_web.pdf?MOD=AJPERES&CVID=nVKABZX.
18. Ibid.
19. Coco Zhang and Padhraic Garvey, "Global sustainable finance market: changing for the better," ING Bank, 20 August 2024, https://think.ing.com/articles/global-sustainable-finance-market-changing-for-the-better/.
20. ESG Analytics, "Where did the term ESG come from anyway?" Blog, Insights, https://www.esganalytics.io/insights/where-did-the-term-esg-come-from-anyway.
21. United Nations, "Do you know all 17 SDGs?" https://sdgs.un.org/goals.
22. Lucas Kitzmueller, Brian Stacy and Daniel Gerszon Mahler, "Are we there yet? Many countries don't report progress on all SDGs according to the World Bank's new Statistical Performance Indicators," World Bank Blogs, August 10, 2021, https://blogs.worldbank.org/opendata/are-we-there-yet-many-countries-dont-report-progress-all-sdgs-according-world-banks-new.
23. United Nations, "Goal 1: End poverty in all its forms everywhere," Sustainable Development, https://sdgs.un.org/goals/goal1.
24. United Nations, "The 17 Goals," Sustainable Development Goals, https://sdgs.un.org/goals#goals.
25. Kitzmueller, et al., "Are we there yet?".
26. Ibid.
27. Ibid.
28. https://www.climatebonds.net/market/data/
29. Kitzmueller.

30. Keiron Greenhalgh, "Colombia issues first Latin American green sovereign bond in local currency," S&P Global, HIS Markit, October 1, 2021, https://cleanenergynews.ihsmarkit.com/research-analysis/colombia-issues-first-latin-american-green-sovereign-bond-in-l.html.
31. Fiona Stewart, "Charting the right course: How sovereign ESG indices can help navigate capital flows," Private Sector Development Blog, World Bank, November 28, 2023, https://blogs.worldbank.org/en/psd/charting-right-course-how-sovereign-esg-indices-can-help-navigate-capital-flows.
32. Zijia Song and Carolina Wilson, "ESG's Appeal Fades in Emerging Markets as Profit Seeking Eclipses Virtue," Bloomberg, October 15, 2024, https://news.bloomberglaw.com/esg/esgs-appeal-fades-in-emerging-markets-as-profit-eclipses-virtue.
33. United Nations Environment Programme Finance Initiative, "Principles for Responsible Banking," https://www.unepfi.org/banking/bankingprinciples/.
34. United Nations Environment Programme Finance Initiative: Principles for Responsible Banking, "Signatories," https://www.unepfi.org/banking/bankingprinciples/prbsignatories/.
35. MSCI, "Thematic Investing," https://www.msci.com/our-solutions/indexes/thematic-investing.
36. Gary Kleiman, "Opinion: Frontline state refugee bonds can finance Ukraine influx," Business news from Eastern Europe, Eurasia, the Middle East, and Africa (bne) Intellinews, March 15, 2022, https://www.intellinews.com/opinion-frontline-state-refugee-bonds-can-finance-ukraine-influx-238085/?source=hungary;%20https://wrmcouncil.org/publications/report/emerging-market-finance-refugee-crisis-application-rationale-and-roadmap/.
37. MSCI, "Thematic Investing.".
38. Ibid.
39. MSCI, "MSCI ACWI Index (USD)," Index Factsheet, August 31, 2022, https://www.msci.com/documents/10199/a71b65b5-d0ea-4b5c-a709-24b1213bc3c5.
40. Andrew Sharp-Paul, "A theme is not an index," Wellington Management, June 2021, https://www.wellington.com/en/insights/thematic-investing-avoiding-theme-washing-us/.
41. Ibid.
42. VegTech Plant-based Innovation & Alternative Proteins Index (EATVI), https://www.vegtechinvest.com/index.
43. Nessa Anwar, "Global debt has grown to $315 trillion this year—here's how we got here," CNBC, May 29, 2024, https://www.cnbc.com/2024/05/29/global-debt-has-grown-to-315-trillion-in-2024.html.

8

Future Checklist for Emerging Economies and Financial Markets

Economic Model: Past is Prologue

Since the end of the early 2000s commodity boom and with the secular slowdown in global trade pre-Covid-19, governments have fumbled for an updated economic strategy placing more emphasis on domestic consumption and services-technology. The longstanding belief cast emerging markets as a leveraged commodities play, but the winners and losers have always depended on the complex breakdown as importer or exporter and effect on growth. In India, for example, every USD 10 increase in global oil prices is estimated to widen the current account deficit by 0.4 percent of GDP while retail inflation is boosted 30–35 basis points.[1] Conversely, oil exporters in the Gulf can fill their coffers, but they also import food while India's harvest provides a degree of self-sufficiency. The pandemic/war period that started in 2020 accentuated these divides, and Latin America and Africa producers enjoyed short-term windfalls from the scramble for backstops as global supply chains seized up and with the imposition of sanctions on Russia, but the calculus for rebalancing remained intact even if it shifted in national security terms. China is the most prominent example of the attempt to strengthen the consumption pillar, which entails raising education-health as well as income standards to create a middle class and boost productivity. Covid underscored this lesson, with disease toll and lost schooling leaving long-term scars.

The IMF estimates that a vast swathe of the developing world may not reprise 2019 level of economic output until mid-decade or later without dramatic strides in neglected areas like structural reform to improve the banking-business environment. This overhaul was a prevailing theme in

B. Morrissey and G. Kleiman, *Emerging Economies and Financial Markets*,
https://doi.org/10.1007/978-3-031-85669-3_8

the first twenty years of the asset class, and lost momentum in the same interval since. Official lender exhortations can provide traction, but as with the 1980s/1990s debt crisis period, formal program arrangements will again motivate the process as it comes full circle a generation later. Pakistan and Sri Lanka are examples of once active privatizers promising again to revisit state company selloffs that in turn can revitalize equity markets and foreign direct investment. In banking an entire youth population has grown up since the initial wave of reforms accustomed to digital online practice, and the combination of non-government ownership and advanced technology can contribute to an era of economic reinvention.

Portfolio/Direct Investment "North–South" Banish

The first cut at portfolio and direct investment flow tracking is from developed to emerging economies as a baseline in current account and international reserve data, indicating whether a country is at risk of crisis. Pure financial flows are often deemed "hot money" with a pro-cyclical tendency, especially with swift reversal at times of single country or global economic stress upending currencies and local markets. In the past foreign direct and private equity commitments were seen as more durable signs of long-term business and policy confidence. This perception unraveled after the Russian invasion of Ukraine. The rapid unwinding with the mass exodus of hundreds of Western firms from Russia was a singular exception to this assumption as their presence came under boycott name and shame pressure. The early months' pullout cost banks and corporates billions of dollars in write-downs and losses, but share prices generally rose as indefinite brand damage was avoided. For example, McDonald's which opened in Russia in 1990 to great fanfare, took a one-time charge of some USD 1.4 billion when it shut down in the country three months after the outbreak of war.

"Intra-emerging markets" flows are also embedded in the exercise of investment tracking with priority emphasis over time. Chilean pension funds with their pioneer heft and reputation started to invest abroad in 1990, and by 2003 nearly one-quarter of their assets under management were outside the country, largely in regional mutual funds.[2] Elsewhere in Latin America, Brazilian investments in Colombia stand out historically. From 2005–2010 Brazil's FDI there surged from USD 93 million to USD 775 million, concentrated in manufactured goods, mining, and construction, with blue chips Petrobras and mining company Vale among the biggest investors.[3] From

2017–2022 the number of Brazilian companies on the ground had doubled to more than 100.[4]

Regional allocation and expansion in the immediate neighborhood is common. In Central Europe, Hungary's giant OTP bank has branches and units in ten countries,[5] while in Asia Malaysia's biggest bank, Maybank, has operations in 18 ranging from Laos to the United States. [6] (See MTN case study) A third category defying hemispheric definition is "extra-regional" flow often highlighted with China's vast inroads into Africa as described in the case study in Chapter 5, or Gulf Cooperation Council member strong two-way commodity ties with the continent.

Case Study: South Africa's MTN's Anti-Hemisphere Bias Pattern

Thirty years ago, reflecting academic literature at the time, direct and foreign portfolio flows to emerging markets were labeled in "north–south" shorthand, reflecting the respective hemispheres, and presumed developed economy sourcing. In the early days of market opening this movement prevailed when, for example, large European and US banks followed clients into new locales, but the trajectory has shifted over the past thirty years. In the mid-1990s emerging markets-based banks and companies unleashed a lasting trend of cross-border operations, with parent companies listing shares in New York, London, or Hong Kong to reflect their global footprint.

A frequently cited example is South African telecom giant MTN. Established at the end of apartheid in 1994, today MTN has operations in 18 countries across Africa and by 2024 had more than 287 million subscribers.[7] Shares are traded over-the-counter in New York on the NASDAQ and for years have been ranked the number one African brand.[8] Started as a pure mobile phone provider, it diversified and now offers fintech and a full range of information and communication technology for businesses and individuals.

Sub-Saharan African markets surged ahead of developed country counterparts in adopting payment platforms on mobile phones, an area MTN embraced. Citizens across the region simply "skipped" a generation of technology. They went from no landline access, largely due to the inability of state-owned telecom providers to connect them, straight to mobile use. The first time we saw a mobile payment through the pioneer M-Pesa service was in a Kenya grocery store in 2009, years before it reached our Washington office base.

MTN separate country units are listed on numerous local stock exchanges. With its primary listing on the Johannesburg Stock Exchange, in 2019 a public offering was a major event in its largest market, Nigeria, where by 2023 it held about a one-third market share.[9] A year earlier it launched an IPO in Ghana, and in late 2021 raised USD 150 million in Uganda and USD 364 million in Rwanda as the exchange there celebrated its 10th anniversary.

MTN is only one of dozens of instances of well-known South-South or "intra-emerging market" investments in Africa. Nairobi-based Equity Bank, the largest in Kenya, has expanded to the Democratic Republic of Congo, Rwanda, Tanzania, South Sudan, and Ethiopia. After its 2006 initial public offering on the Nairobi Stock Exchange, it also listed on the exchanges in Rwanda and Uganda. Johannesburg-based insurer Old Mutual similarly has listings in Malawi, Namibia, Zimbabwe, and London. Togo-based Ecobank has a pan-African network, and Morocco financial institutions are spread through the Sub-Sahara.

Familiar bellwethers are South Korean companies like Samsung with the reverse tendency to list equity, issue debt, and derive the bulk of earnings from developed countries. Just as multinational names like Apple or Nestle based in the US and Europe offer exposure to business and consumer streams a broad range of emerging economies, banks and corporates from these economies have become household names.

Macro-Structural Factor Makeover

Traditional decision-making criteria—GDP growth, inflation, debt/deficits—are mainstays, with ESG and sustainability layered on for sovereigns and corporates as qualitative metrics. In the meantime, simple measures of poverty, unemployment, and income inequality will be in the shared vocabulary of investors and development-relief professionals as they conduct due-diligence and research, rather than unevenly identified concerns or an afterthought. Political risk is also a crucial factor. A change in administration through an election process can quickly derail or reverse sound economic management and reform processes. Included in any assessment is measuring statistics transparency and corruption. The Russian invasion into Ukraine, growing trade tensions between the West and China, and Mideast war escalation that can upend oil and commodities markets with higher delivery costs even with steady supply have starkly shown that global geopolitical issues sway decision-making.

Another new issue paradigm is the break from the earlier goods and raw materials export-led economy model, toward technology and services directed to the home consumer and industrial base. Brazil is an agriculture commodity giant, but exports are only 18 percent of GDP while services, including the rapidly growing information technology and communications sector account for nearly 60 percent of GDP and agriculture only about 6 percent.[10] In India, in the immediate aftermath of the global pandemic tech start-ups raised USD 38 billion in capital in 2021 and several went public on the stock exchange, with foreign investors clamoring for the digital economy

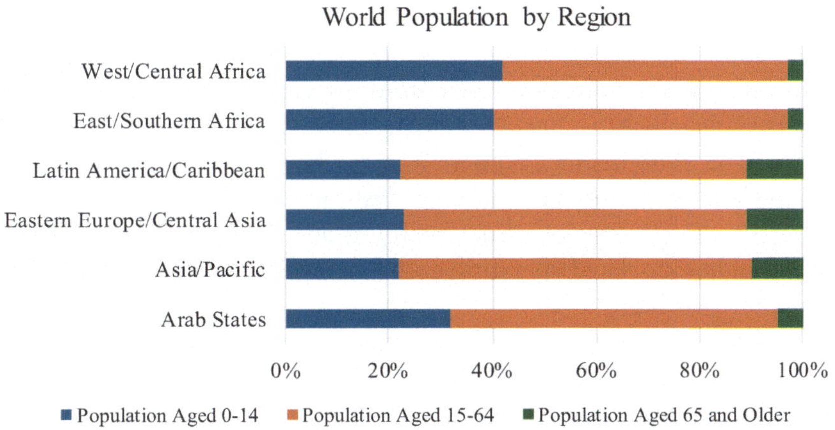

Fig. 8.1 World Population by Region (*Source* unfpa.org/data/world-population-dashboard)

story.[11] After a two year lull in issuance on rising global interest rates in the first nine months of 2024 tech start-ups raised USD 1.8 billion on the local exchanges.[12] Spending on research and development is in catch-up mode, in the same way long-term per capita income convergence was an original rationale. World average spending as a percentage of GDP is 2.62 percent, led by Israel and North America at 5.56 percent and 3.32 percent, respectively, while for lower- and middle-income countries it is 1.98 percent.[13]

Demographics are destiny, and the young population has long been an emerging market advantage, but it too is graying in pockets. South Korea's working age cohort peaked in 2017 and has steadily fallen since while China's crested in 2014 under decades of the one-child policy. While for now the impact is barely felt, over the medium-term aging populations will weigh on growth and government finances. Healthcare cost and quality are standout components brought to the forefront during the global Covid-19 pandemic. Recent data shows that emerging markets' spending on healthcare at 7 percent of GDP compared with the developed world's over 10 percent (Fig. 8.1).[14]

Sovereign Debt Workouts Final Sprint

Previous chapters illustrated the ad hoc nature of sovereign debt crisis negotiations and outcomes in the absence of formal bankruptcy procedures, which the IMF proposed in the mid-2000s against stiff opposition by the US Treasury in particular. It and industry representatives preferred legal changes in documents that would allow a two-thirds majority to bind all creditors in so-called collective action clauses, now standard in emerging market bonds. The co-chairs of the Sovereign Debt Working Group of the Bretton Woods Committee, of which we are a member, stated the problem succinctly in a 2022 op-ed in the Financial Times: "the mechanisms in place to deal with sovereign debt problems have become dysfunctional."[15] Covid-19 weighed on finances in every region, but emerging and frontier markets were hit hardest. Pandemic-related spending and a slump in tax receipts pushed total debt to a 50-year high.[16]

In the first debt crises, sovereigns negotiated with the Paris Club of wealthy creditor nations and/or large international banks which formed the London Club. Today, more than 20 distinct creditor categories are opposite the table with bondholders, including non-traditional lenders such as trading houses with advance arrangements for years of commodities.[17] Traditionally bilateral and multilateral agencies took the lead with restructuring or forgiveness, and then private banks and fund managers were invited to offer comparable terms, a murky concept they often rejected in high-stakes cases. Since the 2008 global financial crisis Argentina was the standout episode where litigation had a featured role, with a distressed fund ultimately collecting a several billion-dollar payout. Otherwise, restructurings were rare events always managed in improvised fashion, following voluntary codes of conduct and baseline legal provisions. Mozambique was a spectacular example of fraud against all creditors including the IMF through the so-called Tuna bonds, with international underwriters found to collude. (See Case Study).

Case Study: Greece's 2012 Debt Restructuring[18]

Although a member of the European Union, Greece over the past three decades has bounced from being classified as an "emerging market" to "developed" and back again. When it spectacularly was unable to service its debts in 2011 official and private creditors agreed on a debt reduction/restructuring. A few months later a special public–private sector group convened by the industry group Institute of International Finance (IIF) to adapt emerging market sovereign debt workout principles to Greece highlighted glaring weaknesses in the initial case in basic tenets such as data and information sharing, good-faith negotiations, and equal creditor treatment. European officials and banking executives were prominent on the committee, which also included US, Asian, and Latin American representatives. The IIF coordinated the investor side for six months of negotiations that concluded in the April 2012 exchange which featured a headline 75 percent haircut. It got an initial 83.5 percent acceptance which rose another 15 percent with the application of domestic law collective action clauses. EUR 205 billion in bonds and loans were covered, and the deal was considered voluntary even as official parties providing their own assistance periodically threatened unilateral action.

The IMF's debt sustainability analysis attempting to reduce the medium-term ratio to 120 percent of GDP was followed as economic indicators continuously shifted and deteriorated over the period. Numerous deviations resulted in an "inefficient and sub-optimal" process impeding commercial access normalization and financial stability. Bonds held by the European Central Bank, national central banks, and the European Investment Bank were excluded, with such subordination of private claims implying adverse effects. Contract sanctity was in turn placed in question by the retroactive insertion of Collective Action Clauses in instruments governed by local Greek law.

On sustainability, private steering committee members criticized heavy emphasis on a nominal quantitative objective and limited consultation on policy and performance parameters that could have stressed cash-flow relief and maturity extension. The IMF's independent judgment should be subject to input and views of interested outside parties to promote both analytical and monetary burden sharing. Information confidentiality should be respected by all sides, and the sovereign should be asked to contribute to the costs of ongoing advisory and statistical work. On a positive note, the enhancements used, in particular GDP-linked bonds which offer higher value for achieving growth thresholds, could be encouraged as a template.

After the outbreak of the global pandemic the IMF and World Bank announced the Debt Service Suspension Initiative (DSSI) as a repayment pause periodically reviewed for low-income borrowers. It was endorsed by the G-20 to bring in Brazil, China, India, and Saudi Arabia as new emerging market creditors, and extended to all official lending through 2021. The DSSI was accompanied by a pick-up in multilateral lending but only 48 of 73 eligible markets participated for around $10 billion in standstill results. Private lenders and bondholders were "encouraged" to join, but ratings agencies were clear that any interruption in payments constituted a "credit event" so no countries pursued a commercial break at the same time.

In 2020 the G-20 devised a collective formula to handle long-term unsustainability with the Common Framework for Debt Treatment. It intended an updated version of comparable terms from all official—Paris Club members and others –and private sources. Zambia was the first candidate, and commercial creditors immediately balked over lack of transparency about China obligations in particular. When it defaulted at the height of the pandemic, the total amount of external borrowings was unknown, as references like the World Bank's annual International Debt Statistics readily admitted the absence of Chinese bank data. The World Bank has noted that the new

Common Framework appears to have failed as a sweeping solution, with only Ghana, Ethiopia, and Chad subsequently entering.[19] Official creditors first group in a committee, with no enforcement mechanism or incentive for later private participation.[20]

The World Bank has proposed two steps to rein in protracted negotiations and standardize the process. The first stage would gather all official and commercial creditors at one time to speed up talks and gain a common understanding of the borrower's plight and policy credibility. The second proposal is to establish a standard formula for determining burden sharing across the board.[21] Twenty years later these aspects of the IMF's mandatory mechanism blueprint were resurrected under its Sovereign Debt Roundtable. So-called contingency instruments where payments are tied to future debt service variables like GDP growth and oil prices also follow longtime expert recommendations for smoother, more viable workouts. In the latest wave, this menu choice appears in Zambia, Sri Lanka, and Ukraine. Non-financial clauses binding future governments to deal legality and full creditor information sharing are also boilerplate in updated practice.

In the meantime, ESG-friendly answers have also surfaced for debt busts, alongside the reduced repayment formulas in swaps involving principal/interest "haircuts" or maturity extensions. Belize is an illustration of a "blue" remedy on large scale, although debt for nature arrangements have been around from the Brady bond days as minor alternatives. Reliant on tourism revenue from its tropical Caribbean beaches and barrier reef, it has undergone five restructuring rounds in less than two decades. Climate change resulted in a series of natural disasters and then overseas visitors dried up during the pandemic. Throughout the same large single obligation, dubbed the "superbond," has been the main commercial obstacle, as debt/GDP continuously veers toward 100 percent/ GDP on fiscal profligacy.

In 2020 Belize was in default for USD 533 million, and the non-profit Nature Conservancy funded coverage at USD 0.55/USD on the condition it expand marine conservation investors could also monitor. Belize won USD 250 million in debt reduction and bond holders won kudos for contributing to environmental protection.[22] The model may be repeated in other cases as Sri Lanka's advisers are promoting it as an eventual feature. It may be viable as a sweeping template for poorer countries where the amounts are relatively modest, and the IMF separately chips in through its $40 billion climate facility trust. Since Belize's debt-for-nature swap, many other countries have used the mechanism that cuts debt in return for climate commitments. For example, in 2023 Barbados completed a swap to upgrade its water infrastructure with guarantees provided by the European Investment Bank and the InterAmerican Development Bank. The International Institute for Environment and Development estimates debt-for-nature swaps could free up as much as USD 100 billion to restore nature and mitigate climate change.[23]

Global Crises' Redefined Growth Advantage

When this work was first at outline stage, US inflation had just topped 5 percent, and emerging markets' fate was tied inextricably to recovery from the economic ravages of the Covid-19 global pandemic. Getting shots into arms and untangling global supply chains was the shared mission as the world re-opened and the disease shifted to endemic, with debt overhang from fiscal stimulus looming for developing economies able to afford it. The US Federal Reserve and ECB were on track to tighten slowly in measured steps, hardly the well-worn crisis recipe for full-scale flight to safety as the emerging and frontier universe was again projected to grow at a faster clip.

As we complete the manuscript, inflation has retreated from a 4-decade high in the US and the US Federal Reserve and European Central Bank have started to reduce rates. However, Russia-Ukraine is the biggest war in Europe since 1945 and the Israel-Hamas war is raging. Post-Covid supply chain bottlenecks have improved but attacks on ships in the Red Sea by Houthi rebels expressing solidarity with the Palestinians in Gaza are weighing. Shipping costs are rising due to the Red Sea crisis and the impact of climate change on the Panama Canal.

After hitting a record high in the aftermath of Covid-19 and the result of Russia's war on Ukraine, food prices had fallen 14 percent through the third quarter of 2024, according to the United Nation's Food and Agricultural Organization's Food Price Index. However, the impact of wars and climate change have kept prices higher than pre-Covid as several emerging economies banned key agricultural exports to ensure domestic reserves. India reduced wheat exports and Indonesia briefly suspended all palm oil shipments as half the world's harvest (Fig. 8.2). (See case Study).

Case Study: Russia's Ukraine Attack Relationship Ripples

Russia's reprehensible behavior as a core emerging market placed it squarely with rogue states such as North Korea, Iran, Myanmar, and Venezuela in the broad international community diplomatic consensus. Commercial isolation is much easier for the latter group as minimal global economic contributors. However, Russia's sweeping commodity ties with trade and financial partners reflect the co-dependency and complexity that underscore rather than

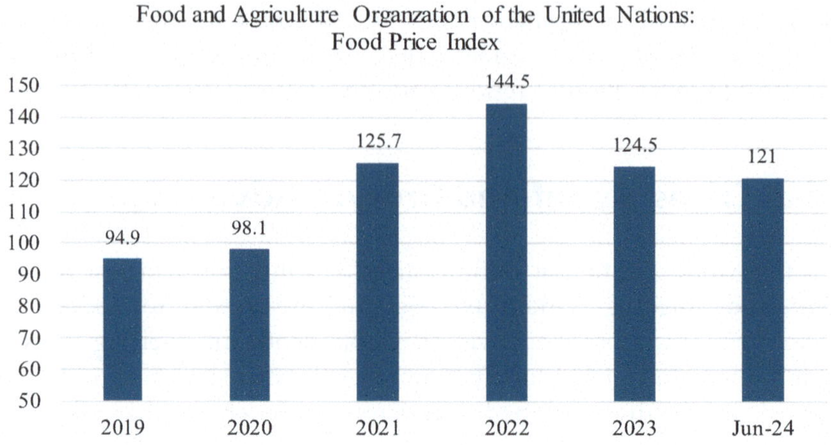

Fig. 8.2 Food and Agriculture Organization of the United Nations: Food Price Index (*Source* https://www.fao.org/worldfoodsituation/foodpricesindex/en/)

undermine globalization as a future overarching theme, with ad hoc coalition formation following policy and practical imperatives.

From a financial markets perspective, the immediate aftermath of global sanctions and Moscow countersanctions led to a tug of war over sovereign and corporate debt repayments, where they were delivered and then refused at the transaction chain end. Central bank assets were frozen in an unprecedented G-20 member move, and most state banks were cut off from the SWIFT international payments network, but loopholes allowed currency intervention and cross-border deals to continue with multiple layers.

Iran as a precedent is an inexact but useful guide to the shifting panoply of actors never fitting decisively in uniform blocs. Banks from the west, UAE, Turkey, and China helped Tehran evade the same SWIFT and central bank lock-up, and longtime US ally South Korea was a major oil importer in defiance when a waiver was unclear over the period. Several niche Europe-based funds were prominent on the Tehran stock exchange, and the EU tried to work out a dedicated cross-border euro-rial mechanism for trade. As an IMF member, majority shareholders could veto a Covid emergency loan, but they could not stop SDR distributions as with all other recognized governments despite pariah status.

The splintering commercial-financial connections with Russia follow a similar pattern. Eurasia Economic Union members like Kazakhstan and Armenia sought to preserve banking, currency, and remittance ties. Initially Chinese financial institutions largely remained in place willing to open FX and ruble accounts, although they later reduced ties worried that they would come under Western sanctions, while India and Indonesia devised local currency settlement mechanisms for oil import discounts. Dubai and Turkey lured wealthy business executives with citizenship promise over time. None of these alignments represent permanent bifurcation into pro-Moscow or anti-West camps but illustrate the multi-dimensional underpinning to the global monetary system that will persist throughout the Ukraine horror and reset again with its resolution. During the period, an ultimate irony could be an Iran welcome back to the fold with a new nuclear for sanctions swap under a "moderate" President and technocrat economic team, and discovery of the country's large young consumer base shunned for a decade. Eventual turnaround in the Russia relationship, especially under new leadership, could also be on the horizon. It will entail return to core emerging market status as a capital and commodity linchpin and overlapping often contradictory foreign policy and business loyalties that escape the simple Putin regime friendly-unfriendly taxonomy.

Despite global economic and geopolitical turmoil, the IMF in October 2024 forecast global growth to remain steady at 3.2 percent for both 2024 and 2025. However, advanced economies are projected to grow 1.8 percent in both years while emerging markets are forecast to grow far faster at 4.2 percent.[24] The simple faster GDP growth-return "argument" for investing in emerging markets endures, far from the breakneck pace of early days, but the softer aspects of living standards now receive development lender attention and fund manager allocation weighting beyond headline output numbers (Fig. 8.3).

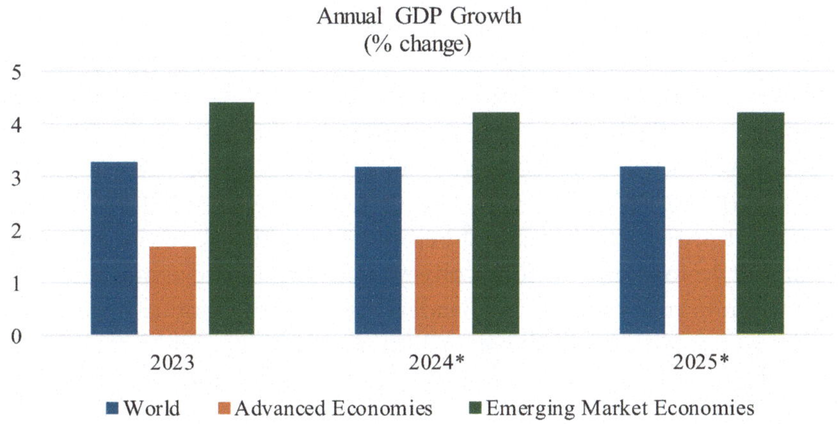

Fig. 8.3 Annual GDP Growth (% change) (*Source* IMF, world economic outlook, October 2024)

Final Words

In all these areas, you as readers will help reshape the specific contours of emerging markets next era. Based on conversations with students and professional speakers from our certificate workshops that motivated this reference, the foundations and vision are well in hand. ESG is now second nature despite some political pushback, and a mainstream pursuit as a banker-fund manager or official lender/charitable organization representative. Geographic assumptions place economic superpowers in the Global South, and tech/e-commerce are digital linchpins with as much heft as second wind physical commodity exports in an unprecedented wartime period. The post-pandemic lesson is more attention to growth quality, as reflected in education and health dimensions that have been the missing key to raising productivity. State bank and enterprise privatization is back as an efficiency and equity market driver for a fresh crowd attuned to past abuses.

On more insider technical aspects, we are already immersed as independent participants in a vigorous debate for performance index permutations unifying local and external, corporate and government debt in one benchmark, and mixing fixed income and equity. Private equity and credit gauges are on the horizon, and derivatives will integrate with straightforward products as the coming generation engineers updates to credit default swaps. The same innovation strides are imminent in the perennial sovereign debt restructure quandary, with the wholesale search for climate swap clearing and trading mechanisms as a fresh device and harnessing of big data to create readily accessible inventories of all borrower and creditor exposures for a common base at the outset. We close with the expectation that predictions in this chapter are at least partially realized before a second book edition comes out, and that our lessons and history conveyed readily find classroom and real-world adoption and application. Readers running the gamut from aspiring university to seasoned professional analysts should be confident that in future volumes they are in a position both to automatically absorb and add their own contribution.

Notes

1. Aakriti Bhalla, "How much will high crude oil prices cost India economy; this much hit likely on GDP growth, inflation, revenue," Financial Express, March 7, 2022, https://www.financialexpress.com/economy/how-much-will-high-crude-oil-prices-cost-india-economy-this-much-hit-likely-on-gdp-growth-inflation-revenue/2453134/.
2. The World Bank, "Chile: Technical Note: Pension Fund Sector," Financial Sector Assessment Program, November 2004, https://documents1.worldbank.org/curated/pt/951971468014980189/pdf/791840WP0Chile0Box0377369B00Public0.pdf.
3. Raul Zibechi, "Brazil and Colombia: An unexpected alliance," Foreign Policy in Focus (FPIF), November 29, 2011, https://fpif.org/brazil_and_colombia_an_unexpected_alliance/.
4. Brazil, Ministry of Exterior Relations, "Republic of Colombia," August 7, 2015, updated March 29, 2022, https://www.gov.br/mre/en/subjects/bilateral-relations/all-countries/republic-of-colombia.
5. OTP Bank, "OTP Group," https://www.otpbank.hu/portal/en/AboutUs/OTPGroup.
6. Maybank, "Maybank Around the World," https://www.maybank.com/en/maybank-worldwide.page.
7. https://www.mtn.com/about/.
8. https://brandirectory.com/rankings/africa/.
9. Martyn Warwick, "MTN of South Africa, the biggest operator in the continent, to focus entirely on pan-African market," Telecom TV, Business Models, March 22, 2021. https://www.telecomtv.com/content/business-models/mtn-of-south-africa-the-biggest-operator-in-the-continent-to-focus-entirely-on-pan-african-market-41099/.
10. Central Intelligence Agency, "The World Fact Book—Brazil," October 28, 2024, https://www.cia.gov/the-world-factbook/countries/brazil/.
11. The Economic Times, "India will have over 250 unicorns by 2025: report," ETtech, April 18, 2022, https://economictimes.indiatimes.com/tech/startups/india-to-have-over-250-unicorns-by-2025-report/articleshow/90915480.cms.
12. The Economic Times, "New-age tech IPOs make a comeback after three-year lull; raise RS 15,000 crore in 2024: report," September 28, 2024, https://economictimes.indiatimes.com/tech/tech-bytes/new-age-tech-ipos-make-a-comeback-after-three-year-lull-raise-rs-15000-crore-in-2024-report/articleshow/113762639.cms?from=mdr.

13. The World Bank, "Research and development expenditure (% of GDP)," https://data.worldbank.org/indicator/GB.XPD.RSDV.GD.ZS.
14. OECD Data, "Health spending (indicator) 2022,". https://doi.org/10.1787/8643de7e-en.
15. William Rhodes and John Lipsky, "Act now to prevent a new sovereign debt crisis in the developing world," Financial Times, March 23, 2022 https://www.ft.com/content/faf73649-4e4e-481c-a245-55862ea644cb.
16. Indermit Gill, "It's time to end the slow-motion tragedy in debt restructurings," Brookings, Future Development, February 25, 2022, https://www.brookings.edu/blog/future-development/2022/02/25/its-time-to-end-the-slow-motion-tragedy-in-debt-restructurings/.
17. The Editorial Board, "The Covid aftermath requires sovereign debt restructuring," Financial Times, February 15, 2022, https://www.ft.com/content/ee97ec19-5b37-4c89-83eb-e69ec17cdf89.
18. Adapted from a Kleiman International confidential client analysis submitted on October 26, 2012.
19. Rhodes and Lipsky.
20. Simon Hinrichsen, "Why countries should restructure debts sooner rather than later," Financial Times, February 10, 2022, "https://www.ft.com/content/7489e312-085f-44f6-b9cd-9b19ceb45bd5.
21. Indermit Gill, "It's time to end".
22. Fran Slayton, "The Weight of the World: can international institutions and nations work together to tackle global problems?" Spring 2022, https://www.law.virginia.edu/uvalawyer/article/weight-world.
23. World Economic Forum, "Climate finance: What are debt-for-nature swaps and how can they help countries/" April 26, 2024, https://www.weforum.org/stories/2024/04/climate-finance-debt-nature-swap/.
24. International Monetary Fund (IMF), "World Economic Outlook Update, October 2024," https://www.imf.org/en/Publications/WEO/Issues/2024/10/22/world-economic-outlook-october-2024?cid=ca-com-homepage-AM2024.

Index

B. Morrissey and G. Kleiman, *Emerging Economies and Financial Markets*,
https://doi.org/10.1007/978-3-031-85669-3

The manufacturer's authorised representative in the EU is Springer Nature Customer Service Centre GmbH, Europaplatz 3, 69115 Heidelberg, Germany. If you have any concerns regarding our products, please contact ProductSafety@springernature.com

Printed and bound by CPI Group (UK) Ltd, Croydon, CR0 4YY
01/10/2026
02225957-0019